AHMEDABAD

Praise for *Ahmedabad*

'This book deserves reading not just because of what it reveals of Ahmedabad but of what Ahmedabad reveals about India' *Biblio*

'A thoughtful, well-crafted book. Shrewd, tough, topical and anecdotal, its style is almost symbolic of the city Shah captures so joyously and creatively' *India Today*

'Shah has the poetic gift of discovering metaphors' *Mint*

'A riveting picture of a city' *The Independent*

'No book on the city of Ahmedabad has been written with such elegance and evocativeness' *The Wire*

'Combines solid research with literary grace ... Both a political and an intellectual journey ... elegantly crafted and gripping'
U.R. Ananthamurthy

'This perceptive, sometimes bitterly funny, book portrays Ahmedabad uniquely, giving us the long view without ever lapsing into abstraction or diluting the immediacy of the present moment' Amit Chaudhuri

'In this richly researched and elegantly written book, Amrita Shah explores the paradoxes of Ahmedabad: a city that is at once nativist and cosmopolitan, caring and hedonistic, austere and exhibitionist. This fine study should serve as a model for other works on the rapidly changing cityscapes of twenty-first century India' Ramachandra Guha

'Shah penetrates this unusual city as it hasn't been before'
Aakar Patel

AHMEDABAD

A City in the World

Amrita Shah

BLOOMSBURY
NEW DELHI · LONDON · OXFORD · NEW YORK · SYDNEY

BLOOMSBURY INDIA
Bloomsbury Publishing India Pvt. Ltd
Second Floor, LSC Building No. 4, DDA Complex,
Pocket C – 6 & 7, Vasant Kunj,
New Delhi 110070

BLOOMSBURY, BLOOMSBURY INDIA and the Diana logo are
trademarks of Bloomsbury Publishing Plc

First published in India 2015
This edition published 2025

Copyright © Amrita Shah 2015, 2025

Amrita Shah has asserted her moral rights to be identified as the author of this work in accordance with the Indian Copyright Act, 1957

Every reasonable effort has been made to trace copyright holders of material reproduced in this book, but if any have been inadvertently overlooked the publisher would be glad to hear from them

All rights reserved. No part of this publication may be: i) reproduced or transmitted in any form, electronic or mechanical, including photocopying, recording or by means of any information storage or retrieval system without prior permission in writing from the publishers; or ii) used or reproduced in any way for the training, development or operation of artificial intelligence (AI) technologies, including generative AI technologies. The rights holders expressly reserve this publication from the text and data mining exception as per Article 4(3) of the Digital Single Market Directive (EU) 2019/790

ISBN: 978-93-69522-47-7
2 4 6 8 10 9 7 5 3 1

Typeset by Eleven Arts
Printed and bound in India by Gopsons Papers Pvt. Ltd., Noida

To find out more about our authors and books, visit
www.bloomsbury.com and sign up for our newsletters

Long since, in history's mirror,
we became accomplices,
awaiting the day we might
seep down through the layers of stone
into subterranean pools
to contemplate darkness again.
—Bei Dao, 'Accomplices'

Contents

Preface to the Paperback Edition   ix
1   Meraj   1
2   The River   29
3   Old City   56
4   Working Class   94
5   Highway Dreams   124
6   New York Tower   155
7   Bombay Hotel   174
(*Coda*) The Kite   196

Notes   201
Select Bibliography   205
Acknowledgements   215

Preface to the Paperback Edition

Attacks on minorities. The arrest of civil rights activists. Tax raids on media houses. Threats to cartoonists and stand-up comics. India is going through an unprecedented churn. Demoted from pride of place on international indices and tarnished with new labels such as 'electoral autocracy' (by the Swedish V-Dem Institute) and 'flawed democracy' (by the Economist Intelligence Unit), the country once touted as the world's largest democracy is undoubtedly losing its sheen.

Influential opinion makers and political analysts in India and overseas unvaryingly attribute these developments to the authoritarian personality of Prime Minister Narendra Modi and his appeal as a fundamentalist Hindu leader. Conventional wisdom within the liberal intelligentsia in India and overseas, articulated in numerous books, documentary films and media columns, has it that the Hindutva rhetoric of historical injustice and hurt pride has turned millions of Indians into adulators of Modi and the promise he holds out for majoritarian rule.

I believe this explanation, axiomatic for many, is erroneous.

The diminution of democratic freedom and of secular rights in present-day India is undeniable. But its cause is far more complex than is commonly suggested and has its origins in processes set in motion over three decades ago. In 1991, India abandoned the largely socialist and mixed-economy path it had followed post-Independence to embrace capitalist reforms. I argue that India's present turbulence has its makings in the changes and aspirations triggered by this watershed event. And it is within this context and the hyper-capitalist world economy that India seeks to join that current trends can be understood.

My perspective, as a writer who combines journalistic research with deep scholarship, is based on a close observation of the sociopolitical trajectory of post-liberalisation India and a focused study of the state of Gujarat, which has often been described as a laboratory for Hindutva.

Ahmedabad started out as a book about Gujarat. Travelling there frequently for a book project around the time of the 2002 post-Godhra attacks on Muslims, I was deeply disturbed by the brutality but also by accounts of ordinary Hindus joining attacks against their own neighbours, of people arriving in cars to loot consumer goods from showrooms and by the visible absence of empathy for suffering victims of the mass violence. I thought of writing a book looking into the recent past for conditions that had enabled the fostering of such a deep and widespread anti-minorityism.

My initial inquiries informed me that what was widely identified as the worst episode of communal violence in post-Partition India was preceded by a long and sustained campaign by Hindutva organisations to effect both a political and an ideological capture of the state. But as I travelled back and forth from Mumbai, where I lived, to Gujarat's commercial capital, Ahmedabad, I realised that the subject I was intending to research had been overtaken by another phenomenon.

Something peculiar was taking place in the city. Every few weeks when I went back it seemed something new had come up: a giant convention centre, a luxury hotel, a flyover, a mall, a highway. The modest, provincial city I knew was transmogrifying before my very eyes.

To call what I was witnessing 'development' would have been a misleading way of communicating the complex set of strategies that were at play there, of which the physical structures were only manifestations. It was a new kind of politics being practised by the state's then controversial chief minister in the aftermath of the 2002 violence, a model if you will. I had a strong hunch that it was going to catapult Narendra Modi to national prominence and find replication at the Central level. I decided to continue looking at Gujarat's recent past but to change my focus and study this model. In doing so I realised also that the conventional frameworks of political understanding would not be able to explain what was happening. I had to look outside them for newer ways.

The first step was to try to make sense of the unusually fast-paced construction underway in Ahmedabad. I learnt that what had struck me so vividly on my visits to the city was not a coincidental coming together of random projects but a planned operation. After the ebbing of violence in 2002, Narendra Modi had presented the adverse coverage of the riots in the national and international media to Gujaratis as a calamity, a blow to the state's *asmita* (pride) that needed to be redressed. He asked the state's people, particularly its business community, to join him in an exercise aimed at changing the negative perception of the state.

In *Shock Doctrine: The Rise of Disaster Capitalism* (2007) Naomi Klein describes how leaders often exploit a crisis to introduce potentially unpopular free market policies counting on the fact that populations may be too traumatised to participate in or resist the change. Sometimes this is done in tandem with developers keen to profit from the mandate for reconstruction.

India's 1991 shift to a capitalist economy was propelled by a fiscal crisis which required an emergency loan of $2.2 billion from the International Monetary Fund (IMF). In 2001, development and government agencies flocked to build a new modern city of Bhuj from the rubble of an earthquake. A couple of years later, Modi embarked on an ambitious exercise to package Gujarat as an attractive business destination. The exercise involved measures such as a biannual 'Vibrant Gujarat Global Summit' for potential investors, the refurbishment of ports and highways in the state and, most conspicuously, the makeover of Ahmedabad.

This last-mentioned feature of Modi's game plan was undertaken against the backdrop of the Indian government's urban upgradation schemes (the 1993 Mega City programme and the 2005 $10,950 Jawaharlal Nehru National Urban Renewal Mission or JNNURM) to encourage the reform and speedy planned development of major cities in keeping with the IMF's credo that cities are the 'engines of growth'.

The atmosphere of fear and grim uncertainty following the protracted mob violence of 2002 and the mythology it built around Modi enabled the packaging exercise to be pushed through with minimal oversight and resistance and with a speed that would have been unimaginable in other circumstances. In 2014 glowing claims about this exercise paved the way to his prime-ministership.

These claims were made most visibly by national television anchors in the lead-up to the 2014 parliamentary elections where they referred repeatedly and with breathless awe to the 'Gujarat model', painting it as a picture of a high-growth, hyper-capitalist model (albeit with poor indices on conventional measures, such as health and nutrition). Had the media done a more in-depth study or looked at available scholarship on the subject, it would have found that the Gujarat model was not only about 'roads, highways and GDP', as it vaguely claimed, but a much more elaborate global process.

Place marketing is a process evolved in the neoliberal era of making spaces, particularly cities, attractive to people and companies with money to spend, mainly transnational corporations, business travellers and tourists. Scholars have identified a number of strategies that are associated with the process, the most common of which is gentrification. Airports are made over, select neighbourhoods are beautified, and special business enclaves and recreational areas with nightclubs and cafes are created. There are several other strategies that cities use to market themselves, including staging large cultural events, sprucing up historical sites or monuments to attract tourists and fostering a service or industrial specialisation.

By 2005, Ahmedabad had acquired the status of a megacity. The state government increased the area of the Ahmedabad Municipal Corporation from 198 square kilometres to 500 square kilometres by merging seven municipalities and expanded the total area of the urban agglomeration to 1,300 square kilometres. Eleven-kilometre-long concrete banks with plans for highways and residential blocks came up alongside the river that snaked through the city. A Gujarat International Finance Tec-City ('double the size of Paris's La Défense and eight times more built up than the London Docklands') was conceived. Ahmedabad's pharma industry and its hospitals, some established as charitable institutions by local philanthropists, were reoriented to brand Ahmedabad as a destination for medical tourism and its old walled city was refurbished to bid for UNESCO World Heritage certification, which it was awarded in 2017. Some of the projects had already been discussed or were underway when Modi became chief minister, but by bringing them under his ambit and clubbing them with new projects, he created an impression of a wide-ranging developmental plan under his leadership.

The Ahmedabad makeover borrowed every rule from the place marketing playbook. But there was a twist in that every element in the Ahmedabad makeover was infused with a Hindutva ideal. For instance, a high street emerging as the new centre of the expanding city acquired a distinctly Hindu ethos while Muslim ghettos on the city margins swelled with refugees escaping mixed neighbourhoods from the city after the 2002 violence. Public space was commodified with a distinct bias towards the Hindu middle class. A new heritage walk focusing on violence in the freedom struggle subtly questioned Gandhi's legacy. Even the city's name was differently spelt to rid it of its Islamic associations.

The remaking of Ahmedabad suggested that the key to explaining Narendra Modi was through his ideological commitments. He is committed to the Hindutva ideology of the Rashtriya Swayamsevak Sangh. And he is committed to neoliberalism. And he is committed to both at the same time.

Conventional thinking in the mainstream media projects India's economic liberalisation programme and Hindutva as two opposing tendencies. The former is perceived as being outward- and forward-looking, cloaked in the accoutrements of modernisation and promises of economic growth and world connectivity, while the latter is seen as being insular and primitive in outlook, peopled by saffron-robed acolytes reliving a mythical past. This construct of economic liberalisation/liberalisation-led development and Hindutva as opposites in the popular media is a false binary.

Hindu nationalism made its presence felt in the early decades of the 20th century but made little headway politically for several decades. It was only in 1989 that the Bhartiya Janata Party (BJP) won 86 seats in Parliament, signalling an upward trend which continued in subsequent years (1991: 120; 1996: 161; 1998: 182; 1999: 182; 2004: 138; 2009: 116; 2014: 282), enabling it to form governments in various states and at the Centre.

The congruence between the timeline of the political ascendancy of the BJP and the onset of structural reforms is not a coincidence. That is when the middle class, the BJP's traditional support base, grew in size from 2.5 million households in 1990 to nearly 50 million in 2015.[1] Television freed from government ownership emerged as the trumpeter of this new consuming class which also came to be culturally defined in upper-caste Hindu terms.[2] The communitarian underpinnings of socialism, which provided a logic to secularism by implying that the weak (minority) were entitled to the protection of the strong (majority), were overturned by a vigorously rapacious individualism.

Economic liberalisation provided a favourable climate for Hindutva to grow. And in turn, I suggest, the rise of Hindutva and the climate of religious conflict have played a critical role in realising the project of economic liberalisation.

Three of the country's most pro-capitalist leaders (Rajiv Gandhi, Bal Thackeray and Narendra Modi) consolidated power on the back of citywide riots. The shaping of Mumbai into a world-class city beginning in the late 1990s saw mill workers forced out of the city, fishing communities displaced, the poor pushed into informal work and large stretches of coastal mangroves destroyed. Workers of the Shiv Sena and other Hindutva affiliates maintained an atmosphere of intimidation through those years by attacking vehicles and television studios and whipping up a fury with their angry rhetoric over a perceived threat to Indian culture and national security from sources such as a Michael Jackson concert, Pakistani cricketers and Valentine's Day celebrations.

As Zoya Hasan claims, resistance to the new economic policies of liberalisation was displaced by Hindutva adherents 'from the realm of concrete economic policy to a confrontation with the cultural politics of globalization'.[3]

Violence in a restructuring society then is a far more complicated business than it appears to be. The celebrated makeover of New York in the early 1990s, for instance, was preceded by a war against homeless people, panhandlers, prostitutes and unruly youth by then mayor Rudy Giuliani. Urban geographer Neil Smith called Giuliani's politics 'revanchist', recalling nationalist reactionaries in 19th-century Paris fighting to reinstate the bourgeois order and wreak revenge on the working class which had 'stolen' their vision of French society from them.

Revanchism creates a hierarchy of claims on citizenship. Justus Uitermark and Jan Willem Duyvendak write in their article 'Civilising the City: Populism and Revanchist Urbanism in Rotterdam': 'Revanchism ... is predicated on a belief system that naturalises as universal the interests and cultural codes of the White middle class while at the same time it essentialises marginalised individuals into subjects who cannot be reformed.'[4]

The dehumanising of those whose fortunes are destined to decline in the new economy is a common feature of restructuring. And it explains why Narendra Modi emerges stronger rather than weaker from allegations of extreme insensitivity, beginning with his harshness towards victims of the 2002 violence to his apparent unconcern for migrants forced to trudge miles after his sudden declaration of a lockdown during the Covid-19 pandemic in 2020.

Every display of callousness magnifies his aura as a capitalist-moderniser and empowers him to act without blowback. He feeds off bellicosity and usefully extends it to a growing list of targets: protesting farmers, students, civil rights activists and political opponents. As Ajay Gudavarthy writes for *Scroll.in*: 'The BJP views the defeated Opposition as prisoners of war. They are deliberately ignored, they are insulted, they are sermonised to, and they are dealt with unfairly. This is an essential feature of the script. ... Behaving unfairly towards minorities is an essential strategy for majoritarian consolidation.'[5]

Much of the commentary on India under Narendra Modi is either about the violence against members of religious minorities and Dalits by Hindutva activists or about the administration's intolerance of dissent and the use of state agencies to punish political opponents and other critics. These align with perceptions of Modi himself. Astute political analysts are thrown by his arbitrary diktats and his obduracy towards petitioners. Modi's effusiveness in greeting foreign leaders, his love for the media glare and his penchant for buying bullet trains and building gigantic statues provoke ridicule. The Central Vista project, which revamped the historic colonial-era Central administrative area in Delhi, had one commentator comparing him to a mid-20th-century African autocrat with a vanity project; another compared him to Mungerilal, a 1980s Indian television soap opera character based on the chronic daydreamer Walter Mitty.

A picture emerges of a fanatical, capricious and megalomaniacal leader, a self-aggrandising man who is so consumed by bigotry that it is impossible to know what he will do next.

It is a compelling image but it is a myth.

Narendra Modi is not a conventional Indian politician. He belongs to the league of capitalist-modernisers like China's Xi Jinping, Turkey's Recep Erdoğan and Brazil's former president Jair Bolsonaro. His motivations are systemic not opportunistic (for the most part) and cannot be understood through the familiar matrix of short-term economic gains and losses and electoral politics that is routinely applied by political analysts.

If we apply the paradigm of the remaking of Ahmedabad, which I would suggest constitutes the Gujarat model to Modi's leadership of India, we can perceive phenomena such as Modi's frequent foreign visits, his 'Make in India' and similar campaigns to encourage manufacturing activity and his passion for the bullet train (a shiny symbol of speed) as elements of a place marketing exercise to sell India to the world.

All of Modi's political moves and programmes, including demonetisation, schemes like the Pradhan Mantri Jan Dhan Yojana to expand the reach of banking and even huge political leaps such as revoking Jammu and Kashmir's special status within the Indian Constitution, become steps (ordering, enumerating, expanding opportunity, extending the formal economy) in a project of neoliberal transformation.

Some borrow directly from Gujarat: the 2014 Swachh Bharat or Clean India Mission extended the logic of a 1997–8 USAID programme in Ahmedabad to improve hygiene and create green spaces to aid the circulation of capital and healthy labour. The hasty beautification of Delhi before the G20 Summit is another instance of the neoliberal preoccupation with appearances. And Modi's partiality to industrial giants such as the Ambanis and Adani corresponds to the heroic, entrepreneurial role marked out for the ultra-rich by Friedrich Hayek, the grandfather of neoliberalism.

The recurring violence and violent rhetoric against minorities serve to consolidate the hegemony of the majority even as Hindutva ideals find expression in the architecture of an emerging India. And Modi's reliance on media advertising is of a piece with the surging role of marketing in the public space.

One can say that if analysed through the correct framework, Modi's thinking, far from being arbitrary and erratic, is formulaic and predictable.

India's democratic backslide too is hardly unique in today's world. Over the past four decades, as country after country has fallen into the embrace of neoliberalism, a new mindset has taken over the world. An economic ideology which projects the market as the answer to mankind's diverse needs and holds profit maximisation as its motto subsumes all other priorities. The state as the medium facilitating the neoliberal dream has demanded a strengthening of its powers and large enough numbers have lustily cheered it on.

Across the world environmental protections and human rights are being weakened or withdrawn. Reports of violence against racial minorities and refugees, the brazen killings of journalists from various places and an unravelling of civil rights in Trump's America confirm the fact that citizens' rights, once thought to be intrinsic to democracy, are being eroded everywhere, even in the world's leading democracy.

In India the line of causation for these phenomena is routinely and unthinkingly drawn to majoritarianism. The widely talked about sociopolitical consequences of neoliberalism, which even filtered into an influential journal of the IMF, the bulwark of the free market, rarely enter into the reckoning (for instance, inequality, which is raging in the world and is currently as high in India as it was in the days of the Raj, according to a recent study by Thomas Piketty and others for the World Inequality Lab).[6]

Indeed, outside of a limited circle of academics and developmental activists, neoliberalism finds hardly any mention. The media and ordinary Indians talk blandly of 'development' and 'privatisation' as if they are standalone activities, not part of a powerful, multidimensional ideology favouring unfettered marketisation and a top-down approach currently dominating the world.

Most Indians, particularly the country's fast-expanding middle class (expected to rise to 715 million in 2030–1),[7] are in love with Western modernity, a feature they share with other post-colonial societies. It is a powerful dream: of unmitigated prosperity through capitalism, an infrastructure equal to the West, the efficiency of the private sector in the public realm and glossy cities resembling Asian favourites Shanghai and Singapore.

A 'new' India is in the process of being born, with ports, bridges, transportation facilities and buildings being constructed or upgraded at a rapid pace. India's road network is now second only to the US and seven bullet train projects are in the planning. There is little evidence in the mainstream media of a public debate about the consequences, priorities and costs, both financial and human, of infrastructural development.

Nor has there been much said about aspects of form and aesthetics despite the powerful cultural and symbolic possibilities of place marketing and branding. The absence of public engagement has left a vacuum that Hindutva has stepped into, as one can see from initiatives such as India's successful lobbying for the United Nations to designate an International Yoga Day and from the birth of a new tourist circuit connecting the temple towns of Ayodhya and Varanasi to Kevadia in Gujarat, the site of the Statue of Unity, a 182-metre-high statue of Sardar Patel.

Ahmedabad continues to occupy a critical place in Modi's gameplan. As prime minister, he has hosted major world leaders there, including the Chinese President Xi Jinping, then Japanese President Shinzo Abe, the Israeli Prime Minister Benjamin Netanyahu and Donald Trump in his first term at the White House. Its new attraction is one of the world's largest stadiums, named after the prime minister himself, where India plans to host the Commonwealth Games in 2030.

The historian Howard Spodek called Ahmedabad India's 'shock city' in the 20th century, the place where many of the nation's most important developments occurred first and with the greatest intensity – from Gandhi's political and labour organising, through the growth of textile, chemical and pharmaceutical industries, to globalisation and the sectarian violence that marked the turn of the new century.

Observing the city at the beginning of the 21st century, I found it as prescient about our times as it was about the previous hundred years. Historically, it was the rulers of the north who wielded power through their wars and military alliances. In an age dominated by the market it is natural that one would look for the ways of power to the place where they received much of their funding from, the mercantile west.

One of India's oldest and most resilient cities, Ahmedabad has a long, hoary history of rebellion, adaptation, pragmatism, experimentation and, above all, a relationship with modernity in its many forms and avatars. In it one can see the possibilities and the realities of our chosen futures.

This preface places *Ahmedabad: A City in the World* in the present context.

ONE

Meraj

'THE POLLUTION WAS SO bad, sister, that if you stood at a *char rasta* you would feel suffocated.'

'At the end of the day your eyes would be burning!'

'Now it is good.'

'You can breathe freely.'

My fizzy drink is flat and warm; it tastes like orange candy. I take small sips, watching the level slowly recede. The boys quaff tobacco from small aluminum foil pouches 'Bhagat', 'Surily Sweet Supari' and 'Goa Silver'.

I sit alone on the bench. The boys stand around it, resting a foot on a stone, leaning their arms on the backrest, but keeping, at all times, a respectful distance from me. Sloe-eyed, loose-limbed young men clustered about the cigarette stall ignore us but a woman with a notebook, accompanied by a group of males, cannot be a common sight in a municipal slum and I suspect curiosity lurks behind the expressions of studied disinterest.

There is much coming and going around us. People enter from the main road through a wide gap in the wall and head for the slum quarters, an identical stream flowing in the other direction. Women, richly dressed, appear to be on their way to a fine event, a wedding perhaps, but it soon becomes apparent that the lustre of cheap thread and gilt and the plastic confections in their hair are just part of their daily armoury against the world. The boys are dismissive of the passers-by. 'Lot of new people now here, sister,' they say, conveying the information in a tone of scoffing derision. '*Bekaar log*, low people ... vulgar types. Start fighting over every small thing. And curse—*baap re baap*! Children. Even ladies. You can't bear it.'

Beyond the oscillating thoroughfare rise the weather-beaten walls of a three-storeyed block of apartments. Iron poles thrust into cement prop up sagging balconies and cracks like lightning streaks are visible on the drab facade. The boys tell me that these are signs of the damage that occurred in the earthquake of 2001, the calamitous earthquake in which entire buildings came crashing to the ground in the city. The injured battlements gloomily look over this wide, open space with its ice gola cart, a cigarette and cold drinks stall, a solitary bench and a few tired, low trees. Shreds of kites flap from overhead wires. In front of us, a small fenced-off ground slowly fills up with rubbish. One of the boys gestures magisterially towards it. 'We have a plan to make a garden here. Fill it up with grass.'

'And trees.'

'... and flowers!'

'This Umesh's nana, you know, was head *maali* for the government parks. His mother was going to help us before she expired. She made the garden for Sophia School. We are determined to develop this vatika.'

I visualize the square with its limp fence and drifting litter transformed into a patch of green. Gardens are all the rage now, a prominent feature of advertisements for upcoming housing projects. Across the river, the swish new colonies have mini playgrounds with mock knolls and slides and swings. Perhaps the boys will try to replicate them, painting them in Disney reds and yellows. Or perhaps they will lay an angular strip of concrete, bordering it with beds of buoyant marigold and fragrant chameli. Instinctively my eyes seek out Meraj, curious to know how he is feeling at this moment, listening to a plan for the future in which he has no part. The 34-year-old Muslim embroiderer is quiet. His eyes, sharp as diamonds, are adrift. The avid enthusiasm that had brightened his features and loosened his tongue, releasing memories and anecdotes of a past life not so much as an hour ago, has dissipated, the animation ebbing away like a retreating tide, making pronounced the hollows of his mildly scarred cheeks, leaving him looking haunted and forlorn.

I first met Meraj in early 2008, in one of the ghettos that have arisen on the outskirts of Ahmedabad city to contain the flotsam and jetsam of Muslims thrust out by waves of communal violence. The movement which started as a trickle in the early 1990s became a flood after 2002, when over a thousand Muslims died across Gujarat in a series of assaults that came to be known collectively by the year of their occurrence.[1] I had been meeting Muslims in the city. I had met Salim, sullen and distrustful, a witness in a case involving the atrocities of '2002' in one of the distant bleak apartment blocks built by an Islamic charitable trust. I had been to Juhapura, Ahmedabad's largest Muslim ghetto, where alongside old, close-set hovels were tall arched entrances to new colonies for middle-class Muslims and, across the road, sprawling bungalows with the nameplates of bureaucrats and businessmen who had recently moved to the ghetto.

In the Muslim-dominated neighbourhood of Jamalpur in the old city, I was surprised to see a giant kite with a photograph of chief minister Narendra Modi of the Hindu chauvinist Bharatiya Janata Party (BJP) widely condemned for his partisan role in 2002. In one of the shops in the lane, all owned by Muslims, were regular-size white kites with the slogan 'MODI IS GREAT— HAPPY NEW YEAR'. The owner, a burly man with henna in his hair, muttering 'it is better to eat than to die', admitted that the warmth towards their bête noire was strategic rather than real, and arising out of a fear of renewed attacks at the time of the state assembly elections that had just gone by. As we talked the mock irony in his tone gave way to a gloomy dissatisfaction with the openly anti-Muslim posturing of the state government. 'Write', he said, with a sudden flash of belligerence. 'Write my name! We all have to die some day!'

A rickshaw driver, wiry and loquacious, with pictures of the Taj Mahal gleaming on the sides of his vehicle, told me he and his friends had stockpiled arms in Jamalpur, ready for any attack from the Hindus. 'I may die but I will take ten down with me.' At a meeting organized to discuss the distribution of compensation awarded by the government for damages suffered in 2002, I heard young Muslim volunteers break into song: '*Angrez nahi zameen par/phir bhi hain gulami/ madad karni hain hame apni* (There are no English in the land/but still there's slavery/we must help ourselves)'.

I heard of random swoops by the police on Muslim localities, scenes that seemed to belong to the West Bank, not to a sleepy neighbourhood in western India. A former corporator and Congress party man, Badruddin Shaikh, glumly contemplating his irrelevance in an avidly pro-BJP environment, told me he was thinking of leaving politics and building a hospital. In one of the few remaining enclaves of Muslims outside the ghetto, an elderly professor of English, meeting me in a flat freshly equipped with an escape route, burst out: 'this divide (between Hindus and Muslims) is stifling!'

And then there was Meraj. I met him while visiting a unit of Sanchetana, a non-governmental organisation working on health and education issues among the underprivileged. The local office was run by a group of largely Hindu women and while talking of the victims of '2002' they thought of Meraj who lived across the street and sent someone to fetch him. He arrived in his workaday clothes, a faded red t-shirt and trousers. Wearing a bright shiny smile, he perched on the edge of a chair as if afraid to fully occupy the space or the moment. Of average height, sallow complexion, with short dark-brown hair and a neat moustache, he was the kind of guy that would melt in a crowd. But there was an eager warmth about him that made him instantly likeable.

Meraj had grown up in the working-class neighbourhood of Asarwa–Chamanpura. His family had lived in a compound of municipal workers where his father owned a *paan ka gulla* (a paan shop). Meraj's childhood was the ordinary childhood of the lower-middle-class Ahmedabadi. He went to the local municipal school, played with his friends in the open square in front of the colony or in one of the houses, flew kites on the terraces, participated in ceremonial swordplay with his brother on Id. Growing up, he studied commerce at a college in Kalupur. Education was not a family forte but Meraj says he had had some notion as a young man of becoming a lawyer.

Why a lawyer, I asked. He smiled sheepishly saying it was something he had seen in the movies and fancied. And then, as if to convey to me that it had been a serious aspiration, he explained how it could not come about. In his late teens he faced a number of obstacles, he said. Helping his father at the shop in the mornings meant missing classes. Then, an outbreak of communal violence in 1992–3 meant he had to stop going to college for six months because the route took him through tense Hindu-dominated neighbourhoods. Worse, his father, fearing an attack, had sent everything that was considered to be of value in the house, including his textbooks, to relatives for safekeeping. Meraj failed his second-year exams. 'Once the line is broken,' he said, 'it is very difficult to connect again.'

Like other young men of uncertain means in the city, though, he had taken the precaution of providing for a back up in the form of a trade skill. He had enrolled himself in an embroidery course near the Relief cinema on Ashram Road. There he had learnt 'plain' and 'fancy' embroidery and stitching. He had bought himself a machine and started doing piecework. In 1994 he got married. The wedding was in Mehsana, 76 kilometres from Ahmedabad, where the bride's family lived; the feast was vegetarian out of deference to her Hindu neighbours. Meanwhile business was picking up. There was a great demand for embroidery and finishing on fabrics headed for the Gulf. Meraj did not deal directly with exports but took on orders from the Sindhi traders of Kalupur, Revdi Bazar and Hari Om Market. He would cycle across every few days to meet with his clients, hiring a rickshaw to bring back the raw material or the 'maal' as he called it.

As the orders mounted, he bought more machines and hired workers. His workshop bristled with reams of cotton, polyester and pashmina, saris and kaftans. The orders were getting so voluminous that he was thinking of buying a second-hand Maruti van. By then he had had three small children and a car would have been useful for family outings as well. But he hesitated. It was not his way to give in to momentary impulses. His priority was to expand the business: if the money would be better spent on buying machinery and hiring workers, then comfort would take a back seat. It was the typically Ahmedabadi way, to suppress present gratification for future growth. Meraj was the quintessential Ahmedabadi entrepreneur, living not randomly but according to a sagacious plan for business expansion. 'I was always saving,' he says. 'Saving, saving, saving. I would take the cycle instead of the motorbike to save on petrol. I would sacrifice all the time just to put money back into the business.'

On February 28, 2002, a mob of Hindu militants had burst in and destroyed everything he owned: household conveniences, vehicles, machinery. 'Cha!' he exclaimed, 'Cha!' still incredulous, six years later, at the manner in which the rioters, with their wanton destructiveness, had rendered his pragmatism impractical and foolish. The cheer faded from his face, his eyes. All at once he seemed to be in a shadow. In the Sanchetana office, in a room full of people, he was alone, wrestling with strangers, sudden and hostile assailants; alone with the ghosts of possessions collected with such care and consideration that they had a meaning beyond mere materialism; alone with the chagrin and the fury of having been demoted, for no fault or fair reason, from the bourgeois life he had so assiduously aspired towards. I sensed that no list of damages, however comprehensive, could account for the feeling of betrayal and rankling injustice that rendered him temporarily incapable of speaking. Finally he muttered: 'I should have just enjoyed my money instead.'

The moment of truculence passed. He resumed his story. Sudden flight with his extended family and Muslim neighbours across the railway tracks behind his house, two years in transit between a refugee camp and relatives, and then he went back. 'My neighbours mobbed me,' he said, breaking into a smile, 'someone passed a five-hundred-rupee note from one side, someone from another. It was like I was the chief minister or something. I felt my house calling out to me. I felt *so bad*!' Meraj, his brother, their families and their father, again set up home in Asarwa–Chamanpura. On the face of it things seemed okay but in reality they were living in terror of a recurrence of '2002'. 'Every time something happened, like a bomb blast ... even if it was far away, it made us so anxious and frightened. We were always checking, fearful that the person away from home would not return.' Finally, tiring of the constant state of apprehension, they all decided to move to an emerging ghetto.

Meraj fidgeted. He crossed and uncrossed his arms, smiled shyly. 'I miss living among Hindus,' he said with a sudden beguiling ruefulness. 'I am glad these *bens* are here.' He indicated the Sanchetana activists in their cotton saris worn in the demure manner of Gujarati Hindu women. 'When I see them across the street, I feel good, I feel like I am in my home in Asarwa–Chamanpura again.' The women laughed with gentle neighbourliness. Asarwa–Chamanpura, what was it like, I asked him.

'*Oh, sister!*' It was as if a light had been turned on over his head. All traces of dejection vanished in a blaze of incandescence. His eyes, his teeth, even the sandy streaks in his hair, lit up with a sparky luminosity. He spread his hands, rattled his head, indicating the impossibility of formulating a satisfactory answer. 'My friends ... the food ... all my neighbours, Hindu, Muslim, we were ... what can I say? It was just ... great!'

It was the first time, through the miasma of horror, callousness, opportunism and injustice that '2002' had come to represent that I had heard the thrum of love and longing; an elegiac strain that had not been mutilated by the need to serve a cause, or render the instant. 'Would you take me there?' I spoke without thinking. I did not expect him to agree but he said yes right away.

*

'You didn't come by car, sister?' is the first thing Meraj said when he saw me arrive in a three-wheeler. In the few weeks that had passed since I had broached the possibility of visiting his former home, I had half expected Meraj to change his mind, realizing upon reflection that there was no need for him to put himself through the agony of relived memories for the sake of a stranger. But he had not backed out and had agreed to meet me on his weekly off. The only concern he expressed, not directly but by dropping numerous clunky hints, such as 'you can come by car' or 'I will wait for your car' and so on, was that we should make our visit in an automobile.

Accordingly, and with some annoyance, I must confess, for I was used to going about my work in an auto-rickshaw, of which the city had a plentiful supply, I had hired a car and set out to fetch him from his new home, off the highway, on the outskirts of the city. The morning had begun inauspiciously. The driver arrived late, then caused a further delay by taking a circuitous route through the old city. At Teen Darwaza, the car broke down. By then, having had enough, I left it with a sense of relief and hailed a three-wheeler. I narrated the sequence of events to a disappointed Meraj, expecting him to take the snafu in his stride. But a few minutes later he was still disconsolate. 'You should have told me, sister,' he said complainingly, 'I would have arranged for a private car.'

I was taken aback by his vehemence. I said I had no way of knowing that the car would break down. It was true, of course, and yet I felt chastened. I had done the needful and hired a car but I had not taken Meraj's keenness to arrive in his former home in a certain style very seriously. Despite its hint of bluster, I suspected it was motivated by a need to salvage some perceived loss of dignity, and suddenly it seemed a trivial request on his part compared with the enormity of what he was willing to share with me. Feeling like I had let him down I cast about for a way to make it right. Would it be okay, I asked him, if I called the rental company and had them send a car to our destination to fetch us when we were done? Oh yes, he agreed joyfully. I made the call and to my relief the matter was settled.

We rode north, circumambulating the serenely glittering arc of the Chandola lake. The Shah Alam dargah was on our right, partially obscured by an encrustation of shops and tenements. I had been there just weeks before with Anwar Tirmizi. Anwar was an activist with Sanchetana and had spent three months working at the Shah Alam Relief Camp in 2002. It was a Friday afternoon, the time of the weekly congregational prayer, when we visited the mosque complex. Stopping on the side, Anwar had drawn a wide semi-circle with his arm, taking within its ambit stone buildings with their domes, double screens and arches, a knot of dusty trees, the compound like a mediaeval Arab town with its throng of devotees, hawkers and beggars, among which a black-robed baba with a peacock feather and a metal cauldron moved about trailing a plume of sweet-scented smoke. The sweep of his arm had indicated the length and breadth of a space, the size of a market square, and invited me to visualize it filled and bursting with the terrified refugees of '2002'. Then he had pointed at a flat-roofed structure flanked by graceful minarets, an outhouse for pilgrims, perhaps, or a stable, deeply recessed and supported by arches and pillars, and said: 'That is where the burn victims and the wounded were treated in 2002 by Muslim doctors. The victims, they were without clothes, burnt so badly ... you couldn't ...' He shuddered, '... you couldn't bear to see.'

Just before entering Asarwa the road ascended, providing an aerial view of traffic scurrying in from the old highway, railway tracks headed for Himmatnagar, a petrol pump and a mill compound surrounded by ancient, burgeoning trees: jungli babul, aduso, limdo and peepul. An ugly modern sculpture raised its twisted discordant metal pillars skywards in the roundabout at Chamanpura Circle. We passed women in bright saris, milk booths, hawkers' carts heaving with sugarcane cubes and bottles of kala khatta and hoardings for television brands. Here and there, a shopkeeper, with a smile of quickening recognition, raised his arm to wave at Meraj.

Asarwa was a village before it became a site for textile mills in the late nineteenth century. The old working class district was evident in the dark-blue signboards of housing colonies, but one sensed a state of somewhat confused growth as well: in its bazaars; the small town; in its prolific businesses of steel, medical equipment, paint and textiles; the metro; and in the mill compounds and the sawdust fumes emanating from desolate lumber yards; the industrial suburb. Underlying these was the sense of old habitation, like a pair of shoes smoothened out by wear. Here were the residential quarters of lower levels of police and municipal staff—stable, securely employed government servants. Here were municipal schools and hospitals and cheap public transport. Here were the improvements made by generations of civic authorities: water-supply systems, drainage, electrical lines and bus services. A long compound wall loomed up, behind which the thin, stained facades of civic housing projects formed a continuous refrain. Meraj exhaled as if he had been holding his breath and slapped the side of the auto-rickshaw to indicate we had arrived.

A wide path ran in an arc, abutting a row of houses comfortably spaced out, each with a small yard out front, partially curtained off from the street by grilles and asbestos sheets. Through the porous walls a hen levitated in a flurry of squawks and brown wings, setting her chicks a-scatter. A mother oiled her daughter's long wavy tresses. The aroma of food cooking on old-fashioned coal stoves hovered over the half-paved narrow lanes. At the beginning of the arc, between the public thoroughfare and the residential part of the colony, in what appeared to be untended no-man's land, the loose mud gave way to wild grass. Meraj stopped. He stretched out his arm, pointing at a spot where bent barbed wire poked out from a loose fence post. 'My father's shop was here,' he said. The mob had torn it down. There was nothing there now; just a tangle of weeds. A few yards away was the house Meraj had grown up in. The doors were open and we walked in. A lady's sharp voice called out from somewhere: 'Who's there?'

'It's me,' Meraj called back.

'Oh,' a woman with a *pallu* on her head and a baby at her waist appeared. 'It's Merajbhai!' she shouted out reassuringly to an elderly lady hovering in the back.

The rooms were joined to each other like compartments in a railway coach. The new occupants seemed to follow an easygoing, semi-rustic lifestyle: just laying down a baby on a mattress or stringing beans in a tray on the floor. There was no furniture, nothing on the walls. I recalled Meraj telling me that when he returned to the colony after the violence he had felt his house 'calling' to him, making him feel 'so *bad*'. I watched as he walked about, touching the walls with an eager, possessive wistfulness.

On the path I had suddenly become aware that we were not alone. A rake-thin man in a yellow shirt and a white floppy hat had joined us. He had slipped in next to Meraj, matching his step with ours so unobtrusively that I could hardly tell he was there. Surprised, I slowed down. The stranger had prominent teeth and eyes that loomed owlishly behind thick glasses. No words were exchanged between the two men but I sensed something had occurred, like the sliding into place of grooves and ridges, the click of interlocking gears, so that though there were two, there could just as well have been one. Meraj introduced us with a vague gesture: 'Umesh', a common Hindu name, particularly among Gujaratis. I smiled, nodded. The men stayed silent, sheepish. The two were evidently close; Umesh had been expecting us. But in my presence, a shyness had set in.

I asked Umesh what he did. I was not surprised when he said he was a tailor. Traditionally a textile manufacturing centre, Ahmedabad had become a supplier of stitched garments. The wholesale market at Gheekanta in the old city, a warren of thin lanes and hole-in-the-wall shops spattered with kid-size jeans, polka-dotted frocks, *salwar-kameez* suits, zari-work *chunnis* and an abundance of men's shirts, was estimated by some to supply half the country's current demand for readymades. We stood for a while talking. Another friend of Meraj's, Satishbhai, a foreman dealing in Compressed Natural Gas, appeared and stood by silently. Then Umesh left and I understood that we were to meet him later.

*

Meraj, Satishbhai and I were at the back of the colony. To our left, barely visible above the jungli babul and peepul trees, was a terrace with a water tank. Meraj pointed. All his life, he said, even at the worst of times when communal tension was running high in the city, he and his family had felt safe knowing that their friend, the influential Congressman Ahsan Jafri, lived so close, right there, in the complex of buildings around the water tank known as the Gulbarg Society. Even that morning, the morning of February 28, 2002, he said his father tried to call and ask for guidance but Jafri had been in no position to help. When the mob arrived at the gate, Satishbhai ran with Meraj and his family through the municipal compound to the back, here where a ditch and a rough path led to the railway tracks. I saw the corrugated tin roof of a railway station and across it a temple shikhara bursting through the latticework of leaves. The signboard on the platform said 'Asarwa'. The tracks raced like slivers of mercury.

'We ran across the tracks,' Meraj said, 'just blindly ran.'

I tried to visualize it. Figures running, footwear scattering, the old stumbling, children wailing. 'Then I saw a mob, another mob coming towards us from there ...' Meraj pointed at a spot further down the tracks. I felt his fear like a knife stab, the flat sunlight hot with menace. It was the first time I had heard of a second mob.

'Did you recognize anyone?' I asked.

'Who looked at the faces, sister?' he said wryly. 'I could only see the swords glinting tim-tim.'

'*Ey, Meraj!*'

A woman's voice called out from the upper storey of one of the drab buildings ranged on one side. There was such delight in her voice, a startled joy at having seen him unexpectedly. We were on our way to the car. A stocky man had come by earlier to tell us that it had arrived and was waiting for us in the small open ground between the houses and the highrises. Almost immediately my cellphone had rung; the driver was at the other end, irate at having been asked to wait inside a 'slum' colony. I told him we wouldn't be long. Now as we struggled towards it, I could see the car surrounded by children touching its metal body and looking at it with awe. The driver stood marooned and morose in the middle of the small crowd. Our group had expanded to include two small boys in soccer sweatshirts and Ramesh, a salesman in a clothes store. At the sight of Ramesh, Meraj had started and embraced him with a cry. Now he explained to his friends with an air of gratification that I had hired a car for the occasion.

Umesh's home was approached through a small open yard. A few steps led to a toilet which stood outside the house. The house itself was tiny, just a room about 300 square feet in size. One side of it was the kitchen, neatly arrayed with gleaming vessels; the other was the sitting area, furnished with chairs and a high bed that doubled as a settee. The walls were decorated with myriad representations of Hindu gods and goddesses. Laxmi radiated rays of embossed silver, Shiva struck a pose of magnificent and graceful rage. Umesh's father, an elderly man with a stiff manner that gave the impression of a physical handicap, was ensconced in a chair. Umesh's sister, a pretty woman in a house dress, welcomed us with eager smiles and set about making tea. Satishbhai left to attend to something outside. The rest of us went in.

Soon the small tube-lit room was reverberating with laughter. Umesh and Meraj ribbed Ramesh about his sartorial style: he was wearing a pair of dark jeans with chains looped at the knee. All three men flaunted signs of their professional expertise. Meraj had an embroidered detail on his shirt pocket and Umesh had gaudy patches on his stitched jeans. Ramesh, they informed me with an amusement the subject seemed to share, had a weakness for metal embellishments and because he was petite and could not get clothes his size in a store he was always buying jeans with metal doo-dahs and cutting them to fit. And then it was Umesh's turn to be teased. 'You see his hat?' Ramesh asked, at which Umesh grinned bashfully. 'He always has it on. Not any kind of hat, only this kind that umpires and wicketkeepers wear.' Unsurprisingly, it turned out that Umesh was the wicketkeeper in their erstwhile weekly games. Like young men all over the subcontinent, these three were passionate about cricket. In the past, on a clear Sunday like this one, they would have been out playing in the open ground in front of the colony with a propped-up thin cement sheet for a stump. Meraj, they told me, was a superb bowler, 'faster than Shoaib Akhtar!'

Meraj, a baseball cap clamped front-to-back on his head, was on the edge of his chair almost rising out of it with excitement. Being back in his familiar environment surrounded by old friends and neighbours seemed to have overwhelmed him, while the invitation to retrace the cherished past for my benefit had rendered him garrulous. He scrupulously supplemented the conversation with such details as he felt necessary for me to better understand his life in Asarwa–Chamanpura, adding zestful observations. The conversation had moved from cricket to schooldays and he was commenting on the lady teachers in his municipal school. 'The make-up they wore,' he said, shaking his head incredulously, 'baap re baap!'

I looked around the cozy room, at Umesh's sister, a woman beyond the conventional marriageable age, enjoying the banter and arranging tea cups on a tray; at Umesh's father whose dour silence I found unnerving though it did not seem to bother the young men one bit and they frequently brought him into the conversation with respectful allusions. Umesh's mother, the woman with the green thumb who would have made a garden for the colony, had died some years previously. It seemed to me an air of tragedy hung over the household; perhaps it was an intimation of ill health for a few months later Meraj would inform me that the gangly Umesh, his close friend, had died of a sudden brain hemorrage; or perhaps it was just an unarticulated sense of loss. On the face of it, it would appear as if the Muslims, Meraj and his family for instance, had suffered by being compelled to leave their home; but in fact, with their departure, a familiar way of life had ended for everybody in the colony.

I realized then that the fact of severance, and more importantly the reason for the severance, had been there all along. Underneath the chatter and the joy of reuniting it was there, like moisture in the air or wires buried in walls, invisible but palpable, unseen but potent, a dull leaden consciousness permeating the everyday and the forever. Time had not altered anything. The consequences of '2002' were real and unrelenting.

As if picking up on my thoughts the young men began to talk about the day it happened, the day the mob descended on the colony in February 2002. 'I kept watch at the gate and when I saw the crowd coming with swords and dharias, I rushed in to tell them that they should escape,' Umesh recounted. Just after they had made their exit the mob burst in. Umesh and Ramesh began to describe how the men took things out of the house and the workshop and piled them up. Meraj got up abruptly and left the room. When he returned minutes later the rims of his eyes were red. To cover the awkwardness he mock-cuffed the small, solemn-faced sweatshirt-clad boys who had accompanied us and were sitting on the bed, making them laugh and wriggle out of his reach. Before the attacks in 2002, Umesh, Ramesh and Meraj had been part of a group of fifteen young Muslims and Hindus who did everything together: roaming around, flying kites, going for movies, marriages, funerals, festivals. 'One time we could not live without each other,' Umesh said. 'Now we are all scattered.'

We are on the bench watching the people of the quarters go by. The sun moves overhead. The rubbish continues to collect in the fenced square in front of us. The boys begin to talk about a boy called Kallu. Kallu was a Muslim. He was Meraj's cousin, an embroiderer in his workshop. Unlike Meraj he opted to stay on in the colony after 2002, though it is unclear whether he actually owned or rented premises or roomed with kindly neighbours. From the way the boys describe him I begin to visualise an individual of Herculean charm. He had rosy cheeks, curly hair and eyes that reeked of mischief, they told me. His fame was spread across the neighbourhoods of Shahibaug, Gomtipur, Saraspur and Meghani Nagar. He was loved by all. He was the kind of guy who got kids together for an impromptu game of cricket; the kind of guy who threw himself into acrimonious situations to make peace. There was an elderly woman in the colony who would not eat till he had come home and an old uncle who nagged him about his excessive drinking. When he was in hospital with a swollen liver armies of children visited him. And he had died, five months ago, at the age of twenty-two.

After he died ... and this is what they were talking about when I interrupted them with questions about who Kallu was and what he had meant to them ... after he died, the colony collected money, two steel tubs of it. And they engaged the city's well-known bhajan singer Hari Bharwad for an all-night performance. The shindig had cost around Rs 50,000. They put up strings of lights. They hooked up a sound system. They organised seating. They even hired a television set to telecast the performance for the additional crowd that had gathered. And right in the centre, they had prominently placed a large photo of Kallu. Kallu was the local hero. The funeral procession had been huge and the people of the colony would have arranged this as well had the family not taken over the body. In any case, the boys claim, Kallu's memory is being further perpetuated by a cricket tournament: matches between local teams with Kallu's picture dominating the proceedings.

I listen to their impassioned narration with some perplexity. 'So Kallu was a Muslim,' I say, 'and he was so very beloved but houses in the colony were attacked not so long ago because they belonged to Muslims ...?' I wonder if there is a degree of compensation here. Could it be that a community that had failed to protect its neighbours, people who had lived amidst them for years, shared their joys and sorrows, felt a collective guilt that was being expiated by the relentless commemoration of a Muslim boy who had died of natural causes? But when I try to shape this idea into a question, the boys look at me uncomprehendingly. The notion is too abstract, too remote. They continue to talk about Kallu instead. 'He had such a good *swabhav*. Like a minister's his funeral procession was! In our quarters all of us felt so bad. Nobody would have thought he was Muslim. There is no feeling of festival after Kallu died.'

*

It is late afternoon when we arrive at the gates of the Gulbarg Society. The three Special Reserve Police personnel deputed to keep watch on the Society regard us with torpid, suspicious eyes. Meraj disappears and reappears having located the man who has the key to the compound.

The Gulbarg Society was built in the 1960s at the initiative of lawyer and politician Ahsan Jafri. Jafri was the son of a doctor who came to Ahmedabad from the Burhanpur district of Madhya Pradesh and set up a clinic in the city's blue-collar district. Jafri, influenced perhaps by his father's clientele of migrant mill workers, gravitated to left-wing politics, joining the Congress in the early seventies, attracted by the socialist rhetoric of its young leader Indira Gandhi. He was not untouched by the entrepreneurial tug of his adopted city, though, and proposed to his Muslim neighbours in Dr Gandhi's *chawl* in Asarwa–Chamanpura, where he lived, that they should take advantage of the liberal housing loans being handed out by the state, buy a plot of land, and construct a society. So the Gulbarg Society came about, a genteel complex of bungalows generously spaced out with spreading trees and a high surrounding wall giving it a measure of privacy and exclusion rare in the shabby neighbourhood.

On February 28, 2002, however, Gulbarg Society became the scene of one of the most vicious attacks on Muslims and Ahsan Jafri the pogrom's most high-profile victim. Accounts of the Gulbarg Society massacre convey the atmosphere of a gladiatorial arena with thousands surrounding the compound in a siege that lasted seven hours. Among the crowd were many Waghris from the neighbourhood. Waghris, members of a backward community stigmatised by the now-defunct British Criminal Tribes Act, were actively wooed by pro-Hindutva organisations and used alongside other marginalised social castes and tribes in 2002 to perform crude acts of violence that upper-caste Hindus might have shuddered at.

The Police Commissioner visited Jafri in the morning and promised to send help. Jafri made calls to the chief minister, the state home minister and local Congress leaders, but to no avail. A mob, estimated variously to have been between 5,000 and 20,000, collected outside the colony and breached the walls and the locked gates. Sixty-nine Muslims, many of whom had crowded into Jafri's house for safety, were killed. Jafri himself was stripped, paraded, his fingers cut off, then his hands and feet, before being trussed by the neck with a forklike object and dragged down the road and tossed into a fire. The Concerned Citizens Tribunal reports that residents of the area saw neighbourhood goons playing cricket with the skulls of the dead.

The most eerie thing about the Gulbarg Society now is the sound of the leaves. They lie everywhere, shrivelled, dry, yellow. They cover the neat wide pathways that run around the low whitewashed houses. They lie on the swelling mounds around the bungalows. They fall from the trees, dropping lightly, incessantly, softly to the ground. The cosy cul de sac is a ghostly place. The three-storey building, at the far end of the compound, a later addition comprising eight flats and a row of shops, looms abjectly. All signs of life—and there must have been plenty of it here once: the colour of wet clothes on a line, the warbling of a television set, the shrieks of children at play—have been stamped out. There is only the sound of crushed leaves underfoot.

There is rubble in the houses and air conditioners bent with heat. The windows are naked with glass panes occasionally cracked. The rooms of Ahsan Jafri's house are bare. The bathroom has a smashed commode. Stones, thick dirt and the drying excrement of stray animals are on the floor. The ceiling and walls are blotchy and blackened with soot. The flames destroyed, among other things, Jafri's library, his collection of books spanning a range of subjects: culture, religion, philosophy. In the now-ravaged room on the ground floor was once his office with a desk, a revolving chair, two sofas and his law books, including bound volumes of the All India Reporter; Ahsan Jafri had returned to the bar after his stint in Parliament and was a familiar figure at the Mirzapur Courthouse. Meraj, coming up behind me, points. 'His table was here ... he used to receive visitors on a sofa there.' He is remembering a time before the brutality, an older time when Jafri was alive and eminent and exuded the expansive comfort of a banyan tree.

In many ways Jafri was a throwback to the past. Photographs of him in earlier days show a handsome man in a safari suit with a broad forehead and a thick shock of hair, standing at the edge of a group around Indira Gandhi, leading an anti-war procession, fasting for communal harmony, joining an official delegation to Kabul in the 1970s, courting arrest in 1977 and so on. In an old interview broadcast on All India Radio he can be heard, talking in chaste Urdu, about the concept of 'watan' (homeland) and the natural beauties of Hindustan. Erudite, cultured (he was president of the Gujarat unit of the Indo-Soviet Cultural Society and wrote Urdu poetry), progressive and international in outlook, he typified the secular, intellectual Muslim that gravitated to the Congress party. His work for the party, as a member of parliament in 1977 and after, had made Gulbarg Society a bastion of the Congress. For Muslims, particularly those from the lower socio-economic class, used to being blown about like chaff by ordinary vicissitudes, he was a pillar of strength. By demonstrating Ahsan Jafri's vulnerability, his assailants had also shown the ineffectuality of an ideology and a party. Indeed they had conveyed the message that, under the new dispensation, to be like him was to court trouble. Like the mafia the old godfathers had to be beheaded before the new could hold sway.

The air rattles with the scraping, scratching, sighing sound of leaves eddying with the breeze. There are no people here, just nineteen empty bungalows surrounded by a wall, a spreading limda tree and a carpet of yellow leaves. There is a proposal, I have heard, to turn the Gulbarg Society into a museum, a memorial against communal violence. I think it could be left just as it is.

One of the SRP constables on duty outside Gulbarg has trailed in behind us. He is a tall, somewhat ludicrous figure in khaki pants that stop above his ankles and a .303 rifle protruding from his stooped shoulders. I feel anxious, concerned that he is about to invoke his authority to ask us to leave before we have had a chance to look around. But he just follows us around shuffling through the leaves, silent and awed. I talk to him a little. His name is Sunil Chavan. He is from Raigad in Maharashtra; his grandfather was in the service of the Baroda maharaja and his father brought the family to Ahmedabad in 1970. He belongs to a family of security personnel. His father and brother are in the SRP and a brother is in the police force. He tells me he has been on duty at the site for some months but he has never been inside before. And then he volunteers the information that his family lives in the SRP camp in Naroda Patiya.

The settlement known as Naroda Patiya was the site of an assault larger in scale than even Gulbarg. Ninety-seven Muslims were killed there on February 28, 2002. It was there too that a pregnant woman's belly was slit open with a sword and her foetus removed and tossed into a fire. The incident, so disquieting in its obvious inhumanity, would become a metaphor for the depravity of the events of the time. I ask him with tense anticipation if he had been there that day. He shakes his head. No, he was on duty in the state capital, Gandhinagar. But, he adds, he did have to rush home that day in a police car. 'I got a message that my mother had collapsed. She had a heart attack when she saw the bodies of victims in Naroda Patiya. She died.' I look for a trace of irony in his trusting eyes and find none.

*

The Naroda Industrial Area came up on the north-eastern edge of the city in the 1980s, developing around the Naroda Industrial Estate, established by the state's Gujarat Industrial Development Corporation at the dreary point where National Highway 8 intersects with National Highway 59. To get to Naroda, one passes through a sea of tarred roads and tin sheds. A dull greyness coats the landscape, unrelieved by the daubs and tints of habitation. In this desolate sprawl, a few kilometers west of the Industrial Estate and a kilometre north of Naroda Patiya, is the township of Kuber Nagar, the largest concentration of Sindhis in Ahmedabad. Sindhi Hindus, a prosperous mercantile community, fleeing from the Sindh province of Pakistan following Partition, arrived in Ahmedabad in large numbers in 1947–8. Ahmedabad, accommodating towards the refugees, established a camp in Kuber Nagar and provided them with space to set up small businesses in the city market. But while they sympathized with their plight and acknowledged their entrepreneurial instinct, Gujaratis apparently baulked at the prospect of social contact with the newcomers. According to Rita Kothari, Ahmedabad-based author of an anthropological work on Sindhis in Gujarat, Jain and Hindu upper castes regarded Sindhis, with their meat-eating ways, their indifference to ritual purity and their use of the Arabic script, as being imperfect Hindus, 'half Muslims' really. For Sindhis, forced to flee their homeland in ignominy by the Muslim, this perception, says Kothari, came to be a source of deep and abiding shame.

The doleful reverberation of banged metal punctuated by the sputtering rev of engines suggests that we are in the vicinity of the Naroda State Transport Workshop. This charcoal landscape is pitted with the illegal liquor stills of the Chharas, a denotified community like the Waghris. It is the kind of place that arouses fear and repugnance in the burghers of the city. Hereabouts, according to various reports, on February 28, 2002, a swarm of Chharas led by leaders and activists of the BJP and its ideological ally, the Bajrang Dal, stormed in and set about killing, raping and burning with a fervidity that seemed to evoke images of frenzied consumption. The assailants would later talk of their female victims as 'fruit' and their acts as 'pickling'. A journalist colleague of mine saw men squirming all over a half-destroyed mosque like 'ants on a sugar cube'. First Information Reports filed with the police would identify as an instigator Maya Kodnani, a gynaecologist from Kuber Nagar, the locality's MLA and Gujarat's first Sindhi minister. Witnesses claim they saw the slim, bespectacled woman moving around on the streets of Naroda that fateful day, distributing arms and exhorting the mob to hunt and kill Muslims.

We notice a chai stall set up against a wall and stop to ask for directions to Naroda Patiya. The men hunched on the long benches in front of it regard us with grim suspicion. There is some hurried confabulation, then a man, without asking, gets into the front seat and tells the driver which way to go. A huddle of rooftops comes into view. The inhabitants of Naroda Patiya are mostly migrants of recent origin from other parts of the country, arriving over the last decade or two, to work as day labourers. This drifting, grimy, out-of-the-way habitation is starkly different from Gulbarg with its settled air and leafy trees. Yet both were sites of highly symbolic assaults. The Gulbarg massacre had as its central motif the subjugation of a threateningly powerful male, while the attacks in Naroda Patiya revealed a manic urge to possess and annihilate the threateningly desirable female.

Naroda Patiya, when we find it, is a warren of sad lanes running past scrawny, close-set houses. The man from the tea stall has accompanied us all the way in and is eager that I meet 'Masterji' who I assume is a person of some education and for that reason a spokesperson of sorts. We find his door locked. My guide is deeply disappointed. He scrawls Masterji's number on a piece of paper, hands it to me and leaves. There is an unusual quiet around us. The dwellings are silent as lighthouses. No curious eyes peek out of windows, no crowds collect. The loose sand gets in between my toes. The sun is in my eyes; I could be walking among coffins. When the attacks began the residents fled in terror to the tall apartment blocks behind the colony. One of the women who managed to make it to the terrace where a few hundred others had taken refuge told a fact-finding team for the Citizens' Initiative of Ahmedabad how she, along with the others, helplessly watched women from her neighbourhood being raped and burnt to death on the road. 'The girls screamed so loud that even now, when I remember, my blood boils.'

Meraj and I make our way to the Special Reserve Police Quarters behind the colony. The houses are markedly different from the humble dwellings we have left behind. They are larger, with narrow porches, and set wider apart. I had read that some of the Muslims running from the onslaught of the mob were sheltered here by a Muslim commandant; the rest were beaten back. I locate the Chavan household. The beam of a television set and a bare-chested man in a dark room are visible through the window but we have to wait several moments before he answers the door. It is Suryakant Chavan, Sunil's brother. I tell him we met his sibling at the Gulbarg Society. He lets us in. The living room has plastic flowers in a vase and an embroidered panel that says 'Home Sweet Home'.

I ask him if he was home on February 28, 2002. No, he says, he was on duty, in the neighbourhood of Shahibaug, a few kilometers to the west. Apparently, Muslims under attack in the Patiya had come running into the SRP enclave to protect themselves and his mother watching from the window collapsed, her low blood pressure aggravated by shock. She died the following day. He was informed and came home immediately, travelling part of the way by train and by police van from Kalupur station. 'We felt very bad about what happened,' Suryakant says about the attacks. 'They were all workers, no ill-will in their hearts. My father and we brothers have seen this sort of thing on duty, but our mother, she had not witnessed this before.' We fall silent. But we cannot stay long. Suryakant's wife and children are waiting to go out. As we are about to take our leave, I ask him if there is a photograph of his mother that I could see. He leads us into the bedroom. Next to the bed is a dressing table with a small bust of Shivaji, the Maratha who fought the Mughals. On the wall is a large photograph of Parvati. It shows a heavy, sweet-faced woman with shiny, high cheekbones. Her large round *bindi* is slightly off centre and the hint of a smile plays around her lips.

*

I hear the driver and Meraj exclaim excitedly as we pass a hoarding. 'Kiran Jadugar!' Meraj cries. 'He is a great magician! He can make mantris and tigers disappear!' All around us is open land pitted with ditches and the occasional creek. Electric wires dance from pole to pole.

The driver who has been quiet through the day is suddenly chatty. He is a Muslim, it turns out, and my interest in visiting the sites of mayhem in 2002 appears to have mollified him. Or so I think. 'I know the graveyard where they buried the Naroda Patiya victims,' he says. 'A journalist had come from Delhi and I drove him everywhere in 2002.'

'Maybe you can take me around as well,' I suggest.

The driver casts a sideways look at Meraj. 'Now you will be of no use,' he says mockingly. 'She has found a new *bakra*! All *patrakars* [journalists] are the same.'

*

'Look at the road!' Meraj says. We are still on the highway and the road is indeed a marvel, a wide ribbon of shimmering tar. '... Perfect!' After a few silent seconds he adds: 'You know Narendra Modi is really a capable man.' I am taken aback, not sure that I have heard right. Could Meraj be praising the chief minister? Meraj, with his keen sense of injustice and hurt, could he be complimenting the person so widely perceived to have abetted the violence against the Muslim community? Meraj continues as if he has said nothing out of the ordinary. 'He is a perfect CM for this state actually ... if only ...' he gives me a confiding look, 'he wasn't such a hardliner.' I am nonplussed. Having heard Meraj narrate his story, having witnessed his fear, his anger, his frustration and his pain at the circumstances and the people who ousted him from his home and demolished the business he had so assiduously built up, I am puzzled by his recommendation of the man responsible for his plight. But Meraj is looking straight ahead as if unaware of anything that should cause consternation or any contradiction that needs to be explained. And I am suddenly reminded of something similar that occurred earlier in the day.

When we were in Asarwa–Chamanpura, Meraj had wanted me to meet a neighbour, a friend of his mother's, but she was not home and we were left talking to a sullen relative of hers, a Hindu man in a stiff baseball cap. I noticed that he had the BJP lotus tacked on the wall and I was surprised that Meraj did not appear in any way uncomfortable with that. I was even more surprised by his response, a few minutes later, when our host, after a few desultory conversational starts, began to express his views on Narendra Modi and Muslims. The chief minister was to be commended, he said, for 'disciplining' Muslims. I looked at Meraj expecting him to be offended but instead found him nodding in agreement. 'Eighty per cent of Muslims are good,' the man thundered on, 'but 20 per cent are bad. They are spoiling other Mohammedans ... See now this boy is hard-working,' he pointed at Meraj, who looked suitably modest, 'but many were openly doing *daaru*, *adda*, gambling. They were talking of bombs, praising Pakistan. The CM stopped it. He is just jailing all troublemakers. But now that he has disciplined them there is order, there is hope.' Meraj, still deferential, continued to nod.

'Ahmedabad is a mega city. See the roads and flyovers! See the BRTS![2] In ten years all this will bear fruit. The future is great!'

*

The high grey wall of the Gujarat Industrial Development Corporation on the Khokra road comes into view. The wall is brand new, as is the gate and the smart awning with A-P-P-A-R-E-L P-A-R-K written in capitals. Behind the walls, where once a leading mill used to be, are thirty-eight pristine hectares of space, a Special Economic Zone for the garment business, unveiled by Chief Minister Modi just a few months ago. Meraj brightens. He bristles in his seat with excitement. 'This is an international market! It will be very good for exports!' I remember that he is an embroiderer of garments for export, that he once aspired to own a large business. His eyes follow the long grey walls covetously till they slip out of sight. The city falls away. We join the rumble of buses and trucks piled high with goods for distant towns. Exhaust fumes thicken the air. Meraj adjusts his cap. I leave him on the Narol Road and watch him walk away, a lone figure, receding into the distance.

TWO

The River

THE PEAKS AND RIDGES of the Aravali rise a thousand to three thousand feet. The hills are humped over a swathe of desert wilderness in the Indian north-west, running over 560 kilometres across Rajasthan, with isolated rocky offshoots continuing all the way to south Delhi. They are rich in minerals, especially rose quartzite. The Sabarmati takes birth in the crystalline heart of this range. It is a deep-digging river at its source, perforating the hillside, throwing up jagged cliffs on either bank. As it flows downhill, its penetrating force is blunted, enabling it to flow languidly over pelted rock and jungle, tripping over shingles and boulders, shuddering over uneven hilly tract before dropping to the plains.

There was a time when the Sabarmati was wont to drain its meagre waters into the west-flowing Rupen. Over time, over hundreds and thousands of years and moving bit by infinitesimal bit, it deviated to chart its own course southwards, forming flat, silver arcs in the arid region of north Gujarat, meandering through the semi-alluvial lands of the south, to debouch through the Gulf of Cambay or Khambhat and thereon into the Arabian Sea. In a land of great rivers, the 371-kilometre-long Sabarmati is a modest entity. Its name, said to be derived from the word 'shvabhra', meaning 'fissure', suggests a cavity, appropriately, for the Sabarmati is marked by recurrent spells of dryness that turn it into a thin, sad trickle of mica and sometimes cause it to disappear altogether. But it is also a temperamental river and there is no telling when it will bloat and billow and froth over its banks, toppling trees and houses and swallowing cattle and people in its furious wake. The shallow, capricious Sabarmati is not navigable. No great pilgrimage centres line its route and no prayers are intoned in its honour. Encyclopaedic references find it worthwhile only to mention that the great city of Ahmedabad was established on its banks in 1411.

The sun beats down on the old city in a photographer's frame, bleaching the stone façade of a sixteenth-century gate. A retreating auto-rickshaw is affixed like a jewel in the shadow of the central arch. An apartment block looms over traffic lights in the distance. A woman, head covered, walks towards an empty vendor's cart. Posters for a Hindi film are peeling off the gate. In the foreground, in the shadow cast by an old house outside the frame, a cow munches something off the street.[1] Settlements rise and disappear repeatedly in the course of history. Cattle bones uncovered in the loamy soil at Thaltej suggest the existence of a grazing ground in the post-Mesolithic era. Late stone-age tools unearthed at Vatva and an eleventh-century Hanuman carving found near the Chandola provide clues to other kinds of life that might have existed alongside the Sabarmati over time. The gleaming contours of the twenty-first century uber city that is modern Ahmedabad rise up on the western bank of the river: flinty highways, pyramids of acrylic and glass. On the eastern bank, one finds the shattered chrysalis: gaunt stone monuments dating back to the fifteenth century when the Muslim king Ahmed Shah founded the city.

The founder of Ahmedabad lies under a high, striated dome, covered by a maroon and green satin shroud. The bleating of a little goat can be heard outside where the clothes of the caretakers living about the rauza are hung out to dry. The sun falls in lazy triangles on the portico. Three pairs of footwear are scattered at the threshold. A bearded man with a prayer cap emerges from the shadowy interiors and watches me moving about the corridor, a camera in my hand. As I approach, he indicates the richly draped mound in the central chamber and says with a ponderous solemnity: 'This is the grave of Badshah Ahmed Shah who founded this city.' He points at the inscription scrawled in Urdu on the lintel and adds meaningfully: 'Ah-*med*-a-bad'. His expression in the dusty gloom suggests that he could say more but he chooses not to. It is not hard for me to interpret the meaning of his gesture and the deliberate manner in which he stretches out the name of the city and emphasizes the second syllable.

In 1987 when the BJP came into power in the Ahmedabad Municipal Corporation, it mooted a proposal to change the name of the city to 'Karnavati', the name of the town or military outpost which may have been established by the Hindu Solanki king Karnadev on the banks of the Sabarmati, preceding the founding of Ahmedabad. The proposal was rejected by the central government. Nevertheless, BJP councilors and party members began to refer to the city as 'Karnavati' in public forums. In August 2010, the Ahmedabad Municipal Corporation began calling itself the 'Amdavad Municipal Corporation' and changed the English spelling of the city's name on its logo and on its stationery and billboards. Even though the new name was not made official, and was made out to be merely a spelling change to reflect the way it was pronounced in the vernacular, there was no doubt that the shift was intended to rid it of its Islamic associations, specifically the fact that the city had been founded by a Muslim king. Now in this high-ceilinged structure it is hard to ignore history.

*

Shifting states of assimilation and separation have been a recurrent theme in the evolution of the region east of the Rann of Kutch between Mount Abu in the Aravali range and the Arabian Sea. Like a rocky outcrop on a beach, in turns submerged and exposed by the tides, the land mass that has come to constitute the modern state of Gujarat has been subject to the alternating intensities of centralised power. Great empires, such as the Mauryas and the Guptas, wrapped their arms around it in the third century BC and fifth century AD respectively, and at other times, under local satraps like the Solankis, who ruled from AD 942 to 1244 and, more briefly under the Vaghelas, it exercised autonomy. In the late thirteenth century Alauddin Khalji brought it under Delhi rule. When Timur Lane launched an attack on Delhi, the Governor of Gujarat was Muzaffar Shah, the son of a Punjabi Hindu convert to Islam. In 1407, in the uncertain conditions created by the attack on Delhi, Muzaffar was persuaded against his inclinations to proclaim himself the Sultan of Gujarat. Three years later he was succeeded by his twenty-year-old grandson and heir, Ahmed Shah, who would build himself a new capital on the banks of the Sabarmati.

The story of Ahmed Shah's decision to build the new city is depicted in oral tales and woven tapestries, paintings and childish scrawls. They show a hare chasing a pack of hunting hounds. Scholars say the visual symbolises an act of defiance by the small against the mighty, an allegory of self-assertion at a time of a weakened empire and rising regional powers. One is tempted to suggest that the move could also be read as a posthumous act of defiance by Ahmed Shah against his grandfather, the reluctant secessionist. Historical narratives hint that he may have handed a poisoned chalice to the elderly Muzaffar to hasten his accession, that his austerity and the long solitary hours he would subsequently spend on the puffy stone floor of his private mosque in the south-west corner of the Bhadra citadel were an outcome of remorse deep and wracking.

Parricide, a malignant leitmotif, recurred through the course of the Gujarat Sultanate; unnatural death, often by poisoning, would claim six out of nine Sultans. That baleful propensity, hanging like a dust storm over medieval Gujarat, would still leave room for instances of protracted rule and expansionist battles. Many of these battles were against Hindu princes and the form of subjugation employed by the Sultanate's rulers, pious Islamists, included destructive raids on temples. In Agra marble monuments speak of love and grace; in Delhi minarets and tombs evoke a past grandeur. In Ahmedabad, the stone monuments of the Sultanate era, the mosques, the *rauzas*, the tanks and the gates, are born of antithesis and miscegenation. In them, the lust for power is bested by the tempering effects of piety, and the violent vanquishing urge manages to carve out a strange, hybrid beauty.

Inside the old Jami Masjid the light filters in thinly from the high clerestory, filling the hall with a pale evening glow. One could be in a cave, a deep sanctuary hacked out of a mountainside. One could be in a forest trampling the dark undergrowth. The mourning, heavy walls recede into darkness. In the gloaming two hundred and sixty pillars are massed, like trees or soldiers, frozen in time. Bare feet traverse an uneven floor of large stone slabs, each a different shade. A solitary mat, long and narrow, lies between the pillars. The dark gathers behind the carved façade of a floating box where once women came in to pray unseen. On a distant wall, a pierced screen flares like a diamond suspended in the dense air. Toranas, lotuses, the curling limbs of the kalpavruksh and other vernacular flourishes chiseled by Hindu and Jain craftsmen, or pillage from temple raids, fill niches and decorate the bases of the swaying minarets which toppled over in an earthquake in 1819. On the threshold of the mosque, embedded in the floor, is a large slab of black marble popularly believed to be the plinth of an image from a Jain temple.

*

In the shallows of the Sabarmati, the Kagdis would stand in pairs, facing each other, between them a bag of macerated pulp made of discarded ropes, fishermen's nets, rags and hemp. Muslims of Arab descent, the Kagdis lived in the village of Kochrab (the name possibly a corruption of the phrase 'kuch i Arab'—habitation of Arabs) by the river. Their paper-making skills were probably acquired from the Chinese and travelled down the ages. Paper was used in Cambay in the early fifteenth century when much of India was writing on leaves. And travelogues from the seventeenth century record the variety of papers produced in Ahmedabad. From the gold-bordered 'fashion papers', much in demand in the Muslim countries of the Gulf and used for issuing invitations by persons of rank and wealth, to the cheap *barigoria* used for accounts and legal purposes.

Gujarat's long, curved coastline, giving on to the rugged terrain of Central Asia, has made for an itinerancy, a nomadic strain, relentless as the ebb and flow of the tide. For centuries peoples have washed over the Gujarati peninsula. Pastoralists, shepherds, hardy horsemen, dauntless warriors, invaders, plunderers, travellers and saints trudging in overland, while the tossing sea brought canny traders, sunburned sailors, shipbuilders, scholars and geographers. One can hear the call of the sea in the emptiness of the vast courtyard of the Jami

Masjid in which the faint lines between the stone slabs seem to run into eternity. The burnished horizon, visible from hundreds of kilometres of the sandy coastline, filled the Gujarati with an awareness of immense possibility. Meanwhile, the items of exchange brimming in the market place—silk and porcelain from China, Indonesian spices, Arabian horses, European wool—agitated him with schemes of profit.

The saliferous air affected everyone it touched with the spirit of entrepreneurship and commerce: Brahmins neglected their traditional occupations of priesthood and scholarship and took up trade, Kshatriyas and Rajputs left soldiery. Akbar, native of the mountainous reaches of Central Asia, first came upon the sea when he took over Gujarat in 1573; the Mughals thereafter would rely heavily on oceanic trade. New commercially oriented Islamic sects like the Bohras originated in Gujarat; the Parsis, descendants of Persians who had fled oppression and taken shelter on the Gujarat coast in the eighth century, were consummate entrepreneurs and even children designed games of commodity speculation.

And the kings too, conquerors and tyrants, bowed before commerce. The Sultanate refrained from interfering in the religious practices of the *vanias* (merchants) and greatly eased their way by battling unruly clans on potential trade routes. The introduction of a centralized system of rule by successive Muslim rulers, a tax-collection bureaucracy and transactions in cash rather than kind, expanded the scope for the operation of merchant capital. Bullion flowed from the Ahmedabad mint as silver coins. New activities like banking came into being and the vast rural hinterland opened up. The flow of money to the villages was channeled through a trader–moneylender known as the sahukar. In his collection of vignettes, *Gujarat and the Gujaratis*, Behramji M. Malabari describes the latter-day version of one such sahukar: an obese gentleman so lugubrious that the train on which he was travelling had to be stopped twice to enable him to get off. In Malabari's opinion this type was a hard-hearted Shylock, but even so it marked a departure from the feudal.

By the eighteenth century these trends resulted in the cultivation of more marketable crops and in the purchase of agricultural land vested till then with the peasant community or given as royal grants. Merchant capital also became more deeply involved in artisan-based production. The town's core competence in the spinning, weaving, dyeing and printing of textiles led the English and Dutch East India Companies to open local trading centres in the seventeenth century. Textile production became more market-oriented. Ahmedabad wove soft silk patolas. It made cuttanee, a kind of satin used in English quilts. It made the exquisite brocade kinkhab that was stitched into royal tents, and a large number of cottons like bafta, chintz and muslin. Indigo grown in the swathe of land between the Sabarmati and the Mahi rivers was processed by local manufacturers and used for dyeing the brimming supplies of calico. The Chippas, traditional dyers, would lay their printed cloths out on the banks of the Sabarmati. In early twentieth-century photographs taken from the air, they looked like bright tops spinning on the sands.

*

There was once, it is said, an Ahmedabadi sheth who, because his delicate eyes could not tolerate brightness of any kind, spent his days indoors seeing by the dull luminescence of jewels embedded in the walls of his house. If history were not about emperors, the vastness of their dominions and the savage wars they fought to retain them but were, instead, about the canny men who encrusted crowns with exotic gems, who maintained the ledgers and who provided money with which the wars could be fought, then the Ahmedabadi *sheth* might have left the dim pearly glow of the backroom to emerge into the harsh limelight of account. In Kiran Nagarkar's novel *Cuckold*, we encounter the character of Adinath Mehta, a 'grand old man' and a financier of princes, one who veiled his considerable clout with a show of social intimacy, one who had 'refined the game of protocol, wherein he had the upper hand but placed himself in the position of a supplicant'.

The inspiration for the shrewd and manipulative Adinath Mehta may well have been the legendary seventeenth-century Ahmedabad merchant Shantidas Zaveri. Shantidas, whose forefathers came from Osian, the ancient Rajasthani desert town where a Kshatriya prince and his people foreswore war to embrace the pacifist Jain religion, had made his early fortune in the humid port town of Cambay. Moving to Ahmedabad, Shantidas established a widespread banking network encouraged by the standardization of currency under Akbar. Banking networks such as his assisted in the collection of taxes and, more importantly, provided resources to finance the emperors' military operations and other state requirements. Shantidas, one of the empire's foremost bankers, came to be deeply imbricated with the personal affairs of the royal family. As a jeweller to the Mughals he had rare access to the perfumed recesses of the zenana, where he advised queens and princesses, many of whom owned ships and relied on merchants to supervise their commercial transactions. Using his privilege and his financial muscle, Shantidas is conjectured to have manoeuvred successions, rebellions and failed coups from the time of Akbar, who died in 1605, to Aurangzeb, who ascended the Delhi throne in 1658.

Civic and community leadership came naturally to merchants of such means and influence. Ahmedabad already had rich urban traditions including guilds of artisans and merchants, called panch and mahajan. On Shantidas was conferred the honorific 'Nagarsheth (head of the city)'. The title, mixing with the fertile influence of religious precepts, established an institutional order of patricians and engendered a concern among the privileged towards urban matters that would make Ahmedabad special among cities.

*

A copper engraving from the collection of the Dutch pastor Philippus Baldaeus presents a rare view of Ahmedabad as it must have appeared in the early seventeenth century. The perspective is wide: the buildings are clustered in a horizontal sliver shrouded for the most part, save for a few minarets and the fort, by vegetation and brick ramparts. Behind the town the flat landscape rolls endlessly with a few small hills to the right. In front of it is the river, deep enough at one end to support a small boat and shallow enough at the other end for two figures to trudge through it on foot. The riverbanks are rife with activity. Clothes are being washed. Sand is being carried to build a levee. Bullocks are led by a man with a stick. Two date palms and a coconut tree thrusting out jauntily in the foreground provide no relief from the merciless sun. Two camels laden with packages clamber over the uneven ground and a man turbaned and attired like a merchant, shaded by a parasol, sits atop one of them.

In summer, temperatures in Ahmedabad shoot up to the forties. Often touching fifty degrees Celsius, the heat leaps out, like an eager pet, felling you with its fiery breath. Occasionally, it builds and builds into the effulgent, dizzying heat wave known as the loo, sapping every droplet of moisture in its way, leaving limp and eviscerated bodies in its wake. Then there is the sand, sweeping in from the salt marshes of Kutch in the west or from the bleak Thar in the north. The light grains swirl and skitter on the sides of the wide streets and blow in gusts coating everything—furniture, cars, people—with a brittle second skin. It was this relentless assault, against which no weapons could succeed, which led the Mughal prince Jehangir, a few hundred years ago, to exasperatedly decry Ahmedabad as 'Gardabad (abode of dust)'. Like the sea, the desert is at the penumbra of the Ahmedabadi consciousness. The lure of abundance emanating from the blue rim is permeated by intimations of parchedness and sterility, creating, it would seem, a terror of complacency. Ahmedabadis greet the outsider with the tense watchfulness of the civet that once commonly staked out the sparsely populated city margins.

A green-eyed, golden-haired savant, Manek Baba, living on the river bank at the time of Ahmed Shah, bristled at the sultan's attempt to muscle in on his domain. Every day, while the king's men attempted to erect fortifications, Manek baba wove a quilt. At night, when the king's men slept the Baba unraveled the threads, causing the walls to collapse. The embattled ruler invited the Baba to show off his magical prowess by shrinking and climbing into a glass bottle. The Baba did as he was bid, whereupon the king stoppered the bottle and proceeded to build the city without hindrance.

Myths about the city hinge on guile and trickery. The Ahmedabadi, caught between the sea and the desert, between the promise of plenitude and the fear of paucity, between the call to enterprise and a pinching caution, puts a high premium on ingenuity. A man who merely succeeds is no match for a man who succeeds by his wits. And even then nothing is quite enough, for triumph is quickly replaced by the anxiety of anticipated loss. Hence judiciousness is advised and demonstrativeness eschewed. The striving for inscrutability, however, is imbued with and accompanied by a serious and apparently permanent state of discontent. '*Polu che te bolyu tema kari te she karigari* [you played the hollow thing, the flute, so what?]' the poet asks, '*sambelu vagade to hun jannu ke to shano che!* [make the wooden pole sing, then we shall see!]'.

The injunction to strive, to innovate, wresting miracles from the unyielding earth, to continually improve or uplift, snags at the Ahmedabadi soul, keeping it in a state of relentless commotion. One can see it in the unsparing tenets of Jainism, in reform-oriented movements and cults, in the asceticism and solemnity with which patriarchs of industrial families once cloaked their fascinatingly eclectic personalities, bearing their wealth, their sprawling business concerns, their enormous families and their admirably large and voluntarily undertaken public responsibilities like camel humps, with an air of stoic resignation.

*

A loudspeaker and a green flag hang on the few bits of stone masonry which is all that remains of Ahmed Shah's citadel, Bhadra. Three long horizontal inscriptions on the gateway and the adjoining arches, in Persian and partly defaced, dating back to 1623, tell of Shah Jahan's unsuccessful revolt against his father, the Mughal emperor Jahangir. There is much coming and going from the Bhadrakali temple in the caravanserai adjoining the arch, the shadowy darkness pierced by the goddess' luminescent eyes.

In the early 1700s, famine and repeated attacks by the Marathas, a Hindu imperial power from the hilly region south of Gujarat, which finally claimed the city in 1758, visited blight upon Ahmedabad. The dwindling demand for craftsmen, soldiers and courtiers drove the city's Muslims to seek work in other towns. Those who stayed were pushed, over time, to the gates by the spiralling prices of land in the central neighbourhoods of the walled city, their properties falling into the hands of the thrifty Hindu and Jain vanias. Under the British East India Company, which took over from the Marathas in 1817, the shift in impetus from the military to the commercial brought about a further decline in their fortunes.

Pigeons flutter and perch on the serrated roof of the Bhadra where a shattered clock says it's always 5.34. Behind the arch a shaky staircase leads up to the local branch office of the Archaeological Survey of India. On the ground floor, massive sombre rooms house publications and official gazettes of the Gujarat government. Opposite the square it faces the baleful stare of the Bhadra Telecom Bhawan.

At the turn of the twentieth century, newly laid railway lines had expanded trade to and from the city and the promise of work in the proliferating textile mills attracted new settlers. Ahmedabad, overcrowded, unsanitary and dirty, was crying for a solution. The British tried and failed to win support for a plan to restructure and expand the urban space from the townspeople. Then, riding on a nationalist appeal, a coterie of dynamic and largely Hindu and Jain mill-owners and professionals led by Vallabhbhai Patel seized control of the municipal board. Patel, not yet the khadi-clad, self-effacing 'Sardar' of his later years but a British-trained lawyer, foppish in a suit, a peaked cap and collars laundered in Bombay, put into action a plan for restructuring and expanding the city. Like the earlier plan of the colonial authorities, which it rejected, this one too aimed to adapt the city for the needs of modern commerce.

It tugged, altered and stretched the tight, winding streets of the old burgh till they began to take on the angular and expansive lineaments of a modern town. It turned the old enclosures inside-out so that road-facing property, instead of houses in the innermost, secluded centre, became more expensive. It linked the railway station and the market. It acquired blocks of agricultural land in the south for new housing. It turned the city centre into a commercial area, attracting the establishment of modern banking and insurance companies. And it engaged in a major land acquisition exercise to propel an expansion of the city to the western bank of the river.

The old town, combining features of both traditional Hindu and Islamic towns, now burgeoned to include a modern appendage on the west. Ahmedabad, though still *dhanukudil* (curved like a bow), was no longer organized according to a ritual cosmography in which the urban centre symbolised the universe. Bhadra, Ahmed Shah's citadel, the old heart and nerve centre of the city, was rendered lifeless, an inert relic of the past, suitable for tourism and for hawkers to hang their wares.

*

Muharram 2008: Most of the entry points to the old city are shut. Domes, filigreed walls and gates like amputated elephant limbs look on arterial roads strangely bereft of traffic. Knots of men in khaki uniforms and berets stand at street corners, armed and uncertain. On the road that winds past the Jamalpur Darwaza, people are moving in a continuous stream. They walk as if hedged in on one side by an invisible rope, though here and there a bulge appears as someone fails to keep pace or quickens a step. There is a sense of arbitrariness in the air, the occasional shout and drumbeat. It is the tenth day of Muharram, the day Shia Muslims mourn the martyrdom of Hussain Ibn Ali, the grandson of the prophet Muhammad, who died in the battle of Karbala in 61 AH (680 AD). Past the timber mart and the fire station, and approaching the flower market, one comes across processions carrying *tazias*, replicas of the mausoleum in Karbala, a holy Shia city a hundred kilometres southwest of Baghdad. The tazias are like birdcages with minarets and onion-shaped domes; they are made of bamboo and paper, some with a marmoreal finish, others pasted with silver and gold foil. The overwrought mood and the thick presence of armed constabulary fills the air with a certain frisson, evoking a wider sense of religious victimhood and recalling strands from the tapestry of the city's agonised past.

It brings to mind, for instance, the years immediately preceding Independence, when the Muslim community, having lost its former dominance, contemplated its future in a Hindu-dominated land with a mix of anxiety and mortification. Uneasy times when the separatist rhetoric of the Muslim League saw its nationwide membership catapult from a few hundred to over two million. And in 1941, when the Ahmedabadi Muslim, over three frenzied days, went berserk and perpetrated such violence that elderly residents still recall those days with a shudder. They talk about seeing bodies of stab victims flowing in the nullah at Teen Darwaza. They recall fires rising from the ground, black fumes floating towards the *pols*, the clustered dwellings of the old town. They recall terrified Hindu families huddled on the terraces, their valuables wrapped in handkerchiefs clutched in their hands.

All at once, the Muharram processions converge at Bhadra, streaming out cacophonously from the inner lanes. Young men in green headbands emerge brandishing swords and twirling sticks in a show of masculinity and religious fervour. The army in khaki observes with narrow, curious eyes. On August 31, 1969, large numbers of Ahmedabad's Muslims had moved through the arteries of the old city, passing Gol Limda, Relief Road, Kalupur, Balochwad and Delhi Chakla and congregated in Mirzapur where a public meeting was held. The marchers were protesting the fire that had broken out at the mosque of Al Aqsa in Jerusalem ten days before. The fire at a site of extreme religious significance for Muslims and perceived, wrongly, it later turned out, to have been set by the Israelis, had sent ripples across the world. In Ahmedabad, however, the incident had had a domestic fallout. The size of the Al Aqsa procession and the slogans which talked of 'meeting strength with strength' provoked anxiety, anger and a great deal of discussion among the city's Hindus. Speculation started that Muslims were massing together to attack Hindus, a lingering fear after the fierce violence that accompanied the partitioning of the subcontinent. The timing, just years after the India–Pakistan war of 1965, seemed to provide a sinister edge to the event.

Some of these qualms surfaced publicly. On September 7, 1969, a political analyst, Vasudev Mehta, in an article for Ahmedabad's largest-selling daily, *Gujarat Samachar*, titled 'Al Aqsa Episode and the Muslims of India', wrote: 'Muslims of India while sharing the anguish with other Muslims made their frenzy more dreadful than Muslims of Pakistan, Indonesia, Malaya—they should understand the limitations as citizens of a secular state like India.' On September 10, another writer expounded a similar view in the newspaper, claiming that: 'While different Indian citizens—Muslims, communists, have international loyalties—Hindus have none. Hence their citizenship is superior.' A few days later, a former president of the Bharatiya Jana Sangh, a forerunner of the present-day BJP, Balraj Madhok, addressed a public meeting at the Ahmedabad Military and Rifle Training Association, where he criticised local Muslims for mounting a protest over an incident that had occurred outside India and at such a distance from the country and talked about the need to 'Bharatiyakaran' or 'Indianise' Indian Muslims before an excited, approving crowd.

On the stretch past the West End Hotel where a part of the ancient fort wall, a decayed remnant, still stands, the policemen form fierce rows. Processions from the old city dribble in. The road, a cul de sac bordered by the river, fills up. Loud whoops and drum rolls sound out, a concatenation of delirious noise. The tazias are released into the cool green waters of the Sabarmati. Tinsel floats to the surface.

*

As a young man Rabindranath Tagore observed the Sabarmati 'with its feeble thin current of the summer months' on a 'vast bed of sands'. In 1878 at the age of seventeen he had come to Ahmedabad to visit his brother Satyendranath Tagore, a civil servant, who lived in a seventeenth-century Mughal palace in Shahibaug. The future poet laureate spent his days roaming the empty rooms of the palace, filled with a 'purposeless curiosity'. On moonlit nights he left his turret room to walk about the terrace overlooking the river and it was there that he composed his earliest songs.

Tagore's contemporary, Gandhi, was also drawn to the Sabarmati. In 1915, returning to India from South Africa, where he had organized the migrant Indian community against unfair colonial practices, he chose to settle in Ahmedabad. 'I had a predilection for Ahmedabad,' he wrote in his autobiography. 'Being a Gujarati I thought I should be able to render the greatest service to the country through the Gujarati language. And then, as Ahmedabad was an ancient centre of handloom weaving, it was likely to be the most favourable field for the revival of the cottage industry of hand-spinning.' Gandhi's commune, the Satyagraha Ashram, came up on a stretch of jungle land on the western bank of the river.

Tagore and Gandhi, the poet and the saint, with their ideas of self determination for societies and men in the early twentieth century, were kindred spirits with varying preoccupations. In his mature years, Tagore was alarmed by the heady influence of nationalism and warned of its closeness to zenophobia. Gandhi, meanwhile, was appalled by the devastating effects of the modern city, which he described as an 'excrescence' serving the 'evil purpose of draining the life blood of the villages'.

Someone is sweeping the leaves off the prayer ground at the Satyagraha Ashram. The heavy branches of Asoka and Neem trees reach over the walls to cast dappled shadows on the margins of the hot river bank. A gentle peace falls between the shadows of the treetops on sands the dull gold of camel skin. And the rustling of a broom, *skrch ... sckrch*, scraping a bare floor.

The bridge with graceful metal loops lies like a coffin within an expanded Ellis Bridge. For a long time it was the only link between the eastern and western banks. Now it is one of seven bridges that lace the two parts of the city together. A line of trees on the east; on the west the distinctive silhouette of a revolving restaurant ('first in India'), now closed, rises like a spaceship on a pylon next to a staggered brown facade encased by metal scaffolding. Two men go by on cycles past the faded pink walls of the Nehru Bridge. Beyond, the Gandhi and Subhash bridges shimmer in the smoky morning haze.

Some days I cross the river several times, shuttling between the east and the west. In the early morning light the banks of the river are flushed, their tossed salmon-pink sands like the spilled contents of a ladies' powder box. Later in the day, a cool, refreshing exudation rises up from the monsoon grey waters and the jangling commotion of the city seems to melt away. The bridges have played a part in history. For generations Ahmedabadis have demonstrated their zeal for a cause by crowding on them. They packed the Ellis Bridge so tight on March 12, 1930, that Gandhi, setting out on the Salt March to Dandi, was forced to lead his marchers across the dry river bed. Then again, after Independence, less than a decade after Gandhi's death and on the anniversary of his birthday on October 2, 1956, the three bridges crisscrossing the river heaved with people surging to lend their support to the movement for an independent Gujarat. 'By serving Mother Bharati [India] we have driven away the English,' Indulal Yagnik, the charismatic leader of the regional movement, had said, 'now the time has come to serve Mother Gurjari [Gujarat].'

*

Parakeets fly over the Ahmedabad Textile Mill-owners' Association; flashes of green in a soft blue sky. The building designed by Le Corbusier has a distinctive angled ramp ascending from the ground like a child's foot rule. Inside, open staircases and immense gaps in the rough grey concrete let in a flood of river light. Le Corbusier came to India in the 1950s at the invitation of Jawaharlal Nehru to design the new city of Chandigarh. In inviting the high priest of international modernism to design the capital of a state born from the ashes of Partition, Nehru was making a conscious break from the past and announcing a vision of the future. The vision, modelled by the architect who once rammed a whole suburban subdivision of Marseilles with its colourful bars and street life into a single high concrete block, expectedly eschewed the curving, labyrinthine lines of old traditional Indian towns in favour of wide boulevards, gridded blocks and monumental government buildings.

Chandigarh was a visual representation of the high modernist ideology that marked the Nehruvian state, an ideology that pivoted on a faith in science and technology actualised in dams and power plants, the much vaunted 'temples of modern India'. This approach, much critiqued in later years for devaluing traditional and indigenous systems of knowledge, for displacing tribals and damaging the environment, seemed at the time to suggest a way out of the messy legacies of the past and a means of empowerment for the future. The Corbusian experiment overwhelmed the course of Indian architecture. The sheths of Ahmedabad invited the wiry French architect to build as many as four buildings (two private and two public structures) in the city. In 1960, when Gujarat became an independent state, two of Corbusier's assistants on the Chandigarh project designed the new city of Gandhinagar that would replace Ahmedabad as the capital. Gandhinagar, a mere twenty-three kilometres from Ahmedabad, is built on the lines of Chandigarh, a town of circles and squares, a sterile diffusion of the noisy, contentious displays of power.

*

Birds flock to the Sabarmati. Rosy pelicans, flamingos and storks. Brahminy ducks, herons, Eurasian spoonbills and Citrina wagtails. River tern, long-billed pipit, the winter wren, redshanks, ruddy shelduck and the common moorhen.

And the peacocks, they are everywhere. The magnificent bird can often be spotted perched on a water tank or a low wall in the city. In secluded green spaces it proliferates and rules. Often you hear them caw, with the harsh dissonance of a brass band coming together for the first time.

The chorus rises and stops suddenly. The air rustles, hot, faintly scented with jasmine. The gated colony I am staying in, an enclave of recent affluence, has houses in Jaipur pink with terraces and sloping naliya roofs, the signature rustic-chic style of the reputed local architect Kamal Mangaldas. Ford Cortinas and Hyundais loom on the paved paths and dachshunds roll with kids on humps of manicured grass. In the early mornings a peacock visits. At first it makes a thorough inspection of the lawn, its velvet blue neck sinuous in the watered grass. Becoming bolder it plonks its way around the back of the house and inserts its small head through the kitchen doorway, leaving a pile of ashy turds on the threshold as a calling card. Next it enters the house, waddling slightly and sweeping its prodigious tail behind it, like a bejeweled dowager come to visit. The peacock is a solitary creature. It wanders alone bearing the burden of its regal train. Sometimes, perchance while picking its way down the tree-lined pathways that run between houses, it sees its reflection on a black, shiny car and, mistaking it for a rival, attacks it with a ferocity that leaves the metal body dented and grazed.

There are peacocks in Amit Ambalal's paintings, curved, resplendent. His favourite bird, though, is the crow. 'It is so alert,' he says with an appreciative glint in his eyes. Ahmedabad's best-known artist is tall, bespectacled and has a gentle manner about him. His father owned a textile mill but, unusually, allowed his son to follow the playful, artistic inclinations of his heart. Amit has a wry sense of humour that takes delight in the oddest things: a gawky Great Dane at a dog show, the smell of moth balls, the soft zing of a mosquito, the freshness of flowers: 'if I need red for balance, I throw in a hibiscus'. Blue is for the god with the peacock crown, for Krishna. 'It is all *leela*,' he says, 'just a play of the gods.' At home, my host, the venerable Kathak danseuse and choreographer Kumudini Lakhia, tells me a story about Krishna. The amorous god brought the parijata shrub from heaven causing a rift between his wives Satyabhama and Rukmini. To placate both, the blue god planted the shrub in Satyabhama's garden while ensuring that the flowers would scatter in Rukmini's. The delicate white flowers on orange stalks fill the night air with a moist, billowing fragrance. At the first sign of light, they are shed and one wakes to find the ground carpeted with stars.

*

At Dharoi in the Mehsana district the Sabarmati descends from the mountains to the plains. A dam was built here in 1978, later supplemented by French collector wells to supply drinking water to Ahmedabad, 168 kilometres downstream. The blushing waters meander gently past ravines and farmlands. At Vautha the Sabarmati meets the Hathmati and five other rivers, a site at which a Shiva linga is believed to have supernaturally emerged. Jain temples appear, small urban settlements, schools, shrines, mosques, a waste water treatment plant, the chimneys of textile processing plants, an outlet to release treated water, dogs scavenging atop a rubbish heap. Rustic settlements cling to the outskirts of the city. On the western bank are the Motera cricket stadium, the Ahmedabad Electricity Company, an overpass named after the former chief minister Chimanbhai Patel, the Sabarmati railway station and jail, dreary lots of housing societies and traffic roundabouts, timber depots, a graveyard and the staff quarters of the Ahmedabad Municipal Transport Service.

There are puddles of yellowish water in the sandy riverbank. The water is red and then thick and black. At one time, around the 1970s, the chemical and dyestuff factories released waste so toxic and hazardous that the courts had to intervene and shut down as many as 700 units. New legislation and efforts on the part of the industrial community put fresh controls in place. But one summer afternoon in 2009, an environmental activist took me down to the dry river bed at Valad to show me sacks of garbage compressed into the river bank and the grooves made in the mud by chromium waste and Azo dye. Dry, yellow pigmented thistles poked out of the soil littered with tiny blue pebbles.

The river cuts through the city like a scythe, flat and still. Trees are dully visible through a sand haze. An ancient mosque goes by next to which a machine releases a gush of black water. The brown blocks of the National Institute of Design, the country's premier design school, on the west, stare across the river at a lapsed smokestack on the eastern bank. Two different lives, two different cities almost, yet an alumnus of the Institute told me that in the early 1990s they could hear the screams of victims of communal violence in the old city floating across the river. All is quiet now but the traffic is rushing past on the Jamalpur Bridge.

*

The steps next to a bicycle stand on Salapose Road lead to the riverfront where a board advertising a primary school with cartoon figures faces a small public garden. A large imposing new temple stands sentinel on the sands. The sand is a warm gold today except for the broad band of shade cast by the Ellis Bridge. At one end of the bridge is a house, a small hut of bricks, with a clothesline strung by the side. In the grey-blue pixilated distance overseen by the logo of Le Meridien and hoardings for Vodafone, the State Bank of India, Torrent Power and Nirma, the sands are being agitated by the heavy machinery of the Sabarmati Riverfront Development Project. Small new walls like concrete biscuits and groves of metal rods have appeared in places. Trucks and jeeps are racing on the banks leaving long scars in the sand.

The Sabarmati flows by architect Bimal Patel's office in Usmanpura. Through the bevel-edged glass one can see a patch of lawn with little purple flowers overlooking the tousled pink sands. An exhalation seems to rise from the river, a heady blue airiness, a tantalising dance of sky and water. It is a view that the occupant of the office would have gazed upon as he sat conceptualizing, planning and giving form to the vision that will re-imagine the Sabarmati as a version of the Thames or the Seine. An exhibition mounted for the 2007 Vibrant Gujarat Summit, a biennial event organized by the Gujarat government to woo foreign investors, illustrates the key features of Bimal's design for the Sabarmati Riverfront Development Project.

In models, wall-to-wall posters and computer-simulated projections the river, flat, glazed, runs through banks manipulated to create a uniform breadth. Water channeled through canals from the recently dammed Narmada river, 200 kilometres away, has turned the Sabarmati's vacillating flow into a perennial fullness. Concrete walkways with steep staircases run along an eleven-kilometre stretch on either side of the river. Pin-sized figures with elongated shadows dot the grey baked ground. On a second level running alongside the river are manicured lawns and tall buildings. Beyond the buildings are highways of six lanes and four lanes known as the 'East River Drive' and 'West River Drive', respectively. Of the variable river and its homely sands, reminder of mountain range and desert, there is no trace. The blazing lights from the buildings, the fluorescent green lawns, the cars racing by and sailboats on the billowing sea of water suggest an attempt at urban imagineering attuned to the neoliberal project of city marketing.

The possibility of developing the riverfront has been discussed since the 1960s when a French architect and Ahmedabadi resident, Bernard Kohn, evoked visions of a Parisian promenade on thirty hectares of reclaimed space on the riverbank. A group of architects and planners, including Bimal's father Hasmukh Patel, came together in the mid-1980s as the Riverfront Development Group, with a pared-down version of the project focusing mainly on improving public access to the river. In 1997 the Ahmedabad Municipal Corporation, emboldened by the prioritization of urban regeneration projects post India's liberalization, established a special-purpose vehicle, the Sabarmati Riverfront Development Corporation Limited, and appointed the Environmental Planning Collaborative, a not-for-profit firm headed by Bimal Patel, to prepare a comprehensive proposal.

The project got underway in 2004 but as its potential ramifications came to light it provoked not an inconsiderable degree of concern among members of the public. Widespread flooding in the city in 2006, for instance, raised anxious questions about the ecological consequences of casing a river. The announcement that almost 20 per cent of the 200 hectares of reclaimed space would be sold to real estate developers and 28 per cent deployed for roads prompted murmurs that public space was being usurped by the state for the use of the rich. Over ten thousand families living on the riverbank were initially promised resettlement on the reclaimed land but were left out in the new plans making for the largest potential displacement in the city's history. And there was the matter of the rising costs, from an estimated Rs 361 crore in 1997 to Rs 1,200 crore.

Bimal Patel's energetic manner belies his close-cropped grey hair, conferring on him a youthful, almost impish aura. He was born in Ahmedabad and studied at the St Xavier's High School, Loyola Hall, in Navrangpura where, he says, the charismatic Father Erwiti opened Patel's middle-class eyes to poverty. Photographs of Jesuit priests are pinned on the wall behind him; a plaque says 'I AM A XAVIERITE I CARE IN DEED'. Post school and a BA in architecture he went to Berkeley to be taught by David Harvey and Richard Walker, urban geographers whose work engaged with the spatial impact of capital, and Manuel Castells, the eminent sociologist preoccupied then with the Marxist approach to urbanism.

He seems to relish the confusion caused by his résumé. He suggests that he might have undergone an ideological realignment: in his architectural practice he says he moved from a search for a vernacular idiom to an embrace of internationalism; similarly he has come to feel that India's socialist past served her badly by tying her up in obstructive laws. His own breakthrough moment came in 1994 when he was invited to redesign a city street, an early urban entrepreneurial project with corporate participation. He tends to return to this experience often in conversation, dwelling on it in a way that suggests a level of gratification surpassing that which he may have received from other accomplishments including, perhaps, winning the prestigious Aga Khan Award for Architecture early in his career. Again and again and with an unwavering gusto he describes the challenges of the project: the procedures and strategies for countering naysayers, sceptics and bad publicity; the overcoming of obstacles put forward by aldermen, politicians, the media, and the public.

The thrill of the backroom fix is evident too in the way he deals with criticism about the Riverfront project. Despite the chief minister's ownership of the venture and the involvement of senior officials, Bimal, as the designer and executer, has become its most visible spokesperson. He defends the project at seminars and in interviews. He counters concerns about potential ecological damage, claiming that narrowing the river is as hazardous as pinching a garden hose. He pacifies community representatives by promising to accommodate informal markets threatened by the enterprise. He moves with agility, sometimes arguing, sometimes mollifying, sometimes throwing his hands up and saying he is bound by orders, sometimes shrugging and saying you cannot please everybody. He talks little about design or engineering difficulties or his motivations as a professional for undertaking this mammoth responsibility. He appears to simultaneously own and disown the project. At times he conveys the impression that his overriding interest is just that it should get done. At other times he suggests a deeper impulse, a vision of a public space 'without walls', a public space where 'we agree on adjusting with each other'.

On one occasion we talk about books. I tell him about Robert A. Caro's monumental biography of Robert Moses, the man lionized for his visionary plans to develop New York until people counted the costs: the extravagance, the thousands of families, mostly poor and black, he displaced to build his highways, bridges, tunnels, showpiece buildings and parks, projects that prioritized the needs of car owners and of the rich, and would forever limit the city's ability to respond to its growing size in an environmentally sustainable and humane way. Bimal has just finished reading about Hitler's architect, Albert Speer. Speer gave shape to the Fuhrer's monumental fantasies: the Zeppelinfeld, a vast parade ground ringed with searchlights for instance, was Speer's idea. He was the only senior Nazi to accept responsibility for Hitler's regime but many saw his expression of remorse as a strategic move to escape the death sentence at Nuremberg. I buy Gitta Sereny's fascinating biography of the man but find that despite the writer's extensive research, Speer and his motivations remain a mystery.

The last time I visit Bimal's office he shows me the new publicity material that is being prepared for the Sabarmati Riverfront Development Project. It is another attempt to diffuse criticism about the project, this time through a change of visuals. The large poster on the table is vastly different from previous stark images. For one it is colourful because it foregrounds people rather than cold structures. Ordinary people, men, women, children, are sitting, walking, enjoying the riverfront. Then Bimal takes me to the terrace of his office building to present a bird's eye view of the riverfront. Under the blue winter sky I see the heavy machinery, the fifty-foot deep diaphragm, the retention walls, the dull grey promenade. I remember something Bimal said to me in one of our earlier conversations. 'People are not used to seeing so much concrete,' he said. 'But to carry four million people, a city needs to be hard.'

The setting sun has disappeared behind the clouds casting a purplish shadow over the river bank. The river is murky like the dipping water in an artist's bowl. The lights from the buildings across the river make thin silvery lines in the water flanking a block of green glimmer from a hoarding. The sky softly explodes with colour. Soft, feathery clouds against a brilliant, luminous orange.

THREE
Old City

JAWAHARBHAI, THE MANAGER OF the bookshop at the Gujarat Vidyapith is excited that I have enquired about *An Economic Survey of Matar Taluka*, a pioneering 1931 report by the Gandhian economist J.C. Kumarappa. 'First time in two years!' he informs me, his eyes agleam behind thick glasses. He is a small-built man in a long kurta that reaches his shins. When I tell him that I write, he says, with evident satisfaction: 'There is no money in that!' *An Economic Survey of Matar Taluka* is a plain, slim volume with a quote by Gandhi and the emblem of the Vidyapith—an open lotus—on the cover. 'A re-*markable* investigation into conditions in one of India's most backward areas!' Jawaharbhai pronounces as he hands it to me, gesturing dismissively when I ask about the price.

We are on Ashram Road, the road that runs parallel to the river on its west flank mimicking the gentle curves and variable proportions of the Sabarmati. Two-wheelers dodge outstation-bound buses painted with axioms and holy pictures. Bunches of fruit hang from restaurant awnings; in their dark interiors are plastic chairs and small shrines on the reception counter. In shop windows busty mannequins, apparelled in saris that belong to another era of fashion, make demure gestures of welcome. Many older buildings, including single-screen cinema halls and the offices of the *Times of India*, have the squat, wide-bodied dimensions of the early 1900s International style. Most striking of all is the pervasive whiff of officialdom, a relic of the post-Independence socialist era. One sees it in government buildings like the Income Tax Office, the Reserve Bank, All India Radio and the Regional Transport Office. One also sees it in showrooms of the Handloom House and the Gujarat State Emporium, legacies of state intervention to support hand-worked textiles and ethnic crafts. It is hard to believe that this arterial road with the dated look of a television re-run was once the pivot of revolutionary India.

Due north on Ashram Road, where the river bends and flows underneath the Subhash Bridge is the Satyagraha Ashram, the city's most important tourist attraction. Less than three kilometers down the road is the arched entrance to the Gujarat Vidyapith, a 'national' university for Gujarat, launched by Gandhi, to provide a nationalist alternative to the colonial system of education. In *Hind Swaraj* or 'Indian Home Rule', an influential tract he wrote in 1909, Gandhi had expressed the view that Swaraj (freedom or self-assertion) in its true sense would not be achieved if the British were merely replaced by an indigenous set of rulers who shared their objectives and their principles of modern civilisation. For Gandhi it was important not only to fight the British politically but also to challenge assertions of Western modernity, including its strong belief in the merits of industrialisation. To that end he was preoccupied with evolving an educational system which respected manual labour, engendered compassion towards the weak and, above all, awarded primacy to the mother tongue. The Vidyapith was a laboratory to test these concepts.

The Vidyapith's twenty-one-acre campus is laid on an angular grid. Sun-dappled paths run by high monastic walls with signboards for 'Ahimsa Shodh Sansthan' or the 'Institute of Studies in Quest of Non-violence', the 'Institute of Equity and Development', the 'Institute of Indian languages' and 'Gandhi's Bible Room'. Aphorisms are painted on the fences: 'TO COUNTER LAZINESS BE CONSTANTLY EXHILARATED'. Young Indian men and women in pale salwar-kurtas mill about. Three girls go by with carpentry boxes. The Vidyapith became a deemed university in 1963. But increasingly it is international scholars—one sees Caucasians, East Asians and Africans, sedulous, in khadi, moving about with an easy familiarity—who evince an interest in Gandhi's teachings. Public membership of the august central library, a repository of rare manuscripts, documents and thousands of books including Gujarati translations of ancient Indian, Eastern and Western thought, has been steadily dwindling.

The vice-chancellor Sudarshan Iyengar, an academic with a specialization in natural resource development and the non-governmental movement, is saddened by the steady decline of Gandhian values in contemporary India. Seated cross-legged on the floor, he deplores in particular the rise of material aspirations observing that: 'the multiplication of wants at the individual level is outside our Indian tradition.' Once the intellectual and cultural hub of the city, the Gujarat Vidyapith now seems a forgotten corner of the world sprayed by dust from buses pausing at the stop outside its walls.

*

The pink dust rises. College girls cover their heads and their faces with *dupattas*, their arms with long gloves, to protect their skin. They look like bandits on scooters riding into the hazy streets. Beyond low walls, boys in white flannel are playing cricket. On the pavement hawkers wait languidly with cold drinks, snacks and sliced guavas. The eye travels unencumbered in this part of town, for this vast open spread, some six hundred acres just southwest of the Gujarat Vidyapith, belongs to the Ahmedabad Education Society (AES). In 1935 the city's rising elite, which included mill owners, prominent professionals and local politicians, started the AES to provide for a future in which clerks, accountants, secretaries, technicians and other personnel would be required in large numbers to service the expanding industrial sector. Tucked away in shady lanes behind playing grounds and walking paths and buzzing with teenagers are modest structures that house the HL College of Commerce, the LD Arts College, the MG Science Institute, the LM College of Pharmacy, the AG Teachers College and the HK Primary Training College, all established between 1936 and 1956. In the vicinity are institutions like the Ahmedabad Textile Industry's Research Association, established in 1947 to develop indigenous expertise in industrial manufacturing processes, the Indian Institute of Management, India's top management school, set up in 1962, the Physical Research Laboratory, a significant centre for space sciences, and the Centre for Environmental Planning and Technology, and further south at Paldi, the National Institute of Design.

Sardar Vallabhbhai Patel, the first home minister and deputy prime minister of free India, was a moving force behind the AES, and Jawaharlal Nehru, India's first prime minister, inaugurated many of these institutions. Accounts of India's nation formation invariably tout a rivalry between the two men: the Sardar, Gandhi's trusted and doughty lieutenant; Nehru, his chosen heir. The men had personalities and styles of leadership that were at a variance. Ideologically too they appeared to part, one being perceived as a right-wing authoritarian figure, the other as a left-wing democrat. Such were the differences between the two around the time of Independence that Gandhi had to intervene to make peace. There is a photograph of the three leaders, the younger men on either side of the bare-chested father of the nation, making a triangle of consensus that has come to symbolise this moment of conciliation. Gandhi was the glue, the soldering iron that forced the two separating tendencies to join together at the birth of the nation. Or so it would appear from narratives of modern Indian history.

And yet, looking at Ahmedabad, at the Gujarat Vidyapith in its dusty corner, at the Gandhi Ashram with its wandering tourists, and comparing them to the lively AES sprawl embedded in the very heart of the city, one cannot help feeling that the chronicles may have been misleading. Gandhi was not the soldering iron. The ageing visionary, with his ideas of an education for liberation and his conception of a self-sustaining village economy, was the one out of joint. Nehru, Sardar, the industrialists and rising professionals who supported the AES, and presumably the common man as well, were all united by the happy, dazzling prospect of an India, ruled by Indians, but nevertheless enveloped in European modernity, aspiring to the scientific and technological prowess of the advanced West, its scale of mass production, industrial expansion and individual prosperity.

*

Long, thin, yellow leaves like origami waste litter the sides of the lane that runs from the Community Science Centre past the MG Science Institute. Despite the summer heat the bougainvillea blooms, a scatter of magenta above bamboo stalks. Around Amdavad ni Gufa, a subterranean art gallery protruding like a giant mollusk from the ground, young adults sit on cane chairs sipping iced tea listening to the plinkety plonk of jazz issuing from loudspeakers. It is so unusual, this whiff of cosmopolitan urbanity, I have to remind myself that I am still in Ahmedabad.

Those who know the city's peculiar history will probably demur and refer to Ahmedabad's long encounter with cultural modernity. And they would be right.

In a grand old haveli down in Gheekanta, a neighbourhood where vats of clarified butter were once weighed on a public scale, one can find Umang Hutheesingh, the scion of a mill family. In a sterile, mercantile town he is that rare thing: a self-styled aristocrat, rubbing shoulders on the pages of a French magazine with Charles and Camilla, King Abdullah and the royals of Scandinavia, turbaned and resplendent under a headline that identifies him as 'Le Lord l'Ahmedabad'. Umang's stock in trade is family history, a colourfully captivating narrative of ancestors who hobnobbed with the Vanderbilts, supplied fine goods to Tiffany & Co., studied criminal psychology in Zurich, supported the Tibetan struggle and shopped for high heels in Scotland.

A few kilometers north, in Shahibaug, on the vast, dark grounds of a high-walled twenty-one-acre property known as 'The Retreat', Anand Sarabhai, biologist and scion of another well-known textile family, lives in a Corbusier-designed house, a house without doors, with a slide swooping from a roof garden into a pool and a scattering of artistic whimsies such as a sculpture of mounted telephone directories by a Chinese artist and a photograph of Watson and Crick touched up in gold leaf by Anand's partner, the outré American sculptor Lynda Bengalis. Back in the 1960s the Sarabhais had invited avant garde artistes Merce Cunningham and John Cage to perform in Ahmedabad.

Kumudini Lakhia recalls the Cage show at the Town Hall. The New York-based composer of *4'33'*, a piece that showcased the normal sounds of the immediate environment, had asked for all the doors and windows to be opened. The sounds of the street washed over an expectant audience. Cage entered with a mud pot and dropped it. It rolled.

Gadgadgadagadgad.

He said: 'Sound ... is in everything.'

The strains of a synthesizer rose behind him, playing a popular Hindi film tune.

Man dole mera tan dole.

Lakhia hums the song with an exaggerated quaver to mimic the snake charmer's flute on which the song is based.

'And I thought to myself,' she says, 'if a musician of his stature can look outside himself and his milieu, why not us?'

By the 1970s, that streak of cosmopolitanism, engendered by the city's global connections, by prosperity and by the city's remarkable openness and curiosity, was challenged by a virulent nativism. There had always been about the Ahmedabadi a bluff independence and ethnic loyalty, evident in the absence of a comprador class such as that which existed in other British-administered cities like Bombay and Calcutta. Gandhi's emphasis on the mother tongue had deepened native pride and given it a pan-regional underpinning. As democracy took root in post-independence India and new political elites struggled for dominance, the tendency towards nativism, so far benign, was whipped up into a sharp parochialism. The movement for the statehood of Gujarat in the 1950s, played out largely on the streets of Ahmedabad, created a heightened sense of victimhood and grievance. In 1961, a local clique of upper-caste Congress party men battling for control over the Ahmedabad-based Gujarat University, appealed to chauvinistic proclivities and successfully marginalised the English language by removing it from primary and middle school syllabi and replacing it with Gujarati as the medium of instruction at the university level.

One can speculate that in different circumstances the purging of English, the encouragement of the native tongue, of native customs, could have led to a creative surge, a cultural efflorescence and a strong sense of selfhood. But in a society that continued to modernise along old lines, privileging commerce and commercial success above other activities, and to travel to distant lands in their pursuit, the move against English, the medium of social mobility, had quite a different fallout. It created insecurity and defensiveness and provided a reason to huddle closer, against the rest of the world. Contributing greatly to this enervating diffidence was the diminishing quality of education in the state. Between 1950 and 1971 the number of aspiring students grew ten-fold; the burgeoning demand for education led to a host of privately run colleges sprouting overnight. Motivated by profit rather than a long-term vision or social responsibility, the promoters demonstrated their rapacious intentions in various irresponsible and detrimental ways such as opting for colleges in the Arts and Commerce streams merely because they were cheaper to start and to run or by hiring part-time teachers and delaying salaries. The rampant commercialisation of education in Gujarat, with its potential for creating armies of aspiring youth, occurred against a backdrop of growing despair in the country over economic stagnation and high unemployment. *Hartals, bandhs, gheraos*, fasts and self-immolations had turned the country's large cities into battlefields between nameless mobs and state authorities through the 1960s. Scholars believed the discontent stemmed from growing inequality, mass politicization, unplanned urbanisation and a general crisis of faith in the system.

Around this time, a figure that was to become extremely familiar not just in Gujarat but also across the country was that of the Gujarat chief minister Chimanbhai Patel. Thin lips, a bald, round head that seemed to rise directly from his shoulders, professorial glasses and a vest worn over a kurta and churidar was how Chimanbhai appeared in his photographs. Caricaturists widened the lips, narrowed the eyes behind the glasses, made a parrot's beak of his nose. Those in the business of coining headlines for newspapers and banners came up with disparaging monickers: 'Chiman *Chor*, *Chaalu* Chiman (Chiman the thief, wily Chiman)'.

In 1974, Chimanbhai Patel, who was a former college principal, a textbook publisher and a patron of over fifty colleges, wriggled his way into the chief minister's post by holding legislators hostage on a farmhouse outside the city. His political machinations, his deplorable interference in academics and his role in fuelling a steep spike in prices sparked off a widespread rebellion in Gujarat that captured the imagination of the country. The movement started with a protest against the rising food bill in a college mess in Ahmedabad and spread like wildfire, gathering up angry students, disaffected teachers, disgruntled housewives, newspaper editors and nameless others. Buses and other public property were attacked on the streets of the city. Soon students in other towns had joined in and the whole state was on fire.

Manishi Jani was twenty-one at the time, an Arts postgraduate and a student representative on the all-important University Senate. He was the undisputed leader of the student movement. In the years preceding the agitation he and other students had staged street plays using irony and farce to criticise politicians. One of their stunts involved getting a shoeshine boy to launch a booklet on hunger; on another occasion they presented a broom to a central minister to 'clean up the system'. Now with 'Navnirman' (regeneration or new birth), as the 1974 movement came to be called, they were clear that this was an issue that went beyond the campus. 'We were saying, "Shut the university *till society changes.*"'

The Gujarat University has a warm sandstone façade with roseate borders, arched tall windows and a clock tower topped by a small dome. The modest, handsome structure, the heart of the Navnirman movement, now has high, fat, mottled pillars, a gate and a wall freshly painted in flat grey, barring free entry to the campus. These new additions with their plastic kitsch tones clash with the refined lineaments and subtle shades of the university building and appear to have been built ham-handedly, without any sensitivity to the surroundings. The fact that the country's premier architecture school, the Centre for Environmental Planning and Technology, is right across the road makes this display of flagrant bad taste even more mystifying. Manishi claims that the wall came up around the university soon after the Navirman agitation. 'The first thing they did was to put up the wall,' he says, suggesting that the intention was to police unruly students. Nobody else I ask seems to remember when the wall and the pillars appeared or even to have registered, with any degree of disquiet, their jarring quality. It is easy to get used to ugliness, I guess.

In 1990, a decade and a half after a chain of anarchic Navnirman-inspired youth agitations in the country had been crushed by the repressive 1975 National Emergency, the much-hated, much-reviled Chimanbhai Patel was back as chief minister of Gujarat. There was no hesitation or apology in the manner in which he assumed leadership of the state that had once risen against him. His bearing bespoke confidence. The scholarly spectacles had been replaced by aviator shades, a Cross ball-point pen peeped stylishly from the pocket of his pale raw silk vest. That he had not mended his ways was clear from this quote in a national magazine which described him as being 'willing to not merely bend, but break every rule and norm of politics, subvert every institution, distort the meaning of every word in the democratic lexicon to continue in power'.[1] But this time his opportunism provoked no adverse reaction. There was no large-scale criticism, no snowballing protests. His minions hailed him as the 'Chhote Sardar', a flattering comparison to the towering leader, the late Sardar Patel. Newspapers and civil society overwhelmingly supported his vision for a 'Naya Gujarat' (New Gujarat) with its centerpiece, the Narmada Dam.

*

Ashwini Bhatt is what people call an 'asli [real] Ahmedabadi'. He grew up in Pakharia ni pol in Raipur in the heart of the old city and studied at the Gujarati-medium CN High School ('it is good to study in the mother tongue,' he says, 'it makes your basic concepts very strong') and now, in later life, divides his time between the United States, where his son lives, and his apartment in Ambawadi. As a writer of thrillers he is a household name among Gujaratis, most of whom have read his books as they were being written, serialized in the popular press. It is said that sales of the newspaper *Sandesh* would jump by 50,000 on a day an installment was due and stories are legion about people choosing to miss their train stop just to get to the end of a cliffhanger.

Then, sometime in the 1980s, Bhatt made it known that he opposed the construction of a dam on India's fifth-longest and Gujarat's longest river, the Narmada. The Narmada Valley Project (NVP), a mega river development scheme, had been proposed in 1959, the heyday of the Nehruvian era. Twenty years later, when Gujarat was about to commence building the NVP's biggest dam, the Sardar Sarovar Project, public perceptions had shifted and the widespread enthusiasm for large-scale infrastructure projects had come to be tempered by scepticism. A popular movement that drew people from all over the country and persuaded the World Bank, a key funder, to withdraw its support in 1993, opposed the dam on grounds of large-scale displacement of tribals and small-time farmers and for its environmental implications.

Ashwini Bhatt had his own reasons for opposing the dam. 'I saw the Narmada for the first time forty years ago,' he tells me in a tone of wonder. 'And the image has never left me. It was just a ... beautiful river!' In 1984 when Bhatt visited the Narmada to do research for his novel *Othar*, construction of what was the world's second-largest gravity dam had begun, and the effects on the river shocked and deeply depressed him. 'It had changed, become sluggish, like it had been raped,' he says, filled with emotion. 'I couldn't bear to see it like that.'

His apprehensions found no response in his home state where a countervailing campaign was underway to convince Gujaratis that the dam was a 'lifeline' for their drought-prone state. Under Chimanbhai the campaign grew more frenzied with newspapers, business groups, civil society organizations and politicians across party lines hammering home the message that construction of the dam was synonymous with Gujarat's progress and that those who opposed it were enemies of the state and its people. Bhatt and the civil rights lawyer Girish Patel were two rare prominent figures to take a public stand against the project. 'A local newspaper abused Girish and me and said we should be beaten and thrown out of Gujarat,' Bhatt recalls bitterly. 'My house was ransacked several times. I was beaten by workers of both the Congress and the BJP, taken to a police station, even thrown out of a running jeep. An organisation in the United States wrote a letter condemning the attacks on me. But not one journalist or intellectual here stood by me.'

*

The screen is strewn with plastic cut-outs of the Gujarati alphabet. A man in a light-coloured jacket with brown trimming sings 'ho-ho-ho' into a microphone. 'Ho, ho, ho'. Accompanying him on a harmonium is Saumil Munshi, dapper in a denim jacket. When I had met Saumil in his office earlier in the week he had been more conservatively dressed, looking like the chemicals salesman he once used to be. Brothers Saumil and Shyamal, Ahmedabad's most famous singing duo, also run a music company called 'Touching Tunes'. They produce Gujarati songs often with a contemporary twist, introducing a faster beat, or reinterpreting the old Krishna–Radha theme as a romance through SMS between a college boy and a college girl.

There is an air of melancholy about Saumil which is belied in conversation. When I told him I was writing about Ahmedabad he thought for a moment, then said, 'Be sure to capture its *gati* [pace]. It has a gati, you know, maybe it is the roads and how they bend.' Now I watch him, a Chaplinesque figure on stage, asking someone to alter the bass. He raises his hand then lowers it. To his left half a dozen men sit with tablas, a faint percussive sound rising from them like running water.

The theme of the evening's show is 'Be Zabaani ni Musical Maitri (Musical Friendship of Two Languages)'. The songs are to be in Gujarati and Hindi. Saumil told me that Ahmedabadis were getting over their reluctance to spend money and were going out, though there were few places to go to on an evening in the city. I go sit by Shyamal in the empty front row. Shyamal, a plastic surgeon, younger and taller but with less hair than his brother, is dressed for the performance in a blue blazer and jeans. Between attending to the synthesizer levels he repeats his brother's complaint. 'There are no varied cultural events. Other cities have books, theatre, hobbies; here there is very little.' The brothers' show for a local Listener's Club this evening then is something of a treat and the foyer is fast filling up with middle-aged couples.

Upstairs two guitars are brought on stage and someone strikes the bars of a xylophone. And then the tablas again release a light drizzle ... *Trrrrrrrrrrrrrr*. Saumil's wife, also a singer, is going to join the brothers on stage tonight. She waits in the wings in a stiff, white organza sari, holding a small handbag. A rustling begins in the auditorium as people enter and take their seats. Lights flicker onstage, green and yellow. 'Hindi is our *rashtra bhasha* [national language],' says the compere into the microphone. 'And Gujarati! How sweet the memory of the language of our homes. Like *puran poli*. 1–2–3-*start*!'

*

We have tramped for close to two hours on a heritage walk organized by the Ahmedabad Municipal Corporation through the streets of the old city. We have seen sights, beautiful, like the extravagantly chiselled brackets on haveli walls, and unexpected, like the Buckminster Fuller-inspired geodesic dome that once covered the Calico showroom—an Ahmedabad sheth's folly— appearing suddenly on Relief Road, a thing of metal shards and angular curves now in delicate decay like a stork's broken wing but still startlingly modern. The tour over, we are standing outside the Friday mosque, just a few of us: an elderly White couple, a trio of Maharashtrians, a Gujarati family from Wisconsin, myself and the guide. Disoriented still from our foray into the musty past, we are reluctant to depart. So we stand about, warming ourselves by the pale light of a winter sky, listening to the market rustle to life. And we make small conversation with our guide. Chitchat about the state of conservation, of heritage sites and of the city corporation's plans. And then I hear him say something that jerks me out of my mildly beatific state; something about a new Walk being planned. A 'Freedom Walk', to commemorate those 'who used violence'.

'Our freedom struggle and *violence*?' I say in consternation. 'But Gandhi .... ?' Shock renders me inarticulate. I struggle to say the obvious: that the Indian freedom struggle was led by a man considered the apostle of non-violence. He throws a tart, pitying look my way. He is a reedy-thin man probably in his twenties, who volunteers his morning hours, free of cost, to the city.

'Of course there is Gandhi,' he says in a manner that is meant to be placatory but manages to convey contempt. 'But enough said about Gandhi. What of the other freedom fighters? Did you know,' he asks, the warmth returning to his voice, 'that there was a bomb factory here, in the city?' Polite murmurs greet his revelation.

A friend from a newspaper calls to tell me about an elaborate wedding-invitation style card that has landed on her desk. It is a summons to the inauguration of the refurbished Mehta House in Desai ni pol in Khadia in the old city. This is not just any house but one with claims to a historic role in the anti-British struggle. 'You should go,' she urges. I arrive late. A festive air hangs over the scene with bystanders squatting aimlessly on neighbouring *otlas* (small porches). Empty chairs scattered with flower petals are still ranged in rows in the chowk outside the house but the VIPs, state legislator Ashok Bhatt, local historian Ashutosh Bhatt, and the mayor, have spoken and left.

The significance of the house, or rather of its owners, dates to the early years of the twentieth century when the effects of colonial economic policies had created discontent among the Gujarati elite and provoked an interest in indigenous political developments in other parts of India. The Swadeshi movement in Bengal from 1905 to 1908, coupled with the electrifying presence of the revolutionary Ghosh brothers, Aurobindo and Barindra, who were in Baroda in the early 1900s, evoked a more widespread response, particularly among the Gujarati youth. At meetings in various towns, there was talk of freeing the motherland from foreign rule. At the 1905 Congress session in Benaras in north India, Congress leader Lala Lajpat Rai introduced a resolution to boycott British mill-made cloth, but in the absence of textile machinery and know-how the resolution was moot. A delegate from Bengal bemoaned the lack of training institutes. Then Keshavlal Mehta, the weaving master from Chunibhai Baronet's mill in Ahmedabad, who was present at the session, spoke up with an offer to house and train volunteers from Bengal. Sixty-odd Bengali youths came to Ahmedabad and were lodged in Dhobhi ni pol in a house that came to be called the 'United Bengal Home'. In return for their tutelage on the looms, the visitors initiated Gujarati boys in the art of bomb-making. A Gujarati, Mohanlal Pandya, was suspected to be behind a December 1909 bomb attack on the Indian viceroy and his wife, Lord and Lady Minto, in Ahmedabad. The Mintos escaped unhurt. Sometime in 2003 or so, the weaving master Keshavlal's grandson, Jagdip Mehta, approached the AMC's heritage cell with a plan to restore the two-storey house in Desai ni pol that had belonged to his grandfather.

*

Keshavlal Mehta has a small, soft-featured face, a thick moustache and heavy-lidded eyes. He wears an adaptation of a Western-style jacket with a tie and a barrel-shaped dark cap. Another sepia-tinted picture shows a group of young men posing between the pillars of a pol house with 'United Bengal Home' chalked on the carved lintel. A *Times of India* clip of an article on Keshavlal's son Satyendra Mehta is tacked on a softboard on the wall. The article describes Satyendra as a 'freedom fighter', active at the time of the Quit India Movement in 1942. It mentions that he frequented Gandhi's Sabarmati Ashram in his childhood but that 'the peace of the ashram was no match for the revolutionary influence'. 'Even today,' it quotes Satyendra as saying, 'I believe in revolution.'

Satyendra's daughters, Jyoti and Pragnya, invite me to stay for lunch. Relatives have travelled from other parts of the city and other towns as well. Jagdip, a portly man with a harried air, is busy dealing with flower vendors and the chair-hire men in the outer room. The inner courtyard is humming with low voices, interspersed with the swish of saris and the tinkling of steel plates. The daughters talk about their father, drawing a picture of a dour ascetic disillusioned with free India and its embrace of consumerism, taking solace in music. In the evenings the family would gather over the harmonium, the tabla, the violin and the jal tarang, and play Rabindrasangeet, an old tradition from the days of the United Bengal Home, when the Bengali youths from far away yearned for a taste of home.

In the hushed courtyard of the 200-year-old house I feel the powerful allure of the east, imbibed and reproduced by generations of cultured Gujarati women donning Bengali saris and painting the alpana outside their doors and by men in their admiration for the figure of the romantic revolutionary. The social scientist Ashis Nandy maintains that 'for the last hundred years or so, the so-called non-martial races of the subcontinent, Bengali babus, Kashmiri Muslims and Gujarati upper castes, for instance, have had a special fascination for violence.'

After lunch I ask Pragnya if she will sing one of the *bhajans* from those long-ago days. She nods. The elderly women at the table lean forward, attentive. After a silent moment of preparation, Pragnya begins. The younger relatives seated on the floor stop chattering and look up. '*De de langa ranga bhanga ... jaya jaya arati tomar ... arati tomar.*' I carry her slow, rich voice into the dark needle lanes of Khadia.

*

At the Nehru Memorial Library in Delhi I come across a book titled *Gujarat In 1857* by Dr R.K. Dharaiya of the Department of History, University School of Social Sciences, Gujarat University.

The reference in the title is to the mutiny against the British East India Company. The rebellion had been for long rendered in history books as an isolated, failed uprising. Then, in the contested terrain that is history in contemporary India, with multiple sources including mass media involved in its interpretation, the event became reconstructed in the popular mind as part of a continuum: the first step in the struggle that would eventually oust the colonizers in 1947. But though the significance of the uprising has been opened to debate, there is no dispute I am aware of regarding the geographical scale of the revolt, which played out mainly in the Gangetic plains and in central India.

The slim volume is packed with testimonials. Umanath Joshi in the foreword writes that it is 'generally believed that nothing significant happened in this part of the country during the 1857 fight for freedom against a foreign power. Dr Dharaiya's diligent research ... produces a document which shows how agog with activities certain parts of Gujarat were during those days of turmoil'. Quotes from others including Dr R.C. Majumdar, Chief Editor of the Bharatiya Vidya Bhavan history series, and C.S. Patel, Executive Vice Chancellor of the CMS University of Baroda, further endorse the contents and the author's scholarship. Shambhuprasad writes: 'Dr R.K. Dharaiya in his book 'Gujarat in 1857' has proved beyond doubts that Gujarat had neither lagged behind not (sic) remained an imbecile and dumb spectator to this great popular upheaval.' Imagining so, he claims, would be a 'gross misunderstanding'. In his preface the author too expresses hope that whatever '*misunderstanding* [emphasis mine] about the martial spirit of Gujarat prevails will be removed'. The primary intent of the book, supported by a number of influential local academics, is to prove that Gujarat participated in the mutiny of 1857. The compelling motive however appears to be not so much a matter of achieving historical veracity as much as defending a certain image of Gujarat.

I read the book and find a rousing tale of Gujarati mutineers being blown from the mouths of guns, encountering betrayal and facing death with calm composure. The story in brief is that Ahmedabad became 'infected' by news of insurrections in 1857. Mutineers from the north moving on the Indore–Mhow Road towards Ahmedabad in June 1857 caused great excitement in the city. Indian troops stationed in Ahmedabad 'became restless' and people 'began to bury their costly articles and ornaments in the ground'. Seven horsemen of the Gujarat Irregular Horse revolted on July 9, 1857 but their plan to seize arms failed due to a misunderstanding and they escaped in the direction of Sarkhej. The *Times of India* of October 19 reported thirty-five mutineers in an Ahmedabad jail. The British suppressed the incipient revolt by mercilessly slaughtering the rebels and bringing in a force so large that it created what the author believes may have been a false impression of peacefulness.

I hear a similar version of 1857 from Ashutosh Bhatt. The elderly gentleman who is routinely sought out by newspapers for his views on urban history meets me in his beautiful old home in Khadia. As I observe him in his old-fashioned Western-style clothes and take in the elegance around me, the fluted columns, the burnished floor tiles, and feel the peace that rises like a soporific vapour from the street, it is hard to believe that I am in the most notorious of all neighbourhoods in the old city.

Khadia is a middle-class locality. At one time it had a preponderance of Nagars and Brahmo-Kshatriyas, highly educated Hindu castes that dominated the administrative services under the British. Despite its upper-caste, elite socio-economic profile it has a reputation for extreme volatility. Police records and reports of various judicial commissions of inquiry into mass violence over the years have noted with consternation the proclivity of Khadia's residents for rioting and creating mayhem. Most instances of belligerence, which include rowdiness and stone-throwing, have been against law enforcement authorities, but the locality, the site of the first Jana Sangh office in Ahmedabad, also has a reputation for visiting violent attacks on Muslims.

The most prominent figure in Khadia is the local legislator Ashok Bhatt, its representative in the state assembly since 1975. I met Ashok Bhatt in May 1985 when I visited Ahmedabad to write about the protracted turbulence in the city: caste clashes had given way to Hindu–Muslim riots, a newspaper office had been set on fire, and the police had staged a revolt. Ninety-two cases of arson, fourteen murders, eleven attempts to murder, and a hundred incidents of rioting had been reported in just one week towards the end of April. In the fortnight preceding my arrival, an ugly confrontation had taken place between a company of the State Reserve Police and the residents of Khadia. The residents alleged that the paramilitary company had used excessive force and damaged their property; the State Reserve Police claimed that the residents, women and children included, had targeted the law enforcement machinery with stones, burning rags and Molotov cocktails. A few days after the incident, one constable accompanying a team sent by the High Court to investigate these charges was waylaid and fatally stabbed and another was shot in a backlane.

Ashok Bhatt was named as an instigator in the killing of one of the policemen and had gone underground. I was taken to meet him in the house where he had taken refuge. 'Throwing stones and getting bullets—what kind of justice is that?' is what he said when we met. I remember him well, a lanky, stooped man with darting eyes and a puckish manner that seemed to suggest that he wasn't the kind of person to take things too seriously. Now, nearly three decades later, Ashok Bhatt is a grey eminence and he and Ashutosh Bhatt run the Khadia Itihaas Samiti (Khadia Historical Society).

Ashutosh Bhatt shows me some of the books the Samiti has brought out. I catch snatches from blurbs: 'The fire of Bharat in peaceful Gujarat', 'Whenever there is a wrong Gujarat fights for justice' among others. Ashutosh Bhatt has a genial, abstracted expression. When he proceeds to narrate a history of Ahmedabad, his words flow smoothly, with no pause or hesitation, as if there is no possibility of doubt or contestation. Yet, even through the lull induced by his lilting cadence, the departures from the history of convention and the patterns of revision are clear.

On the occasion of its formation, the poet Umashanker Joshi eulogized Gujarat state as 'the land of milk'. Poet and academic Niranjan Bhagat writes in the October 1998 issue of *Seminar* that Gujaratis have traditionally displayed heroism and prowess, 'on the sea as seafarers, not on the land as warriors', causing, according to him, even martial races such as Rajputs of the north to abjure 'their weapons and war mania' after settling in Gujarat. The basis of this representation of Gujarat can perhaps be found in anthropology and geography. But one can also trace it back to the late nineteenth century when upper-caste Gujarati elites, participating in a cultural project to define the region, assiduously fashioned a description in their own image. Claims like Gujarat had 'always yielded a rich harvest of merchants', that these 'children of industry and enterprise' were 'soft and gentle at home' made by the best-known writer of the time, Govardhanram Tripathi, author of the magisterial *Saraswati Chandra*, were typical.

Now, in the twenty-first century, a dramatic refashioning is underway. Contemporary revisionists seem determined to alter the widely acknowledged idea of Gujarat as an Arcadian realm. And if Dharaiya's book and Bhatt's revelations are any indication, the feature judged most in need of amending is the reputation for peacefulness, for softness, a quality, some might say, of effeminacy. The revisionists, it seems, would like to infuse the pliancy with a metallic hardness, the aim being to produce an alchemy, not metaphorically but *literally*, as one hears in Bhatt's vivid evocations.

In Ashutosh Bhatt's narrative, Dadichi Rishi, the mythical sage who offered his bones to the devatas to refashion the celestial weapons he had swallowed, 'represents' the tradition of Gujarat. Sardar Patel, the 'loha purush', or Iron Man, is equally representative. And then Bhatt begins to speak of Gandhi. And here subtly the emphasis shifts from the man to his environment. This is not the Gandhi the world is familiar with: maternal, complex, original, but an entity that comes to a land forged by the discipline of Jain strictures and toughened by the *akhadas* or gymnasia that sprouted in Gujarat after the Bengali Ghosh brothers spread the gospel of violent revolution. From this hard, metallic terrain, in Bhatt's narration, Gandhi derived his ideas, his strength, his force.

The other powerful and overarching strand in Bhatt's discourse is Ahmedabad. In various ways, in the wealth and capability of its burghers to support progressive causes, in its enlightened traditions, in clever contrivances such as the huge underwater tanks called *tankas* in the old city, he perceives his town's eminence. Building on this superiority, which stems from the man in the pol, his sensitivity towards all living beings (implied by the presence of bird feeders), his understanding of the private (that is the courtyard inside the house) and the public (symbolised by the community square), Bhatt constructs a trajectory of national pride. A fierce love for home is the building block of a fierce love for the country.

*

Since 1928 when Pritam Nagar, the first housing society patterned on the lines of co-operative housing societies that were coming into vogue in Europe as a result of housing shortages after World War I, came up in Ahmedabad, co-operative societies have proliferated west of the river. The neighbourhoods of the new city were organised according to principles derived from the British-led Town Plans. They had modern sanitation, wide roads and lights. Unlike in the walled city, where mixed use was the norm, in the new town, residential areas were separated from commercial areas. And houses were designed for single families. 'I live here now,' says Mohan, gesturing at the plastered walls of his apartment and beyond, where the buildings with their matchbox apertures rise like stalactites and the bleating, smoking traffic beats through the busy road. 'I live here but I *don't like it*. Whenever I get a chance, I go running back to Khadia.' His wife, a blowsy, attractive woman, listening silently, jerks her head in indulgent confirmation.

'Festivals and weddings! I miss the celebrations!' Mohan's high, nasal voice rises. 'Here there is nothing! Nothing! There you have sound! You have colour! And everybody participating!' He looks about him disconsolately. 'In these big buildings, in this modern city with all the traffic, you don't get it, it is only there in the walled city that you get *hoonf*.' 'Hoonf' in Gujarati indicates a sense of inner security, of peacefulness, such as, I imagine, one finds on the faces of sleeping infants.

In the *pichwais*, devotional cloth paintings created by the artists of Nathdwara, a pilgrim town 300 kilometres north of Ahmedabad, the god Krishna is depicted as a seven-year-old child, Shrinathji. Blue-skinned, fish-eyed and precocious, Shrinathji holds up the Govardhan mountain to protect his people from the torrential rain sent down by Indra, the god of thunder. He lives in a splendid mansion, adored and cosseted. Feasts of fifty-six dishes, the celebrated 'chhappan bhog', are prepared for him. Attendants spray each other with butter balls for his amusement. Beautiful gopis with henna on their palms play musical instruments and dally with him in verdant fields under an overcast sky. His head is adorned with peacock feathers, flowers and *jhumkas*; his neck with bejewelled chains, his feet with anklets, his hand with a long-stemmed lotus. His robes change with the seasons and the festivals, sometimes a translucent orange, sometimes a shimmery gold, sometimes striped and worn like pyjamas in the Moghul style, sometimes patterned with motifs. He basks, the playful boy-God, in the indulgence and adoration of his adult acolytes.

The worship of Krishna probably started in Gujarat around the twelfth century. Till then the Gujarati Hindus were primarily devotees of Shiva, the almighty destroyer. The shift to Vaishnavism became most pronounced four hundred years later with the emergence of the Andhra preacher Vallabhacharya, whose sect, the Pushti Marg (Way of Grace), acquired immense popularity. The phenomenon ran parallel to the rising prosperity of the merchants in this coastal region. Not surprisingly, for Krishna, the God of sensuality and pleasure, was far more in keeping with the mood of an advancing mercantile community than Shiva, the God associated with skulls and bones and the macabre rituals of the graveyard.

The exuberant spirit of sixteenth-century Vaishnavism pervades the old city of Ahmedabad. Indeed, according to myth, Krishna in his role as architect, designed it in imitation of his own legendary town of Dwarka. Celestial intelligence, perhaps, and certainly an exultant zeitgeist, moulded this habitation so like a toy town, with its dainty carved houses, curling pathways and chabutras, elaborate bird feeders mounted on pillars rising like traffic lights in the middle of chowks.

A Hindu woman emerges with startling suddenness from a doorway in one of the pencil-thin lanes of the old city. Her eyes are closed, her head covered by her sari pallu. Her lips move silently, ceaselessly. She raises her arms high overhead, letting water fall from a small metal *lota*. The imminent possibility of my being splashed does not deter her. It is unlikely she has even registered the proximity of a human form, so engaged is she in her communion with a higher being. She returns, as abruptly as she came, leaving a water stain on the path.

It is cold, though blocks of sunlight have formed on the tops of houses. In the empty chowk a cricket stump is chalked on a wall below a poster for Hutch telecom. A baby watches me from behind a candy-pink *jaali*. I notice a man, barefooted and effeminate in a robe draped like a sari over one shoulder, moving swiftly through the hushed lanes. I trail him, stray dogs nuzzling my hand. I follow him into a small local Jain temple. Unexpected treasures are known to lurk in these modest structures inserted like doorstops into niches. Curtains when parted reveal engraved silver doors; a torchlight in a dark corner lights up an inlay of rubies and mother of pearl. This *derasar* has a ceiling of carved teak, a cupola full of burnished figurines, animal forms, flowers and musical instruments. Below it an elderly nun with a cloth flap tied around her mouth performs her ritual devotions watched by the multiple unblinking eyes of the metal Tirthankaras.

In the era of the Sultanate, citizens lived in *puras* or independent suburbs established by noblemen. Historians are not sure when and how the pol, the term given to the later style of community life that would become a distinctive and defining feature of the city, asserted itself. A pol comprises a cluster or several clusters of tightly packed houses connected by an internal network of labyrinthine lanes and fronted by a gate that could be shut at night, closing it off from the outside world. Sometime between the fifteenth and the eighteenth centuries, pols germinated like spores within the town walls. The walls had come up in 1487 in the rule of Mahommad Begda. Twentieth-century scholars would estimate the existence of 365 pols accommodating a further 600 sub pols in a 220 square kilometer area. It was a form of high-density living accompanied by a highly organized social structure that had, with the exception of a few mixed pols, Hindus, Jains, Parsis and Muslims living among their own with further subdivisions on grounds of caste and profession.

Was it an external fear that caused this implosion? Did the expectation of assault by an invader and his marauding artillery cause this huddling of bodies, this shrinking of streets, the bulwark of gates and the drilling of mazes dotted with secret escape routes? This is a view held by many old-time residents who believe the congealing of lived space to be an eighteenth-century phenomenon in response to frequent raids by the Marathas. Under their plundering ways, which earned them the Arabic sobriquet 'ganim', the town for several decades fell into steep neglect, leading a visitor in 1781 to write about the town's 'nodding minarets, decaying palaces and smouldering aqueducts' and to compare it to the fallen glorious cities of Nineveh and Babylon.[2]

This is not the only explanation, however, and architects have amply proved the possibility of the urban form evolving in response to the climate rather than a human aggressor. The tall shadows of close-set facades, the narrow, tubular forms of the houses and multiple perforations gently ameliorate the harshness of summer, giving the intertwined glut of pathways the lulling protectiveness of a womb. Here, in this dim corner of the world, every action, every sound, is significant. When people talk about life in the old city, it is no wonder that they invariably foreground the quotidian. The humdrum ordinariness of everyday life is evoked as a fount of incomparable richness and satisfaction. The daily ritual of cleaning teeth with a neem stick, performed at the leisurely pace of masticating cows, followed by a perusal of the newspapers, with views exchanged across the street, members of many households all similarly occupied on their otlas ...

Young men gathering at street corners to confer over weighty matters such as a googly bowled in a cricket match; the climax of a film viewed at one of the clutch of movie halls nearby: the Cinema des France, Model, Alankar, Kalpana, Rupam or Relief; and girls, neighbourhood girls, they do not identify by name but covet with all the ardour of their approaching manhood. Housewives returning home from the temples; children playing hopscotch; calamities and change in the world outside being avidly debated by elders on wooden benches by the light of a brazier on winter nights; routine and connectedness providing strength in this tightly circumscribed world. This I imagine is what people here mean when they talk about 'hoonf', a peace that comes from feeling truly at home.

> DON'T EARN SO THAT YOU COMMIT CRIME
> DON'T SPEND SO AS TO GET INTO DEBT
> DON'T SAY THAT WHICH WILL GET YOU INTO A FIGHT

The admonitions in Gujarati are on a wall abutting a compound shared by a temple and the B. Ranchodlal Chotalal Girls High School in Khadia. Like most of his friends, growing up in the decades when English was marginalised in Gujarat, Mohan went to a vernacular-medium school, a fact that caused no dip in his swagger as he moved about in the pols and labyrinthine streets of the walled city. The first time he travelled outside Gujarat, however, his sense of self worth came crashing down. He had gone to stay with relatives in suburban Mumbai. His big-city cousins laughed at his lack of English and made fun of his dress and his manners, calling him a 'poliyo' (a pejorative term for someone who came from the pols). 'I felt I knew nothing at all!' Mohan recalls with haunted eyes. 'I felt the difference between them and me. And I felt so ashamed.'

We negotiate our way through a swarm of little girls in school uniforms. Somewhere in these lanes, the 'passport-*iyo*' Hanuman temple is said to be remarkably efficacious at granting prayers from American-visa seekers. Advertisements for the Unit Trust of India and the Life Insurance Corporation are plastered on kiosks and pillars. The first modern banks and insurance companies came up a stone's throw away on Richey Road. The conversion of the central part of the walled city from a traditional mixed use area into a commercial district commencing in the 1940s and the large-scale migration to the west created blight in the old city. Neglect is evident on the intricately carved facades of many of the old pol houses. Some have been pulled down and replaced with gaudy concrete—the work oftentimes of a powerful builders' cartel. From the 1980s onwards the demand for *jharokhas*, brackets and pillars from stripped pol houses, grew in other parts of the country. Many old houses became godowns where the Marwari shop owners of Gandhi Road could store electrical goods. The recurrence of communal violence led to waves of expulsion of well-heeled Hindus and Muslims. New colonies in the west perspicaciously advertised 'a riot-free environment'. Girls from genteel families refused to marry boys living in pols. West of the river, the old city came to be talked of as a diseased organ, a slowly putrefying part of Ahmedabad.

Mohan bids me to ignore the clackety clack of the machines of the printing press on the first floor as I follow him up the steep staircase of the narrow multi-storey pol house in which he grew up. His chatter evokes images of the sun-patterned rooms filled, as they must have once been, with parents and grandparents, sisters and brothers. I imagine the voices of the past floating up the atrium, all the way to the top. Downstairs, on the ground floor, the main living quarters of the household are arranged in a straight line. The toilet is next to the entrance. '*Outside*,' Mohan emphasizes. 'Everything that is dirty is *outside*! Inside is all *pavitra* (holy).' We walk through: the outer room, the kitchen, the puja room. By now Mohan's face has taken on an unhealthy pallor. 'My grandmother was *very* particular! That line …' I see a line of white tiles bordering the kitchen and the puja room. 'That had to be kept shining at all times!' He hops from foot to foot almost beside himself with agitation. 'You understand? At … all … *times*!' I look at him all flushed and overwrought. I remember how during an interview with a trader at the National Cloth Market, my interviewee, a large shambling man in his sixties, noticing that I had not taken off my shoes outside his office, turned black with menace and started talking threateningly, though as if hypothetically, of me as a third party he could throw out of the room.

They say that homesick sailors returning to Gujarat used to pine for the reassuring glimpse of Mount Girnar, silhouetted purple against the clouds. I wonder if this hyper-anxious preoccupation with rules and purity and psychological borders is connected with the peripatetic proclivity of the Gujarati. For a mercantile people, used to a life of constant shifting and adjustment, home, perhaps, had to offer the security and fixity of a mountain peak.

*

Mohan and I are walking about in a maze making me feel I am participating in an elaborate subterfuge. This is guerilla territory. Everything is and is not. One can imagine an invader, well-armed and puffed with might, disconcerted by surprise and sleight of hand. The houses, the streets here, are hard yet elastic. Unseen passageways provide a way out of cul de sacs. The rooftops packed close together are a parallel topography providing routes for transport of essentials and escape. This cunning, with which the outsider can be tricked and deceived, is also applied inwards for maintaining social norms, as I have seen, and to hide wealth from covetous eyes. The narrow frontages of many houses open out like accordions on entering, exposing unexpected spaces, courtyards splashed with sunlight, glossy floors, steep staircases and chambers as large as nineteenth-century ballrooms, and furnished with Belgian glass. It is a hamlet that can burst into life or curl into itself like a tortoise, preserving itself with this mercurial adaptability for hundreds of years.

'I can't *bear* Muslims,' Mohan is saying. 'It is from the beginning, this prejudice. I look over a wall and I see a topi and I feel *sick*! I smell that meat smell and I feel like vomiting. I can't *bear* it.' He looks ill indeed, a red flush climbing up his face. 'All of us in the pols feel this way. I tell my son also, any community is okay but not *that*!' Since 1969 when the first episode of large-scale communal violence exploded in the city, clashes between the two communities have been a routine occurrence. 'Anything can spark it off,' Mohan says, 'a fight over a kite, a scooter knocking against someone from the other community. A minor thing becomes major. For small things pebbles are thrown, tubelights are thrown. From the beginning we are taught that we can't *tolerate*.'

A provocation, a rumour, a news item can release a Hindu mob almost instantly into the treacherous porous streets where the police are scared to venture. 'We cover our faces with handkerchiefs and take the mob to the "border". At such times we forget that we could die. If you are stabbed you don't realize it because "they" [the Muslims] put something on their knives to numb the pain.' He shows me a scar from a cut on the side of his forehead. 'We pick up stones and start pelting. The police come and we run. We were afraid of the police. They would come in-between the two sides—then you can't do anything.' He continues without pausing or altering his tone, 'But in 2002 the police gave us licence for one day. And in the nine months of curfew that was declared at the time, there was sharing in the Hindu pols, money, food, even cigarettes over the rooftops!'

Mohan's protruding eyes are bright in his shiny face. 'From the time we were children this was our life. Ashok Bhatt would teach us how to throw stones. Any Khadia man can throw stones. We learnt how to loot shops. We learnt how to make bombs with our bare hands. We learnt to lift bodies. We never thought about becoming doctors or engineers. What we used to aspire to was to throw a stone at the red light on the police commissioner's car. We would talk about it endlessly and agree that whoever broke that light would be the champion among us. We thought the more we do this kind of thing, the more fame we would have. I ruined my career ...' I hear despondency in his voice, remorse over wasted time, and I am surprised by the glimmer of self-awareness, of introspection. Yet, as abruptly as he started on this unexpected train of thought he breaks off, seized by an uncontrollable fury that brings a flush to his face and reminds him that he cannot *bear* it.

*

'My suggestion was we could do *leepan* on the floor here. I could even do it myself ... *What? What?* ... You don't believe me?' Ashok Bhatt spins around, his eager pressing glance encompassing us all, the small knot of people he has led to the first floor of a 300-year-old house he is restoring in Rameshwar ni pol. It is 2008 and he has aged by a quarter of a century since I last saw him, with silver hair to show for it. And he has risen from a lowly legislator to become a minister several times over. Yet he retains the jejune air of our first meeting.

'I have done leepan, you know!' he announces with a flushed face and gesticulating hands. 'In the village every year we would bring in the fresh cow dung and spread it out, all over the house.' The current mayor, a large, swarthy man with a sandalwood mark on his forehead who answers to the greeting 'Jai Jyanendra', seems unimpressed. But the deputy mayor, the two officials from the Heritage Department and the lady member of the Standing Committee burst into indulgent titters at the thought of their cabinet minister and senior leader of the BJP doubled over smearing the floor with cow dung. Ashok Bhatt's daughter, a grim, stout woman, joins in the hilarity, shaking her head at her father's incorrigibility.

Bhatt looks gratified. The amusement validates his chosen attitude of flippancy. It is hard to pin anything particularly terrible or serious on this man with his pixie features and wandering eyes. Even the accusation that he was in the police control room on February 28, 2002, on a day when policemen appeared unwilling to stop the incidents of heinous crimes against the city's Muslims, seems to lose its grim force. There is no security presence outside his house in Rameshwar ni pol, just a couple of desultory guards at night. He chooses to live in the space where he grew up, eschewing the ministerial perks he is entitled to. He dresses in kurta pyjamas; his manner, shoulders stooped, hands clasping and unclasping, oozing unction. He greets visitors personally, stepping out onto the otla to usher them in, and is known by one and all to have a yen for the savoury treats of the Raipur Bhajia House. The image, no doubt real but also assiduously cultivated, is of the boy next door, the person to be counted on, at once unassuming and influential.

It is an old RSS[3] trick, a local journalist tells me, to use a 'kitchen entry' as he puts it, which consists of a show of self-effacement and helpfulness that is extremely appealing, particularly to the women of the household, to insinuate oneself into a community. But what perhaps at one time was political strategy has now acquired new ramifications. The homeboy, the inciter of Khadia in the 1980s has become, at the dawn of the twenty-first century, the autochthon, the native, the indigene. And around this shift is the slow but steady transformation in the imagining of the old city.

The reimagining of the old city began gradually in the late 1990s with the percolation of Western-inspired ideas of heritage conservation. On the Heritage Walk of the Ahmedabad Municipal Corporation, started in 1997, one can see these influences in the preserved facades of landmarks, identified by small, neat plaques, in statues in lifelike poses that turn public squares into exhibition tableaux. The effort snowballed through the 2000s, involving stepped-up conservation activity and local communities, artists, photographers, dancers, students, including those at the city's premier design and architecture institutions, quasi-historians and the media, in an annual cultural festival, culminating in a quest beginning around 2010 to be listed by UNESCO as a World Heritage City.

The marketing of culture and local history has been a significant strategy in the place wars fought among cities internationally and reflected most vividly in the course correction made by Shanghai and Singapore in the 1980s and 1990s. Departing from its policy of 'out with the old, in with the new', Shanghai restored the historic landmarks and traditional shikumen or stone gate houses in the narrow alleys of the district of Xintiandi while Singapore focused on the conservation of its colourful ethnic quarters such as Chinatown, Little India and Kampong Glam. The new protectiveness towards the traditional and relatively messy form of habitation stemmed from a need to balance the antiseptic nature of the rapidly modernising city and, more critically, to reclaim the cities' Oriental charms in order to arrest falling tourist traffic. But, as urban scholars have acknowledged, Cultural Imagineering, as this form of urban engineering is called, has the potential to conceal social complexities and polarisations of various kinds—ethnic, gender, social and so on—by 'mobilising every aesthetic power of illusion and image'.[4]

In 2007, at a time when Gujarat was under harsh criticism, nationally and internationally, for the vicious anti-Muslim violence of 2002, a Brazilian Kathak dancer performing for the Ahmedabad Heritage Festival amidst the rubble in the old city sensitized Ahmedabadis to the pain of their destroyed heritage. The language of the heritage movement, terms and phrases such as 'conservation', 'restoration', 'revitalisation', 'revival of Ahmedabad's pride', seemed designed to bring solace to a city under attack. By displacing both shame and solace to the plight of a building or a bird feeder and by making possible the reclamation of the Islamic, as poetry, architecture and craft, but not as a community or a religion, the heritage movement seemed to play into the agenda of militantly pro-Hindu politicians. The celebratory air, encapsulated as in the brochure of an annual heritage festival—'In India festivals are a way of life'—overlaid the traumatic social fissure with a determinedly happy layer of forgetting.

Similarly for the Ahmedabadi media, the preservation of Ahmedabad's historic core provided an advertiser-friendly upbeat subject with a veneer of commendable inclusiveness. Stories about Ahmedabad's endearing folksiness run side by side with reports on its expanding urbanity. This celebration of nostalgia is amplified by every part of the burgeoning media, including by homesick bloggers in the diaspora. The heritage movement has given Ahmedabad a fuzzy aura of welcome and sharing. It is 'maaru [my] Amdavaad', 'aapnu [our] Amdavaad'.

In Ashok Bhatt's house in Rameshwar ni pol, the bouquets are piling up. Bhatt has been elected Speaker of the Assembly and visitors are calling on him to offer their congratulations. Three Bohra men, conspicuous in their stiff white caps, enter the house, while Bhatt is busy with a visitor who has come to invite him to an art show, and find seats at the edge of the room. The Bohras, a Muslim business community, made peace with the Modi government soon after the incidents of 2002. The presence of the trio is clearly a continuation of the olive branch approach. Bhatt acknowledges their arrival with a nod and from time to time his eyes settle speculatively on the group.

Images of Shrinathji are scattered in profusion all over the room. Also conspicuous is a photograph of Narendra Modi with a declaration in Hindi: 'I dream but I also have the will to realise it!' Cellphones erupt into bhajans (*Shri Krishna Sharnammumah*) or patriotic songs (*Vande Mataram*). Visitors come and go exchanging 'Jai Shri Krishnas'. The mayor announces that he is off to Japan in a few days. He is to go, he says, to a place 'where the Americans killed many people'.

'To invite a man of *ahimsa* to a place of *himsa* is wrong,' Bhatt says, widening his eyes to convey a hint of mockery. A titter ripples through the room. The Standing Committee woman and the Heritage department officials are still there, drinking tea from small cups with a floral pattern. As I get up to leave, Bhatt comes to the door to see me out. Outside, in the bitter winter morning, a crew from a local TV channel is waiting to interview him.

*

The moon is still in the sky, a wispy, cottony half disc. Rubbish bins, grey and overfull, line the exit pathways of the city. Soon even those disappear. The empty road unspools for miles. The windows are up but the cold air finds a way in. 'Wear Seat Belt' says a sign on the road. 'Better Late Than Never' says another. A sticker on the windscreen of my borrowed car repeats the instruction on seat belts in Gujarati. I am doing what scores of upper-class Ahmedabadi children aged six to fifteen do every weekday at the crack of dawn: going to school.

The schools that are in present favour with the haut monde of town are located well outside the commercial and residential areas of the city. They are in places where tractors are stirring the red earth and filling up water bodies, hacking settlements out of the pliant countryside. They are by the sides of highways or on stretches of new road, flat and glistening all year under the harsh sun. They are filled each day by an efficient feeder system, a legion of school buses fanning out into the city collecting their human saplings with sleep still in their eyes.

Nothing keeps parents of social eminence awake at night as much as the concern that they are not doing enough to assure their children their rightful place in the coming world. Reared in easier times, when a slipshod mix of chance, enterprise and privilege was enough to put the Merc or at least a Hyundai in the garage, ensure crystal on the table, holidays in Tanzania and business options in Lagos and Tokyo, they deeply fear the stampeding of their exalted habitats by the aspiring hordes. The only way, the *only way*, to ensure a seat on the bus for their progeny is the right education.

Early rays light up the pink dust on the Sanand Highway. On my right, hundreds of cars like stabled horses pack an open stockyard. A large tractor showroom goes by, then more cars and two wheelers, new, awaiting disbursal, in an open field. A tanker of the Bharat Gas company lumbers around a desolate traffic island. In 2008, the Gujarat government procured 1,100 acres of land in Sanand on the city's western margins to entice Tata Motors to set up a plant to produce its low-cost Nano car after it was ousted by violent protests from displaced farmers in leftist Bengal. I hear that much of the agricultural land hereabouts has been sold to developers in the expectation of an emerging auto hub.

The letters G-O-K-U-L-D-H-A-M are spread out on a bank of grass beside the road. Across a temple sponsored by a Ford workshop, I turn into a long, narrow lane bounded by a brick wall behind which the grass grows tall and wild. Occasionally a yellow school bus, like a rogue camel, crashes past, snorting, raising dust.

The right education: in the era of globalization it is a ragbag of features. It consists, at the very minimum, of a high standard of spoken and written English, an internationally approved curriculum, tie-ups with American universities, preferably Ivy League, sufficient acreage for field sports, diverse extra-curricular activities and infrastructure in the form of computers and air conditioning. Innovations such as a no-examination policy are seen as being fashionably progressive, while for many parents, particularly those who have lived abroad, the active propagation of 'Indian values and culture' is an essential requirement.

The intense prioritization of schooling has attracted a flamboyant new breed of entrepreneurs to education: men and women with professional skills and corporate experience, well-versed in management jargon, bandying phrases like 'branding', 'top-down reverse appraisals', 'quantitative assets' and 'people growth plans'. The difference between them and corporate honchos and them and the run-of-the-mill promoter of educational institutions is that they perceive themselves to be idealists involved in the delicate and significant task of social transformation.

In the Eklavya School the bell has not yet rung for the start of day. Some senior-school students in white uniforms are sweeping the concrete path to clear the litter of dry leaves that has fallen through the night. A few have stationed themselves on the edge of a small pond and are dipping a net to collect leaves from the water. Their lack of experience shows in their awkward moves. The leaves keep blowing back or slipping out of the net. This is the kind of activity I often hear touted as a progressive measure in this sort of school, an example of how children softened by luxury and plentiful domestic help are taught humility and the dignity of labour. At Swastik's Sattavikas school, the director Raja Pathak tells me how he designed the walk from the school gate to the classroom to be long and open to the elements in order to put children, used to air-conditioned cars and other comforts, in a suitably modest frame of mind for learning. And also to make them alert. 'Openness converts you into alertness,' he says. 'God is watching! God sent many to watch you!'

I think of schooldays for the privileged in my time. An uneasy recollection of neat rows at assembly, stern prefects, house names borrowed from British writers and British flora, marching tunes pounded on a piano. Outside the junior school at Eklavya, children in hooded winter jackets gather around a boy beating a drum, their small hands hidden away in the pockets of their navy-blue and red uniforms. At a bugle call, shivering steeples of hands form and eyes shut. A small boy observes me through his fluttering eyelids. The proceedings are conducted by a pair of older students, a boy and a girl. There is a short speech in Hindi followed by a Sanskrit prayer. Then the familiar strains of the bhajan that is one of Mahatma Gandhi's favourites, *Raghupati Raghav Raja Ram*, are heard and everyone sings along. One little boy in particular has his eyes closed and claps and sways as if to a rock beat.

FOUR

Working Class

JULY 8, 2009: THE newspapers talk of a number of people having died and many more being hospitalized as a result of consuming spurious liquor over the previous weekend. They are calling it 'The Sip of Death'. Young men lie, two to a cot, in postures suggestive of an alcoholic haze; the presence of nurses, saline drips and women in saris, making helpless, maternal gestures provide the only clue to the war raging inside their thin, fully dressed bodies. The death toll mounts.

In the streets of Majoor Gam, where most of these early victims come from, there is outrage. Men and women pelt stones at the police when they come investigating. The bewailing, enraged expressions on the faces of the women and the poses struck by the teenage males, leaning on one foot, taking aim with the practised elegance of a cricket bowler, call to mind quotidian battles on the streets of distant places like Ramallah, Gaza and Srinagar. On the front pages of Ahmedabad's newspapers the following day, however, these scenes appear to me exotic in quite another way. For so long now, the media, increasingly commercial, and driven by the prim interests and pre-occupations of the consuming, advertiser-friendly middle and upper classes, has acquired a certain anodyne character. This is a rare foray into the heart of the gaudy, seething, working-class neighbourhood.

The residents of Majoor Gam slip easily and naturally into their expected roles for the cameras. Like actors in a play, they assume expressions of long suffering and hold up plastic pouches of what looks like discoloured water but what is, as every child in the locality will tell you, desi daaru. There is a penumbra of ludicrousness around this unfolding human tragedy, a shadow, darkly comic, that pulls the gaze athwart the bright beam of suffering. This is not a story about people dying. This is not a story about people dying from consuming spurious liquor. This is a story about the consumption of liquor itself.

Gujarat is a dry state which means that the manufacture, consumption and sale of liquor is prohibited here. The fact that several people have died from drinking exposes the hollowness of the ban. This is the reason why a battalion of vehicles with press stickers and OB vans with their rooftop gadgetry are squirrelling into the warren-like pathways of the labour district. This is why the unfortunate residents of Majoor Gam are flaunting pouches of liquor: to expose the charade of prohibition. What denudes these attempts and the responses they evoke of any seriousness, however, is the fact that what is sought to be exposed is already known. Everybody knows and everybody knows that everybody knows. The easy availability of alcohol in Gujarat is the state's worst-kept secret.

An effect of Gandhi's strong advocacy against liquor was the inclusion of Prohibition in the Indian Constitution as a directive principle. The Constitution left the choice of implementing it to individual states. Gujarat and the northeastern states of Mizoram, Nagaland and Manipur, chose to embrace absolute Prohibition. That Gujarat's policy in this regard remained more or less unchanged over the next half century demonstrates a groundswell of support for the continuance of Prohibition in the state. But the gap between the law and practice, between the idea and reality, has resulted, over the years, in the creation of a peculiar schizophrenia and a miasma of amorality that is rarely acknowledged despite its pernicious consequences. These are evident, for instance, in the informal methods of distribution that have sprung up all over the city.

On the walking path that meanders through the grounds of the Ahmedabad Textile Industry's Research Association, one evening, I hear Lata Mangeshkar's shrill *Ay mere watan ke logon* resound from a fellow stroller's cellphone.

'Anilbhai?'

'Deepeshbhai?'

He makes several calls, to men with common Gujarati Hindu names and, apparently, from the loud bursts emanating from his speakerphone, a uniformly patriotic taste in caller tunes. He is looking for someone to deliver a bottle of vodka that evening. Branded Indian Made Foreign Liquor (IMFL) is delivered at the doorstep. Cheap hooch is sold in the vicinity of roadside stalls where one can find boiled eggs and other tasty 'bitings'.

Back in the 1980s, when Marwari Jain and Hindu jewellers and shopkeepers in the country's pre-eminent commercial city Bombay looked to the Muslim ghetto to supply their needs for smuggled gold and electronic goods, there arose, from the shady streets of Dariapur in Ahmedabad's old city, a powerful bootlegger by the name of Abdul Latif. The son of a tobacco shop owner, and a school drop-out, Abdul Latif started out by assisting a bootlegger, then taking to the trade himself. He was a person with a flair for business, entering into arrangements with liquor dealers outside the state and with underworld figures in Bombay. He also consolidated the bootlegging *dhando*, earlier divided among many in Gujarat, under himself. For this he had a large staff of young Muslim boys and several policemen on his payroll. Under his protection, liquor was sold, of course, but

Ahmedabad also became an entry point for drugs, brown sugar and smuggled gold. His spectacular rise was supported by the Congress, which used his army of able-bodied men for political purposes. In 1985, Latif, possibly acting at the behest of local leaders, triggered an episode of communal violence by knifing Hindu passersby.

Latif, and the Congress' role in his rise, reinforced the distrust of the city's Hindu majority. The press relentlessly played up the image of the Muslim as an inveterate criminal and the BJP adroitly fanned the flames to singe the Congress, describing the party as the guardian of criminals. In 2009, the boot is on the other foot.

*

A dozen or so rough-looking elderly men are collected on the second floor of the Textile Labour Association (TLA) building near Lal Darwaza. They are lined up at the far end of a vast hall, carrying with them their papers and their old gate passes, which they present to two men sitting behind a table busily filling in details in long, blank folders. Downstairs, the sound of a car at the entrance indicates that Manhar Shukla, the 95-year-old general secretary of the TLA, has arrived. Shukla attends office for a few hours most days, though it is clear that there is nothing really for him, or for that matter for anyone, to do.

The composite textile mill industry commenced its slow decline in the late sixties under the combined assault of technological innovation in the shape of the electric powerloom, which favoured smaller-scale, disaggregated operations, and the political exigencies of a callow prime minister who was willing to use legislation to break the back of big business, the mainstay of a syndicate of veteran politicians ranged against her. This decline reached its logical conclusion over the following two decades. Almost all of Ahmedabad's composite textile mills have closed down. There were more than seventy in 1950. The TLA's membership has dwindled from hundreds of thousands to a few thousand and thirty-odd people remain of its five thousand-strong staff.

From underneath the staircase a dusty life-size photograph of an elderly couple peers out at a dog lazily basking on the porch. Anasuya Sarabhai, from a prominent mill owner's family of the early twentieth century, discovered Fabian socialism while living in England and was moved to work for the welfare of textile workers in her home city. With her in the photograph is Shankerlal Banker, scion of a prosperous Mumbai banking family, who assisted her in founding the TLA in 1920. Gandhi, who appears on a frieze outside on the façade of the building, provided the inspiration for and the guiding principles of the TLA. Gandhi's approach to labour relations derived from a traditional Hindu–Jain ethos according to which workers and mill owners were part of a family, settling disputes through mutual consideration and compromise rather than confrontation. His collaborative approach would become enmeshed with the unifying goals of the Independence struggle and even influence India's New Labour policy in the late 1950s, but it was in Ahmedabad, in the TLA, that it was sought, most assiduously, to be realised.

The building has the feel of a municipal school in summer. The corridors, the sparsely furnished rooms, are empty. Stray voices and the clatter of footsteps carry through the hollowness. The only evidence of activity is in the hall. The men collected there are ex-employees of the erstwhile Continental Mill and are being assisted in a judicial case for pending dues. In a while, after all the men have had their turn, the officials pack up their records. But still the men linger on. They sprawl on a bench in the adjoining passage, stand around aimlessly, or find buddies and huddle over a chipped table in one of the many vacant rooms. They are not required to stay but they appear reluctant to leave. I hear chatter, the occasional loud exchange and some laughter.

I see a tall spare man, distinctive, with a red *teeka*, a scarf and long wild hair. He looks like he could be a politician. A bystander observing my curious glance tells me the man was in the cloth-stamping department of the Continental Mill and has all the details of the legal case. I tell them I am not here for the case. A stout, coarse-featured man, supine on a bench, straightens up and calls out to me, surprising me with his polished English. He is a former factory manager, a managerial position that distinguishes him from the ordinary workers around him. As if to underscore the fact, he starts listing the names of the places he has worked in, occasionally adding dates and the number of employees and even identifying some mills that he personally closed down. 'Maneklal Harilal ... Rajnagar ... Bharat Vijay ... Bageecha Mills, Monogram Mills, 3,000 men, for fourteen years, then Ajit Mills, 1,200 men, on Rakhial Road for eleven years. Continental Mills for fifteen years ... Closed Arbuda Mill, 4,000 workers ... December 31, 2008 closed down Neptune Spin Fab ...'

There was a Coketown in Ahmedabad, a rash of smokestacks spreading beyond the town walls, far east of the river. But the mills influenced life in all of Ahmedabad. The siren that summoned labourers to work also beckoned the student to school and the housewife to her chores. The trill of the cycle bell pervaded songs. The industrialist, the trader and the late-shift worker ate side-by-side at the night market in Manek Chowk. And everybody found comfort in the massed presences on the street, their cycle lamps wavering on cold, foggy nights like shivering fireflies.

A hundred and fifty years after the first textile mill was started in 1861 by a Nagar Brahmin called Ranchodlal Chotalal, vast compounds are strewn with broken masonry and overgrown with wild weeds and bramble. Silver Mill, Sarangpur Cotton No. 2, the New Hosiery Mill ... mills known to locals by more intimate associations—the 'ganji-farrack' mill, a mill that made vests and frocks; 'pathra' mill, a mill compound strewn with stones; 'batata' mill, where potatoes were sold, and so on—all now in ruins. Every so often one looks up at a traffic light and notices the familiar saw-tooth roof on a facade standing all by itself, an empty shell.

In Girdhar Nagar, across the railway tracks, not far from Asarwa, the names of old mills, Jubilee, Rajnagar and Manjushree, are still landmarks by which people know their way around. In Pritampura Chaali No. 2, a row of identical tiled roof houses, garlanded photographs tell of a time when the boy in spinning at Tarun Commercial married a girl from the bobbin department at the Star of Gujarat. After the locks appeared on mill gates, families split up; some members going back to the villages. Many mill workers died broken-hearted, and their co-workers took their bodies to the crematoria via the mill gates. But life has moved on from those bleak times. Many *chaalis*[1] in Girdhar Nagar have become modern apartment blocks. The progeny of former mill workers have got jobs, in call centres or hospitals, where they mingle 'with good people like doctors'.

Gajraben, who lives in the first house in the chaali, talks to me, with wet dye in her hair, of her many responsibilities, including assisting at crèches run by the local MLA who is from the BJP, which has made considerable inroads in this former Congress bastion of low-caste textile workers. The able-bodied among the former mill workers, too, have long found other occupations. Manilal Parmar, a stocky, loquacious 59-year-old full of colourful descriptions about life in the mills—the crowds streaming in for the morning shift, his 'group' in the Ring Frame Department, the camaraderie over drinks, tobacco or a fashionable Taj cheroot—

works now as a guard in a housing society. 'I don't have to do anything,' he says, 'just sit in a uniform all day.'

The strains of the *Hanuman Chalisa* assail me as I climb upstairs to the second floor at the TLA. Entering Smita Pandya's cabin, I find them growing louder, so loud that I can't hear her. 'What is it, is it a loudspeaker on the street?' I ask, going over to the window. She picks up her cellphone and I realize, with a start, that the booming intonation is emanating from the little instrument on her table. Her finger presses down and the sound ceases, only to be replaced by another chant.

'*Vishnu Mantra*,' she says with an indicative gesture. 'I listen to it every day. It has a calming effect on me.'

I resign myself to attending to her soft voice over the sonorous mantras. Smita is a Project Officer with the TLA. She appears to be in her late thirties or early forties, a brisk-mannered woman and well-qualified, having studied both sociology and law. I had introduced myself over the phone and she appears to have classified me with the numerous researchers and scholars who periodically descend on the deserted TLA building for she begins to tell me about them, particularly about the Dutch researcher who spent months doing interviews and looking at fading papers and the American who was there the other day.

'Here,' she proffers a bunch of photographs. 'After you called I found these, I thought they might be of interest to you.' The photographs are in black and white. There are discolorations on some of them, and blotches where they have come unstuck from each other. There are photographs of activities of the TLA, probably in the nineteen fifties or early sixties. In one photograph, taken from a top angle, women in saris and children are seated in orderly rows in the hall, the same hall in which I saw the men from Continental Mills lined up, receiving instructions of some kind. There are pictures of training camps, of kits being handed out, of rows of people sitting down to a meal and of speeches being made. Over the years the TLA leadership was blamed for an excessive cosiness with mill managements. In the photographs, among the ageing male office bearers, I recognize a rare woman, a young Ela Bhatt, modest and serious. In 1972, Bhatt broke away to found her pioneering Self Employed Women's Association. Despite its shortcomings, the pictures reveal that the TLA, with its welfare approach, was a potent force in the lives of the workers.

The TLA's work in politics and civic affairs in the early twentieth century transformed the conditions in the industrial district. Land levelling, road paving, refuse collection, street lights and other features of the new city across the river percolated to the industrial district. Bus services ended its long isolation. Reading rooms, schools and akhadas or gymnasia further enhanced the quality of workers' lives. An evocative photograph of a TLA meeting by the veteran Ahmedabad-based photographer Pranlal Patel from the 1940s shows a mass of people with the rugged appearance of mill workers gathered on the riverbank. Men and women, Hindus and Muslims are collected, dressed as if for an outing. A smokestack rises in the background. The air is grainy with dust. The mood is relaxed, almost joyful. And each tiny figure appears to be part of a community.

While I have been looking at the photographs Smita has been parlaying with a couple of women staffers who are engaged in some work in the next room. I indicate the photographs in my hand. 'These ...'

'Oh take what you want,' she says.

I am speechless. There is so much history in those pictures. 'Shouldn't they be archived or filed?' I ask.

'They were being thrown away. I retrieved them only to show them to you,' she says with the casualness of someone immersed in more urgent matters.

I look sadly at the pictures, yellowing and bruised. I think of all the pamphlets and records and plaques in the desolate building that must have already been discarded. The former factory manager in the hall had said to me over and over again with regret: 'I wish I could have given you all the papers I had kept from the mills; I just threw them away.'

Smita has finished with her assistants. Fortunately the chants on her phone too have run out so we can talk comfortably. She reminisces about the old days. 'When I first came to work here, the crowds were so large that there was no space left for standing in any of the rooms,' she recalls. 'And then when the mills shut, the workers' wives would come and ask us, what should we do? They relied on the TLA so much.' I can hear voices coming from the next room. 'We are running a tailoring project to make some work for the labourers' families,' she explains.

In the dry afternoon, under a whirring fan, we continue to chat. Talk turns, as it invariably does, in this city, at this particular time, to the state's flamboyant chief minister. 'Narendra Modi is a great chief minister,' she says.

'Why do you say that?' I ask.

Without hesitation, like a child reciting a multiplication table, she reels off a list of achievements. 'Because of him we have paved roads in the city, we have water and lights. Because of him, ladies can move about safely till late. The slums were so dirty, particularly Hatkeshwar and Chamanpura, but not anymore. Because of him, roads have been widened. They had to break houses, temples and masjids and only someone with *kushal vehavar* (good relationship skills) can do this. He has changed the traffic situation, dealt hard with the police. After the recent bomb blast Narendra Modi took all the necessary steps to investigate the conspiracy. After the riots in 2002, Narendra Modi worked for both communities, set up camps for Muslims, provided food, medicine. Narendra Modi thinks of all. If there is no water, he thinks "how can I get water?" He knows how to get work done. He always thinks of bringing the lowest higher.'

*

In the basement of the celebrated Corbusian building that houses the Ahmedabad Textile Mill Owners' Association, opposite a photograph of Gandhi spinning on his *charkha*, portraits of past association presidents hang on the walls: sheths and baronets from 1891–1948 with flowing moustaches, teekas and turbans. These were Mahajans, leading men of the city. Their ancestors had paid off brigands and kings to protect Ahmedabad. In their time, they built an industry, cast a paternal eye over the city, established national institutions and sat on influential committees. The mill owners, along with Gandhi and the leaders of the Textile Labour Association, who would go on to become ministers and formulate national policy, were not only caretakers but also strands connecting the lowly Ahmedabadi labourer to the distant government in Delhi.

Things change. When the end was near, it is said, present-day mill owners behaved with a lack of responsibility that was glaringly inconsistent with their illustrious legacy. Many of them abandoned the mills that had turned into white elephants and diverted their funds into real estate. There were allegations of bad loans, financial mismanagement and of machinery being sneaked out of factory gates. The business community at large and the workers felt equally betrayed. But the mill owners too, I am told, were suffused with guilt. It led them to retreat, to shut themselves up in their big, dark houses, disengage themselves from the life of the city.

On a pavement abutting the old, demolished Silver Mill, a group of four squats on its haunches, tying bunches of yellow leaves into brooms. Their homes are under tarpaulin sheets tagged to a low compound wall. A man sits on a ledge under a tree in the dim glow of a streetlamp. I pass a row of cycles. Men hunched on benches watch me watch them, suspiciously. A cigarette shop; a board advertising Tip Top Tailors for suits; a hairdresser; an electrical repair shop; dingy, dark windows on a house advertising 'Gujarati and Punjabi food'.

I pass the Chamunda Youth Circle, cots standing on their sides, a wood shop, a sizzling pan on a stove, a TV shop. Men on benches, men at cigarette shops, men on the streets—men everywhere, swarming with a surging aimlessness.

In the 1800s, the early years of the mill industry, before the formation of the TLA, the abject living and working conditions of mill workers sometimes drove them to rebel. Suddenly and without warning, labourers would take to the streets. These episodes, usually on a small scale and involving workers of one mill or department, were called *chamaklas*. But sometimes they snowballed, gathering numbers and turning into *hullads*, bursting through the industrial district like shrieking tornados, causing terrified citizens to hurry home and shopkeepers to down their shutters.

I come upon a roundabout, a statue of a woman frozen in the act of pouring water from a pot. Carts mounted with loudspeakers and trumpets stand at a bandmaster's shop in readiness for a wedding. I pass open doors with life faintly visible behind dirty curtains. An empty barber's chair beckons right out on the pavement, a mirror nailed to the wall reflecting the passing traffic. Parked cycles and scooters flank a petroleum shop. Men cluster around a paan ka gulla. More men, loitering, milling about, escaping the confines of crowded, airless homes.

The street rippling with figures, all alike in rumpled clothes with bleary, vacant faces, makes me recall the mobs in 2002. There have been attempts to connect the decline of the mills with that episode of violence. Yet, as former mill workers convincingly point out, through the twenty-odd years of desperation after the closure of the mills, there was no perceptible rise in the level of lawlessness or crime that would give credence to the theory of an anarchic outburst. The labourers just found other work: driving auto-rickshaws, hawking; work less paying, less dignified, less consistent perhaps, but they did it all the same. As one laid-off worker's wife told me: '*jevi-tevi reete samay nikli gayo* (somehow that bad time passed)'.

But with the idea of communal violence on my mind as I am driven through these wide, dreary streets pulsating with aimless males, I ask the driver of my rented vehicle if he was out on duty on February 28, 2002, the day the violence started. He doesn't answer right away and for a few anxious seconds I wonder if he was out with the mobs instead. Then he responds, saying he did not take out the car till the third day and then only because someone had to be taken to hospital. I ask him what he saw. 'All this ...' he says, spreading his arm, '... beating, burning.'

My questions have made him chatty. He begins to identify neighbourhoods by community: 'Muslim area', 'Hindu area'. We leave the surging lanes of the old working district and head north towards the broad roads of Nava Wadaj. It is late and shuttered business establishments loom in the shadows on the sides of the road. 'See those?' he says, pointing at them. 'They belong to Marwaris.' I sense a strong hint of disapproval in his tone. The damp road glistens under the neon lights. A truck rumbles ahead towards the char rasta. 'Marwaris are into the *pasti* [recycling] business,' he says. 'They are into many businesses but they have a monopoly over pasti in this area.' We cross the traffic lights and drive on with a flyover looming on the side. He is still talking about Marwaris. 'They undercut everyone else. They come here, live in huts to save money, and build big houses back home in Rajasthan.'

'Local Gujaratis are declining day by day. The processing

houses are mostly with Marwaris, Haryanvis and Rajasthanis. The Gujarati has ethics but all these do not.' The trader at the New Cloth Market, an off-shoot of the historic Maskati Cloth Market Association, gestures to indicate his dismay at the state of affairs. He is a big swarthy *vaniyo* from the old city. A poster on the wall says: *dhan maate nathi bhog seva maate* (sacrifice is not for wealth but for service). His father was a cloth trader and had a licence without which trading was not permitted; that is, in those days, he says, when rules and codes of honour meant something.

'See,' he says, beckoning me to listen carefully. 'A hundred centimeters make a metre. *They* will deduct two per cent of cloth. They also undercut for heavy profitability.' He snorts in disgust. 'Profit and outward show is everything to them!'

*

July 9: The toll has risen to fifty. Three hundred victims are being treated at three hospitals. Most of these men will die. Stupefied by liquor they are likely to have ignored the initial signs, the vomiting, the stomach pains, the prickling behind the eyes. By the time they have arrived at the hospital doors, likely as not the poison has corroded their insides to an irremediable extent. Illicit hooch contains a distillate of a fermented wash containing methyl alcohol, ammonia, rotten fruit and sometimes copper sulphate. Hospital authorities explain that methyl alcohol is metabolized into formaldehyde when consumed, the poisonous formaldehyde cells affixing themselves to tissues. The process takes three hours. During this time, ethanol, intravenously injected, can prevent the digestion of methanol by the liver and allow it to be excreted without metabolism. But with patients arriving twenty-four hours or more after consuming the lethal drink, chances of survival are low.

The next day the modus operandi begins to unravel with the

arrest of a hooch supplier, Harishanker Kahar. A migrant from Uttar Pradesh and a habitual offender, Kahar, or 'Hariyo', as he is called, is a wholesale distributor of country-made liquor in Ahmedabad. Hariyo's arrest puts the police on the trail of the supplier of the hooch, an absconding dairy owner in Mehmedabad, a satellite town of Ahmedabad. Hariyo confesses that he knew the 700-litre consignment he had received from Mehmedabad on July 5 was possibly lethal when his alcohol meter showed twice the regular concentrate of methyl alcohol. He reckoned he could dilute it more than usual and double the stock. He continued to sell the brew even after learning of the deaths. Hariyo is booked for culpable homicide (not amounting to murder).

Six police officers from Ahmedabad, including four inspectors and two assistant commissioners of police, have been placed under suspension and transferred to other parts of the state. Teams of the State Reserved Police have been rushed to vulnerable border districts to prevent the flow of illicit liquor into Gujarat from neighbouring states. Political scientist Ornit Shani maintains that the widespread phenomenon of policemen abdicating their duties on political orders during the communal violence of 2002 was enabled to some extent by a history of extreme politicization of the police force and its complicity in the bootlegging business.

The hooch deaths which were earlier concentrated in Majoor Gam close to the old walled city are now being reported from further east. Victims are being identified in the newer and more distant industrial areas of Amraiwadi, Naroda, Rakhial, Bapunagar and Odhav. Nineteen have died in Odhav and people have been spotted lying near the canal vomiting. At Amraiwadi, locals continued to protest against the incident forcing the police to resort to lathi charge and tear gas shelling. Meanwhile, unclaimed bodies continue to surface. As more information is uncovered about the zones that the consignment of the brew that has killed over a hundred people has reached, authorities reportedly 'step-up' efforts to track its fatal march. A total of 462 bootleggers have been arrested in raids across the state. The police have seized large quantities of raw materials used in the preparation of spurious liquor, along with containers and bottles.

*

'There have been deaths in Bapunagar also in this *latha kand*,' Tulsibhai says with raised eyebrows. 'I heard of one man from our Market.'

'From our Market?' Dhanjibhai repeats, shocked. 'How can it be ... a middle-class person?'

'Who can tell? This daaru thing is like that. Anyone can get addicted.'

Dhanjibhai reflects on this. Or perhaps he doesn't. I can't really tell. He has a broad, expressionless face. For much of the afternoon, he has been slumped in his chair, head sunk, staring at the floor. I have been sitting with the two diamond traders in Dhanjibhai's office in the Sardar Patel Diamond Market on a hot summer day in 2009. I have come to witness the effects of the ongoing worldwide economic slowdown on the diamond polishing business, one of India's two biggest export-led industries. Outside, in all the offices, on the steps of the three-storeyed Market and in the cubby holes that face the road, middle-aged men, much like Tulsibhai and Dhanjibhai, are sitting stiffly against white bolsters in front of low sloping desks which contain the tools of their trade: an eye glass, pincers and pouches of diamonds. They drink tea, swat flies or do nothing. They are not destitute; they have savings to tide them over. But they are not educated. When they have no work they do not know what to do. Time passes very slowly.

Tulsibhai takes me on his scooter into the backlanes of

Bapunagar. The nerve centre of the diamond-cutting and polishing business—India has ninety per cent of the world share—is in the city of Surat, 265 kilometres to the south. But in the 1980s workshops started opening in Ahmedabad as well, mopping up labour freed from the textile mills and attracting migrants, mainly from peninsular Gujarat, imbuing Bapunagar with a mildly exotic flavour. The *karkhanas* of Ahmedabad are small-scale units doing piecework for the trade that is controlled by immensely wealthy Palanpuri Gujarati Jains living in mansions in Mumbai, Surat and Antwerp. The global recession has reportedly made little more than a dent in the fortunes of these mega millionaire diamond traders; some see it as an opportunity to speculate in the stock market. But for the owners of karkhanas and hundreds of thousands of workers across the state the downturn has spelt doom. On an average one diamond worker has been committing suicide, every day, over the last three months.

In a two-storeyed building with a narrow frontage that housed a busy unit we find a lone polisher scraping a diamond on a *ghanti*. Since Diwali almost all the karkhanas in Ahmedabad have shut shop. The workers, many of them employed couples, have been without work for six months or more. Bapunagar pullulates with 'tension', a much-heard word in the diamond district these days. Blood pressures are high. A gnawing anxiety renders nerves as brittle as leaves in late summer. 'Devu', another word of the moment, means 'debt' and indicates the piling arrears: unpaid rent, school fees and medical bills. Money, even for daily groceries, is scarce.

I meet two former worker couples in a small flat bearing signs of bourgeois gentility: a television set, a refrigerator, school bags on a rack and decorative knick-knacks. The comfortable lifestyle enabled by the diamond business has engendered middle-class notions of respectability. 'We don't want much, just a little help to tide over till the industry picks up again,' has been the common refrain. But, with the days of joblessness lengthening into months and no sign of help forthcoming, the measured appeals have given way to bewilderment. The workers talk about their contributions to the Indian economy, their donations to public causes such as the national war chest for Kargil or Gujarat's earthquake relief fund and express bafflement that they should be so neglected. They understand that the politicians from peninsular Gujarat who have taken up their cause are out of favour with chief minister Narendra Modi but surely, they say, he should be above such partisanship. 'If he is the *raja* [king], are we not his *praja* [people]?'

It is disconcerting to watch their dignified reticence slowly come undone. Unused to organizing themselves as a labour force they struggle to articulate their distress. They write letters to the chief minister. They talk to the media. They seek political support. A veil of disheartenment hangs over these efforts. They wonder why the media carries misleading stories of functional karkhanas. They wonder if it is worthwhile protesting and incurring the further wrath of the chief minister. They wonder if it is better to get by with small subsistence-level jobs, doing piecework embroidery or couriering documents. A worker says in frustration that he will fast to death all by himself at the Gandhi ashram on the Sabarmati. Then, one morning, diamond workers in Ahmedabad, overcoming their doubts, gather outside the Gujarat Assembly building in Gandhinagar and are beaten back by the police. A journalist colleague, newly arrived in Gujarat, is horrified by the brutality and even more by the disrespect shown towards workers, unimaginable, he says, in his home state, the pro-Marxist southern state of Kerala.

*

At the Nehru Nagar Circle, eleven kilometers west of the bleak diamond district of Bapunagar, traffic is at a standstill. Heads poke out of cars. Passers-by stop to stare. The object of their curiosity is a bus. Not any old bus but a prototype for the new Bus Rapid Transit System. In 2007, following discussions spanning two decades on a new public transportation system, the Gujarat Infrastructure Development Board, supported by a central government scheme, the Jawaharlal Nehru National Urban Renewal Mission, began work on the BRTS. In keeping with the chief minister's characteristic flamboyance, the project was given a massive build-up. For many months the news was all about sophisticated gadgetry such as a biometric time attendance recorder, a projector showing real time movement of buses and glass-fronted bus stops, some with air-conditioning, a rare luxury even in private homes. And then there was the bus itself, a sleek marvel, with the sheen of new paint, a pale mauve reportedly selected by the CM, digital sign boards and pneumatic doors. Rather than a system designed for the mundane goal of transporting humans efficiently, the BRTS came to be seen as a symbol of a hyper-progressive Gujarat. It is little wonder then that this, the first sighted bus, should be the cause of hubbub more suited to the viewing of a jaw-dropping artifact.

July 11: The number of casualties in the latha scandal has risen to 136, the highest ever toll in Gujarat. The *Times of India* reminisces, with a certain fondness, about the Latif era, claiming that the ordinary labourer was spared from drinking hooch then because of Latif's cheap, bulk supplies of IMFL. Muslims no longer control the liquor business in Gujarat. The names thrown up in the current incident—Kahar, Parmar, Luhar, Charra—are Hindu and from the disadvantaged or marginalised castes. The police have arrested three boys who used to ferry hooch from Mehmedabad in Kheda district to Ahmedabad and distribute it to various retailers on their scooters. The scrawny boys have fashionable haircuts and sulky expressions. The police point out that they have seized their scooters.

*

The St Mary's Nursing Home where Chandubhai Maheriya was born in June 1959 is a low, sickle-shaped building set amidst orderly rows of cactus on a quiet stretch abutting the locomotive shed in Gomtipur. The nursing home, run by the Dominican Missionary Sisters, is next to the Blind Working Men's hostel, the Salvation Army and the French Church. This tranquil corner is at the edge of the old Silver Mill reachable by a broad road built when the TLA was a force in the Ahmedabad Municipal Corporation, and was sprayed with water daily to settle the dust. By the side of the road, houses unwind, all painted the same shade of blue. Children tumble on wild monsoon-fed grass. There are dogs, the occasional goat, tail-swishing buffaloes and men playing cards on coir mats. Nobody accosts us and the children do not stare or follow us. A peacock preens atop a water tank on a multi-storey building in the distance.

There was a sewage dump hereabouts, south-east of the walled city, some hundred years ago. Chandubhai belongs to the caste formerly known as 'Chamar', among the lowest rungs on the Hindu caste hierarchy. He grew up in the Abu Kasai ni Chaali with others of his caste and poor Muslims like his neighbour Barkat Bibi. At dusk every day, men on bicycles would traverse the narrow lanes balancing pots of *hojri*, boiled entrails, to augment the *khichdi*, a gruel of rice and lentils, that was the staple meal in that *basti* of labourers. In the corners where the rubbish collected, Chandubhai foraged as a child for bones to sell to the bone processing mill. In the market we see the wood shop outside which he would wait for shavings for the kitchen fire.

Chandubhai's father was a mill worker. He was also an

admirer of the Columbia University-educated Dalit leader B.R. Ambedkar. He sent Chandubhai to a nursery founded by the Amhedabadi elite and, after that, the local municipal school. In a wide street edged with mean shops Chandubhai points to where Ambedkar visited and spoke. The bespectacled Dalit icon is not as pervasive a presence in Ahmedabad's labour district as he might be in other cities, in other parts of the country, mainly on account of the greater influence of the Gandhi-led TLA.

At one of the TLA's essay competitions Chandubhai won the first prize and the judge, impressed by his writing, gave him a chit of introduction to a communist leader in his neighbourhood. By then Chandubhai had discovered socialist literature like *Maa*, the Gujarati version of Maxim Gorky's *Mother*—made available cheaply by the House of Soviet Culture and ideologically inclined translators. He also frequented the Maneklal Jethalal Public Library, a seven-kilometre walk, away on the other side of the Ellis Bridge. His brother, a graduate from the prestigious missionary-run St Xavier's College, had a job and the rare means to afford a daily newspaper which he also read with a devouring intensity. Soon he would be writing letters to the editor, launching fervid debates on Dalit issues.

Chandubhai is dark, diminutive and dresses in short-sleeved shirts and old-fashioned high-waisted trousers, Meeting him for the first time one is apt to be struck by the evenness of his disposition. His expression never varies, his tone does not change. Not even when he describes how the teachers at his higher secondary school used to berate him for walking barefoot or for tying a handkerchief around his arm. He simply could not afford footwear he says and the flimsy piece of cloth was his attempt at concealing the boils that periodically erupted on his skin as a result of the unsanitary conditions in which he lived. Did you not feel any rage, I ask him. 'No,' he says simply, with the stillness and deep engagement that is so much a part of his personality. '*Kothe chadi gayu hatu* (I had become used to it).'

Writing was an outlet. One of his best-known essays, 'Mayor's Bungalow', was a sharp, darkly ironic piece about the state of sanitation in the low-caste precinct. The essay was based on a real-life incident. In his own words: 'There were no toilets in our chaali, we used the ones in the next chaali where the Wankars from Mehsana lived. We Chamars from Kheda were much lower than them socially so they did not like it and showed their displeasure. In any case the bathrooms were terrible. In the rains the waste would flood over and rise towards us. Festivals with all the waste clogging the gutters were the worst occasions. However many *agarbattis* we lit, the smell would fill our house. So the community pooled some money and made pay-and-use toilets. In this very poor area, these toilets looked so attractive that we started calling them the 'mayor's bungalow'. Then the young boys of the Vanar Sena [an army of higher-caste youths] came and broke them.'

On December 25, 1980, a land dispute in the village of Jetalpur near Ahmedabad led to the beating and fatal burning of a Dalit boy. Chandubhai wrote a poem 'Kavyanu Mulya' in response to the event. 'If the one word of revolt will knock the ears of /Thakur Vajesang's deaf ears/I feel the value of my poem will be invaluable.' This was a time of intense activity in progressive cultural circles. Ketan Mehta, a filmmaker of Gujarati origin and a part of the emerging parallel cinema movement in the country, had dealt with caste in an imaginative folk idiom in his film *Bhavni Bhavai*. A daily newspaper was carrying a column by the principal of a tribal school. Jinabhai Darji, a Congress politician and ally of tribals and other marginalised communities, started the publication *Naya Marg*. *Aakrosh*, a Dalit poetry magazine started in 1978, and anthologies of Dalit poetry, were beginning to appear; Chandubhai would go on to edit two of them. Despite its coarse, visceral idiom which caused consternation in refined literary circles, Gujarati Dalit poetry had less of the raw abuse that marked the poetry of its neighbouring state Maharashtra, which saw the birth of a Black Panther-like movement in the 1970s. Chandubhai maintains that the tendency for Gujarati Dalits to be anguished rather than angry and less confrontational stemmed from the environment. 'It was very hard to rub out Gandhi,' he explains calmly.

We have left the road skirting the Silver Mill, where a newly employed Chandubhai, walking home from the station three decades ago, would imagine upper-caste men or evil spirits emerging from the dark to attack him. Chandubhai now works in the education department at the state secretariat in Gandhinagar. His home is there too, in a secluded leafy lane in Sector 2B. On weekends such as this he returns to visit his mother and run errands in the neighbourhood in which he grew up. We pause for him to drop off papers at a cyclostyling shop and re-enter the maze of lanes. The sonorous wail of mantras can be heard, interrupted by staccato bursts. Around a corner we come upon its source, a row of Ganapati pandals and a large loudspeaker with a thin raggedy man dozing on a chair next to it.

The three-storeyed post office looms over the tin-roofed shacks of Rajpur–Hirpur. Over the wall of the municipal school Chandubhai once attended, the famous shaking minarets of the Sidi Bashir Mosque are visible in the distance. But the school is now a ghost building guarded by security men and feared to be sinking, its yellow walls being sucked into the swampy ground on which it rose. We are close to Chandubhai's chaali, or *vaas* as he sometimes refers to it, borrowing from rural terminology which distinguished the low-caste marginal habitation from the settled character of the *gam* or village. Much has changed in the chaali over the years. Muslims such as his old neighbour, Barkat Bibi, have moved out to live in ghettos like Juhapura. Many Dalits have moved out of Rajpur-Hirpur as well to rising localities like Chandkheda at the northern edge of town. Some have even become entrepreneurs, using government schemes to make businesses out of their old caste occupations of bone, raw leather and ceramic.

The chaali is in shadow. The peculiar silence that comes from the absence of whirring fans in a slum tells us that the power has failed. Electricity in Ahmedabad is supplied by the Ahmedabad Electricity Company Ltd., a state-run corporation now under the control of the industrial group Torrent. Ahmedabad was one of the first few cities to privatise its electric supply after the passing of the Electricity Act aimed at opening up the power sector in 2003. A concerted drive by the new owner to cut illegal connections has made it unpopular in the slums and the poorer parts of the city. 'The other day some people on the road asked me to sign a petition against Torrent,' Chandubhai says. 'I don't understand it. They were standing outside a Ganapati *pandal* blazing with lights and complaining about the high cost of electricity.'

Chandubhai's old house is sparsely furnished and sports all sorts of spatial contraptions including a pulley-operated window that opens up in the roof. Posters, of a blonde child chasing a goose and a mythological scene with chariots and Hindu gods, brighten the dull walls. A small sticker of the traditional deity of the family is stuck on the side of a cupboard. We emerge on to the two-feet-wide lane running between the houses, paved with rugged stone dating back to an improvement scheme of the AMC in the 1970s. On the electric-green walls, amidst parked cycles and curtains made from old jari-edged saris, the new white meters from Torrent stand out. The power is still down. Chandubhai stops to talk to a man in shorts inside one of the shadowy homes. A girl is sprawled at the doorway trying to do her homework by the daylight filtering in between the close-set rooftops. Her notebook is thrust out to catch the light. Her handwriting is beautiful.

*

In a low-roofed hut, close to the fan, a chair is placed for me. A young woman, the wife, is in the open rectangle to my left that serves as the kitchen. Across from her, on a thin mattress, an older woman, the mother, sits with her head and part of her face covered by her sari pallu. Behind me is a photograph of the deceased. When he was alive, forty-year-old Beejalbhai Solanki did odd jobs—welding, gas work, fabrication, whatever he could find. The work was infrequent, sometimes for an hour, sometimes for half a day. All his income was squandered on drink and the craving for 'non-veg' brought on by inebriation. His wife ran the house on her meagre earnings as a casual labourer. On the morning of Tuesday, July 7, Beejalbhai was sick, vomiting uncontrollably. He died in the afternoon, on the way to the hospital.

The fan ruffles the dark, pregnant stillness. The house is in the heart of the hutment colony in the nondescript back lanes of Kantodiavaas deep in the heart of the labour district, deserted save for two policemen keeping a desultory watch. A short walk would bring a person to the compound walls of the Ankur Mill and the Nutan Cloth Market, close to which one can see the one-storeyed houses of the liquor suppliers. This is where a large part of the hooch, arriving from stills on the city's margins, riding on State Transport buses or trains, ends up. Here are the hands that transfer the liquor into small plastic pouches, an overwhelmingly large number of which belong to women. More than half the bootleggers arrested in the wake of the *latha* tragedy across the state are women.

In Kantodiavaas everybody knows their names: Munni, Kalal, Vimla, Sashikala and Saroj. On July 13, press photographers click the arrest of three suppliers from Kantodiavaas, all in loud, printed saris. Two are reported to be in their sixties. One can't tell because of the black masks covering their faces. They have slack shoulders, clutched fists, bangles and rings like ordinary housewives. But those who know have spine-chilling tales to tell. Of the Waghri women who sit on *charpais* on the street, calling out to men. Calling night and day, like sirens from the deep. Women who loot the drunks and, when someone dies of excessive consumption, carry off the body and abandon it in some dark lane.

In this forlorn, pitiable, desolate corner of the world, the inhabitants, low-caste Dalits, are casual labourers. Any morning if one were to go to any of the several pre-fixed spots in the city, one of which is round the corner at the char rasta near the Paras restaurant, one would find them and their like, hanging around waiting to be picked up for a few hours or, if they are exceptionally lucky, a whole day of work. Informalisation, perceived in the 1970s as a pre-capitalist phenomenon which would disappear over time, in fact, reasserted itself all over the world towards the close of the century. Ahmedabad recovered its ability to generate employment after the collapse of the textile mills, but the nature and circumstances of work for a large section of people was dramatically different from what had gone before. As employers sought to minimize costs and risks in the post global age, health cover, job security and other measures protecting workers' interests introduced by Keynesian-era labour reforms and fought for by unions shrank.

Work participation by both males and females increased during this time but regular employment dropped. Women who may have worked part time earlier were likely to be working full time now. The type of work available was often arduous and degrading—carrying bricks at construction sites or sifting through garbage to separate plastic bags for example. Employers sometimes reneged on payment. And rules regarding holidays and so on were rendered superfluous. For the industrious residents of Kantodiavaas there is no holiday. Whenever work calls, they must go. The heightened insecurity in which the labouring class lives has led labour scholars to suggest replacing the lens of poverty with that of vulnerability which, in urban areas, includes not just intermittent employment but also insecure housing, health-threatening environmental conditions, lack of social networks, violence and other forms of deprivation such as discrimination and humiliation.

The children have collected outside the door. The children of Kantodiavaas walk an extra half-kilometer to school to escape the vulgar taunts of the liquor sellers. They fear the curse of the devi, the vengeful goddess, which the liquor sellers frequently call upon them. They fear the police who harass them for complaining about liquor dens. They fear their teachers when their parents run out of money to buy school books. One boy saw a body in a *nullah* during the last episode of communal violence and has never been the same since. Chandubhai's exit from the low-caste ghetto was enabled by a combination of personal effort, philanthropy, legislation and ideological support. But when the social net is removed, and a free-market economy allowed to reign, I wonder how far the disadvantaged can go. The wife of the deceased man shuffles towards her mother-in-law and begins to weep. There is a rustle of saris as she is taken inside. A wail breaks out from the other room, loud, plaintive, grief-stricken.

*

In this room, with gadgetry enough to match a state-of-the art operating theatre, fabric is checked by colour, weight and shine, tugged by an Electronic Pilling Tester and burned by a Genon lamp. Every step is recorded. Every move is watched by the client on a monitor, thousands of miles away. An external laboratory certifies quality. Another laboratory re-checks, rejects or accepts the fabric. There are daily Damage Control Meetings and stickers of colour for type of damage. Downstairs, soft imported lignite passing through filters to remove sulphur dioxide releases white smoke with particles of a specified size. And in large, high-ceilinged rooms, fabric is stretched on easels and marked for faults and fat bales of grey are bleached in bubbling, steaming vats.

The fastidiousness, like the peaty effluvium of hot cotton, pervades every niche and part of operations. The convivial, lax ways of the old Gujarati-owned composite mill are frowned upon in the processing houses, many of which are owned by Marwari Jains. In this particular house, no smoking, drinking, tobacco, onions, garlic are allowed on the premises. There are prayers at the start of work and, in the holy Hindu month of Shravan, swamis are invited to perform rituals in the nights. The unit manager, influenced by his environment, has given up his habit of chewing zarda and watching television at home. He works '364 days' of the year. He knows that there is no room for error for, unlike the diversified structure and the multifaceted, absentee owner of the composite mill, the processing-house owner is suspicious, watchful, omnipresent and solely focused on the running of his business. Not that the unit manager would have it any other way, not when downscaling and the upgrading of skills has made senior-level jobs like his so very satisfying. It is the worker who has been rendered anonymous.

I wander through the high-ceilinged sheds. In one, Kitango lungis, sarongs for the Indonesian market, polyester lengths of green, turquoise and brown, the colours of nature, are being spun in a machine, shrunk in alkali, aired and neutralized in acetic acid. In another, 2.8 × 2.8m double bedsheets are being printed on what looks like a giant Xerox machine. The Lazy Cat has a big face, big grey eyes and a paw. Half-a-dozen bare-chested men stand on either side adjusting the pigments. A blade slices across and, after a pause, slides forward, repeating the motion till Lazy Cat rises up, paw sliding forward. The men observe the machine's slow, heavy slide silently. Nose, eyes and whiskers turn red, green and white consecutively. A bloody red fills the background. As I leave the premises with their softly steaming, shuddering, UV-lit corners, I imagine a German child sleeping on Lazy Cat.

I am in a car being driven from Ahmedabad's new industrial hub Vatwa in the east with the owner of CTM, one of the largest processing houses in the city. Mohanlal is a Marwari Jain from a family of textile traders in Uttar Pradesh. He moved to Ahmedabad in 1948 and bought first a composite mill, which failed, and then a processing house. Mohanlal is elderly and has an old-fashioned, dour manner which belies his chattiness. He says the Pollution Board, with its stringent requirements, is troublesome. He is worried about fluctuations in the market (*teji-mandi*) and believes it is important to diversify, to keep 'two or three lines' as back-ups. He is thinking of getting into real estate. Despite these irritants and his dull monotone Mohanlal is happy in his environment. 'From the North you read news of murder and robbery. But the Gujarati is *shant* [peaceful], "Gandhi" type, not *ladaku* [aggressive]. And the CM, Narendra Modi, is a good worker. The Mega City will happen. Fifteen or more bridges and roads are coming up. This will be India's Paris once the Sabarmati develops. It will be better than London or Paris. There will be high-rise buildings and boats, the atmosphere of London. Now the BRTS is also starting.' He has a contented look on his face.

From the time of the incident of mass deaths due to liquor poisoning, the state government, except for the occasional announcement about matters like hospital costs, has maintained a studied silence on the subject. The chief minister, perennially omniscient, articulate and full of righteous anger against the enemies of the state, is mute. His views, platitudes (nineteen in total and all in Gujarati), such as: 'many elements are giving the tragic incident political colour and are trying to ruin the peaceful atmosphere in Gujarat', and: 'my government is sincere about eliminating the vice of illicit liquor', however, surface on Twitter, making him appear to be a spectator rather than the principal actor in the unfolding drama. Meanwhile, the Opposition's demand for a debate in the Assembly is disallowed by the Speaker Ashok Bhatt. Unruly Congress members are suspended for the remainder of the Budget session, and fined for damaging six microphones.

Then, as July draws grimly to a close, the state government reacts. The Minister of State for Home Affairs, Amit Shah, introduces a bill to amend the Bombay Prohibition Act, 1949, claiming it to be a 'historic step' towards ending the illegal liquor business in the state. This government is different, it is responsive and unafraid to take extreme measures is the subtext of the hype around the new bill. Indeed, the bill is introduced in little more than a fortnight after the tragedy unfolded. The bill proposes the death penalty for culprits caught manufacturing or selling hooch that takes lives. A new section also proposes making negligence by prohibition officials or police officials punishable by a jail term of up to a year.

FIVE

Highway Dreams

ARRIVING IN AHMEDABAD EARLY one morning, I find the city wrecked by a massive *vavazodu*. The high winds that accompany the south-west monsoon race at speeds up to sixty kilometres an hour. I imagine the air must have howled and shrieked through the dark town, whipping trees, rattling glass panes in window frames, snagging at shop awnings and shanty roofs and sending stray animals scurrying for shelter. I am driven through roads littered with smashed foliage and debris. In the damp tired air, drops of water glisten on the leaves of bent trees. Close to my destination in Ramdev Nagar, in an open plot of land next to a construction site, I come across men, some young, some middle-aged and a few elderly and bow-legged, all dressed in baggy, khaki shorts, shoes and socks, standing to attention like schoolboys. An RSS shakha is in progress.

It is rare to see grown middle-class men in India, and even more so in Ahmedabad, exerting themselves physically at a street corner. Their discomfiture shows in the self-consciousness of their postures and the quick upward flicks of their arms to fend off flies. A couple of them are in rumpled bush-shirts that suggest they rolled out of bed from the adjoining lane. In a few minutes the exercises come to an end. A saffron flag is unfurled and planted in a stand. The group salutes, fist at chest level in the RSS style which is a quick dip and lifting of the head, and prays. A boy removes the flag and folds it with precise movements, taking care to place the stick in its proper groove. A clothed pot, a table and a plastic chair are arranged. The men fall into single file to drop currency notes and cheques into the pot. The group disperses. Some men remain, flopping delicately to the ground. I hear them discussing the vavazodu.

For several months now, the Marriott hotel has been coming up, bit by bit, at the Ramdev Nagar char rasta. Each time I come to stay with friends in this fast-developing western edge of the city, I see new storeys. Naked in its half completion, it towers over the roundabout, a looming, promised presence with no deliverance in sight. On the roundabout is a saffron sign credited to the Bajrang Dal, a militant Hindutva group: 'Welcome to Hindu *Rashtra* [nation]'.

Before the malls and multiplexes on the Sarkhej–Gandhinagar, or SG Road—the 46-kilometre highway that connects western Ahmedabad to the state capital Gandhinagar—sprouted and turned this once far-flung corner into a chic address, Jodhpur Tekra, adjoining the present-day Ramdev Nagar, was the haunt of cowherds, the tribe of Rabaris. Even now one can occasionally glimpse their women in the thick black stoles of the *banni*, gracefully striding on the tarred slopes. Kalubhai, the driver, sharp-featured, laconic like most Rabaris, recounts how a *bawo*, or mendicant, who lived in the wilderness preceding the making of the char rasta, or crossroads, hollowed out a cave temple in honour of Rama, which gave Ramdev Nagar its name. A large group of Waghris from the neighbourhood to the west that people call 'Hollywood', because of their colourful attire, came and settled close to the temple bringing their own gods. One of their shrines, to Sitla Mata, the goddess of small pox, still stands prominently on a wide divider surrounded with tied coconuts and grain for birds. Now the Rabaris' cottages and the Waghris' huts have been overlaid by houses redolent of wealth and modishness. Winter mornings, walking through the deserted streets, I come upon the embers of fires started by security guards of upscale housing complexes, the occasional temple-goer and a stout rich housewife exercising fiercely by walking up and down a strip of lawn.

*

If there is, anywhere in the world, a materialization of the Hindu Rashtra—an actualization of the fantasies that drive the idea of a Hindu state, the ordering, a socialized religiosity—a physical approximation of what such a society would look like, then surely it is here, on the modern threshold of this ancient city, a brave new world. In the south are the high pink walls of the Indian Space Research Organisation, not a furlough from the Ramdev Nagar crossroads. Launched in the Nehruvian era at a time of international space competitiveness, the Indian Space Programme, one of India's rare technological successes, was designed by the Ahmedabad-born physicist Vikram Sarabhai, unusually, to focus on developmental goals. In recent times, and in keeping with India's growing desire for assertiveness on the world stage, the space programme has defied its founder and acquired a showy profile, manifested most vividly in a much tom-tommed moon exploration mission announced in 2003 by the first-ever BJP prime minister, Atal Bihari Vajpayee. Closing the boundary of the proto-Hindu Rashtra at the other end is the globe of Science City, a plasticky planet plonked on two hundred hectares of lunar landscape. Another five hundred and fifty hectacres have been earmarked for it in furtherance of the BJP's plans to develop a scientific temper within an environment of 'knowledge-driven economic growth'.

Science City was inaugurated by the first-ever BJP union home minister in August 2001 to 'provide a perfect blend of education and entertainment'. Under the bulbous canopy is a prodigious wandering terrain, suffused with the spirit of carnival-cum-trade fair. Commercials appear and disappear on LED screens, the air echoing. Stopping by one Sunday evening I see bemused visitors—children with tin foil wafer packets, distracted adults—drift here and there: they queue outside the 3D cinema hall, the hall of space, the hall of science; they stray to the dancing musical water fountains or the car park.

But this is only one of several possible topographies. There are others, each in its own way serving to highlight an aspect of the envisioned State. One, an exceedingly apposite one, would start at the same high pink walls of the Indian Space Research Organisation but on the opposite side of the road, where one finds a phalanx of charitable and spiritual institutions such as the Shree Jalaram Hospital, the Paramdham Chinmaya Mission and the Sivananda Ashram. Behind gates topped with wire mesh are sloping concrete paths, manicured lawns studded with trimmed trees, lampposts, ponds, open spaces for satsangs, indoor meditation halls, and well-positioned words of wisdom: 'Be humble, simple, noble and gentle', 'Purity is the gateway to the kingdom of God'. Continuing past the Satellite Crossroads with its wildly popular corner temple run by the International Society for Krishna Consciousness and managed with the support of the local industrialist Karsanbhai Patel our cartographer takes a sharp rightward turn down SG Road—now pullulating with *shikharas, toranas, ardh mandapas, chhatris,* cupolas, flames, animals, gods and goddesses, to arrive, as if by design, at the showpiece of Swaminarayan, the world's fastest-growing Hindu sect, the monumental Akshardham temple in Gandhinagar.

The edges of towns were hospitable for ashrams in ancient India. Original city plans for Ahmedabad demarcated this belt between Ahmedabad and Gandhinagar on the western margins as a green area but permitted religious establishments. First making an appearance in the 1970s, when weak Congress legislators imposed on the state by an increasingly autocratic Indira Gandhi wooed influential Hindu sects with cheap government land, spiritual centres and temples mushroomed over the next couple of decades. A latter wave was propelled, at least partly, by the realization that religion could be marketed as a popular leisure activity in Ahmedabad and, accordingly, garden restaurants and Disney rides came up alongside or even within the premises of the temple complexes. Inspired by the success of this border theme park, perhaps, and its centerpiece—a faux mountain range replicating the celebrated Vaishno Devi shrine in Jammu—and driven by the aims of the state's Hindu chauvinist government, the snowballing of temples along this vector has acquired a more determined and strategic purpose. The cultural theorist Jyotindra Jain, for one, maintains that 'Gujarat wants to become the fountainhead of all Hinduism (originator and preserver) in India.'

In 2003 alone the foundation stones for replicas of at least two important and celebrated shrines, the Balaji Temple in Tirupati and the Amarnathdham in Jammu, were laid in the presence of Chief Minister Narendra Modi and his senior colleagues from the BJP. The original Amarnathdham is located at a height of 13,600 feet above sea-level. Its centerpiece, an ice stalactite that forms through the winter months, is worshipped as a Shivling, the phallic representation of Shiva. The duplicate Amarnathdham on the Gandhinagar–Mahudi Road in Ahmedabad has a refrigerated five-foot ice block maintained in its frozen state throughout the year. The agglomeration of deities and shrines from other parts of the country offers a convenient alternative to the arduous pilgrimages enjoined by tradition, also serving to advance the BJP strategy of forging a Hindu unity across regional and other differences.

The corridor outside Dilip A. Luhar's office has a bilious hue caused by sunlight filtering through a green canopy over the inner quadrangle. The local unit of the Sadvichar Parivar Charitable Trust, which he oversees, is a multi-faceted operation accommodating within its fold the running of a hospital, several eye clinics and the performing of philanthropic activities such as feeding *shira*, a sweet semolina dish, to pregnant women in hospitals and the transporting of the ashes of dead Hindus to holy sites. Luhar, a thin smiling man in his sixties, given to making unexpected pronouncements like 'a man whose daughter is happy is happy', occupies a large room filled with images of gods and holy men. There is Vishnu, Krishna, Lakshmi, Saraswati, Amba, Sai baba, Dongreji Maharaj, Puneet Maharaj. On his table are booklets of 'good' thoughts and religious instructions printed by the mission. Luhar wears a small orange teeka on his forehead, acquired at the Hanuman temple on SG Road, where he stops by every morning before coming to work. 'Life is very insecure,' he says. 'We are in a cauldron. You cannot predict when someone will pour ghee on it and cause an explosion. You need assistance.'

At his urging, I visit Maruti Dham, the Hanuman temple. A recent addition to the highway pantheon, having opened only in 2004 or thereabouts, the Hanuman temple has become popular because of its proximity to the celebrated Vaishno Devi replica. This hot, dry morning, there is no one about, though. The tiled courtyard, the marble steps and the space around the sanctum sanctorum are empty and gleam with an almost surgical cleanliness. I look down on a neat, still house on a patch of lawn at the back. An air conditioner protrudes over the closed window. I am told it is the occasional residence of the temple's spiritual mentor, a Haridwar-based Swami. Across the road is a *gaushala* where stray cows are cared for. Fifteen cows at the rate of five hundred rupees per cow, per day, are maintained by donations. A man at the entrance hands out coloured receipts to donors.

Opposite the temple a roundabout punctuates the highway. The north-bound road heads to the new centres of higher education established by industrial houses in and around Gandhinagar: the Dhirubhai Ambani Institute of Information and Communication Technology and the Nirma University.

*

The glossy new residential complexes and office towers spreading out on this fashionable border have smooth granite floors, glass walls, rectangles of grass, gymnasia, separate entrances for the domestic staff, and clever contrivances such as a timed drip-irrigation mechanism for watering plants. Ahmedabad's developers, young, ambitious, big-talking men reeking of zeitgeist, have a penchant for affixing numerals to buildings, like a series or a limited edition: Shaligram 1, 2, 3 ... Builders know how to dig into their clientele's heart, a teacher of interior design in the city tells me. They tap into the hidden dreams of customers, then make and offer homes positioned in three price ranges. The advertisements, making the right emotional appeals, create a mounting yet uniform set of aspirations. With their deep, deep pockets and brash entrepreneurialism, real estate developers are the new geographers in town, pushing for development where they plant their flags, here, there, there.

On SG Road a herd of cows ambles across the road. One pauses on the divider, imperious despite its dung-spattered coat, magnificent, sharp horns aloft like a *trishul*. On the right tabernacles of different sizes used in household worship spill out from the wood and marble shops, creating a pigmy Hindu temple town by the side of the road. The relentless march of construction has cannibalised the rural perimeter of the city already beleaguered by the erratic rainfall of the previous decade. Yet, an ersatz pastoral nostalgia blares from the copious signage for new residential colonies. The Godrej Garden City urges one to 'plant more trees and breathe well'. Orange County Green Plots ('where lives your heart') suggests: 'Tranquility in your home reflects in you ... Lifestyle at its natural best.' Verdant longings radiate from hoardings for Nirma University ('Green Ahmedabad'), Ganesh Housing ('Make Gujarat green, greener, greenest') and the emerald lawns of Maple County.

*

Till 2006, SG Highway marked the westernmost extremity of the city. Then the Sardar Patel Ring Road came up, seven kilometers further west. A 76.3-kilometre road barreling through privately owned acreage and twenty-three villages! An idea fated, one would think, to be mired in endless litigation. If it took a mere three years to be executed it is to the indubitable credit of the man people in Ahmedabad know simply as 'Kaka (Uncle)'. Kaka, or, more correctly, Surendra Patel, a veteran RSS man affiliated with various arms of the Sangh Parivar, is now Treasurer of the Gujarat unit of the BJP and a member of the Rajya Sabha. More importantly he is a Patel, from the fertile Charotar region south of Ahmedabad. His community, easily the most venturous of the highly nomadic Gujaratis, spread out across East Africa, Fiji, Trinidad, Surinam, England and the United States, and built the Ugandan Railway in the 1960s.

Kaka studied engineering at the Sardar Patel University, founded by Ahmedabad's first Chief Municipal Engineer, Bhaikaka Patel, and went on to join the family's construction business in Ahmedabad. As chairman of the Ahmedabad Urban Development Authority (1996–7 and 1998–2005) he initiated many of the grandiose projects, including the Sabarmati Riverfront Development Project, that would transform the face of the city. Till he was in his late fifties and had already been chairman of the Urban Development Authority once, Kaka had never travelled outside India. In 1997 he went to Europe and the United States.

I ask him if he was influenced by what he saw. Was it the motorways of the West that inspired him in his second term as the AUDA Chairman? He looks noncommittal. Yes, he says, London's M25 Ring Road made him think Ahmedabad should have one and in America too he saw many ring roads. But, you see ... He shrugs to suggest a need to clarify. Seeing things for oneself is a good thing and it 'solidified' what he had imagined. But the fact was that he did not feel the need to travel abroad because he had already had a vision in his mind of what the West was like. 'Everyone in Charotar has a relative abroad, mainly in London and America,' he reminds me, 'including myself.' His siblings and his wife's family are abroad. Expatriate Gujaratis have donated lavishly to build water tanks, clinics, towers and schools in the Charotar region. And it is this vision, brought home by the diaspora, that has formed his worldview.

The shrewdness that he brought to bear on the realization of his pet project, the Sardar Patel Ring Road, was homegrown. It is widely known that he chose not to court resistance by acquiring land in the conventional manner, under the Land Acquisition Act, and opted instead to revive a form of land readjustment called the Town Planning Scheme in which the owner voluntarily surrendered up to forty per cent of his property in the expectation that improvements made by the authorities would increase the price of his truncated property. 'It was win-win for everybody,' says Kaka gleefully, 'win-win!' It is a rare flash of enthusiasm. In general, Kaka, a silver-haired, bespectacled septuagenarian with a small moustache over well-defined lips, shows little emotion. Indeed he has a way of getting things done without even looking a person in the eye.

I can imagine how intimidating that can be when he proceeds to explain, in his whispery voice, how he dealt with those who did not buy his 'win-win' deal.

The farmer who had planted eucalyptus trees for instance, a stubborn lawyer, a host of other property owners who for one reason or another were not attracted by Kaka's entrepreneurial offer. In such cases Kaka would try various approaches. Threat for instance. 'I would say to the land owner: "this will be to your advantage". I would say that "I have come to *request* you. And my hand is like *this*"', he flashes an open palm. '"If you give, it is good. If not then I will come after two years having prepared my legal documentation and my hand will be like this."' He makes a grabbing gesture. '"The road will happen. That is certain!"' At other times he would use charm. He would make a personal visit, share a cup of tea, apologize, cajole, and somehow diffuse opposition. 'It is because you have come I am agreeing,' the potential dissident was likely to say when this happened. Even for an especially tough opponent Kaka would just put his arm around him and say, 'This is my special friend, his land is my land.' And in that way, he says, opposition was blown away.

'*Vikase bandhyo vishwas* [development generated trust],' observes Kaka's right-hand man, Nimish Joshi, sagely.

Nimish arrives one morning to take me for a drive on the western arc of the Sardar Patel Ring Road. The Rama preacher Morari Bapu's heavy-lidded eyes regard me with soft piety from a wooden panel above the dashboard alongside a miniature idol in a glass case. A gold-trimmed red scarf used in religious ceremonies flutters from the window of the white Santro. Nimish has the stubby, boyish look and spiky haircut of someone in his early thirties and wears a holy red thread on his wrist. We have fixed to meet in Vastrapur, not far from the lake complex with its fountains and faux medieval walls. The Vastrapur lake complex was one of Kaka's showpiece projects, part of his plan to revive the city's water bodies. His proposal met the needs of the BJP's core electoral support group, the Hindu urban middle class, both by answering a growing demand for leisure and the symbolic resonance of water, water being sacred in the Hindu mythos.

We leave the SG Highway and cut across Bopal. Bopal is a cautionary tale, a neighbourhood that attempted to develop on its own without political backing, and reached a point of stagnation clear from the sight of rocky, pitted roads and unfinished commercial complexes. 'It is an urban slum,' Nimish says with a contemptuous wave. We drive further west. On either side of us the bright green grass is interrupted with hoardings, fences, the flat roof of a hotel, an advertisement for a complex called 'The Egyptian' with the painting of a Pharaoh on it, the elegant red roofs of bungalow apartments. Where the connecting road meets the new Ring Road, hoardings for apartments and holiday homes loom up on either side: In its sleekness the Ring Road resembles the motorway of a developed country. We move soundlessly, climbing gently upwards, into a pale blue sky scattered with white fluffy clouds. A truck rumbles past. In the distance the globe of Science City appears, South America stretched over its glimmering, pearly blue rump. There is silence for miles except for the occasional outburst from Nimish's phone which breaks into a paean to the mystical Shirdi Sai Baba every time a call comes through. A strong smell of dry grass rises at Chharodi. The ornate, palatial buildings of the Shree Swaminarayan Gurukul Vishwavidya Pratisthanam swim into view. The SGVP, an international school established by the Swaminarayan sect, sprawls over 52 acres and offers yoga, football and horse riding lessons to its students. We pass a sea of houses in the distance. 'Designed but no infrastructure yet,' Nimish informs me crisply. On a tall arch the name 'Swagat Green Ville II 2006' stands out in a baroque font.

Abruptly Nimish leaves the Ring Road and makes a loop back to show me the reach of 'development'. More housing complexes appear: white, low, glass-fronted. A hospital, banks (Kalupur, HDFC, ICICI), shops, beauty parlours, commercial complexes, a café. Next to the 'Utopia School', which has classes in both English and Gujarati, a ten-storey building is coming up. 'Up to the highway is all occupied,' he points out, 'beyond that people have probably bought holiday homes as an investment.' A Party Plot goes by with two miniature canons on the gate post. Not far from it we come upon a sign that says 'AUDA Lake' next to a low wall made of fabricated boulders, much like a fortress wall identical to the mock fortress appearance of the refurbished Vastrapur lake complex. 'Kaka's style,' Nimish points out proudly. Kaka's style has permeated much of the city. For instance, in his restless desire to beautify the city, he decided to shield a crematorium on SG Road from public view with a giant statue of a seated Shiva. 'Kaka being a *dharmik* [religious] type,' Nimish explains. But then, as he goes on to narrate, breaking into a wide smile, 'the cover provided by the statue started attracting lovers. Lovers in a crematorium!' He laughs, evidently tickled.

It is well-known in the city that Kaka's star has dimmed in recent times. His elevation to the Rajya Sabha was seen as a move by Narendra Modi to get a potential rival out of the way. Kaka seems philosophical about the fact. 'Life is in three parts,' he says: '*bhakti*, *karma*, *gyan* [Faith, deed, knowledge]. I have done the karma, now it is time for the gyan.' Kaka's contribution to 'gyan' is in the form of prayer booklets. They are extravagantly produced, hardbound, peppered with glossy photographs of sunsets and stormy skies, encrusted with glitter and interspersed with trite sentiments ('Music is universal language, it transcends barriers, it unites man with man and man with God'). He plans to start an institute to teach yoga, music, the Gita and the Vedas. 'We have to give direction to our new generation,' he says, 'to think of our culture, to think of the community, not money.'

*

The new ISCON mega mall flaunts its sharp-angled bulwarks. From its smooth ramparts hang images of the cornucopia of sensual delights on view inside. Its palisades, its twin atria mounting the tropical skies, evoke monumentality and aspiration, while its soaring water fountains bring to mind the bounties of paradise. Moving west of the river in the early twentieth century, Ahmedabadis had attempted to create versions of neighbourhoods in the old walled town: caste living with caste brethren, community shrines in the parking lots. Every part of the city was a reconstructed memory, every part a space of belonging. But here, where the long arm of Satellite Road meets the vertical thrust of the Highway, where for long was a no man's land, was a space for new imaginings, new dreams, new fantasies. And here it was, amidst the replicas of religious centres, that the recurring malls would come up: the Mega Home Store and timber furniture mart, the Big Bazaar and the gigantic Acropolis mall. More malls, across the road from ISCON, orderly like a row of potted plants. Vast, hollowed-out towers with escalators going endlessly up and up and up and smooth, glistening floors echoing with the clatter of footwear and the reverberating hum of a distant loudspeaker. Millions of rupees of retail, jeans, sportswear, kidswear, watches, shirts, travel gear, greeting cards, handbags and imitation jewellery. Soft, pastel glass vistas interspersed with the low buzz of the food court and the whoosh of children being swallowed up in PVC slides.

The advertisements for housing complexes are like film reels. I pass a sequence of hoardings that extends for almost a hundred feet. The new cheap solvent inks from China bleeding into miles of white vinyl make the houses so vivid, so real. Digital camerawork brings everything up close. The glitter of gold, the sun on a Peugeot, an unshaven cheek, so close, so personal, as if the contemporary advertiser would enter the consumer's soul.

As evening falls on the Satellite Crossroads, computer-processed visages of film stars frozen in pain or glee, advertising the movies in the multiplexes across the road, are replicated in the multiple plasma screens of television sets in a Croma Electronics store on the ground. A mirrored wall of fantasies that shift, re-form, coalesce. Here, desire is manifest in every glossy, neon-lit surface: the desire for security, for beauty, for love, for revenge, for speed, for possession. And somewhere within this miasma of arousal, escape and urban sophistication, is the benedictory larger-than-life likeness of the bearded, bespectacled leader who presided over the anarchic spring of 2002 and who continues to hold the city and the state in his velvety palm.

The image is repeated, like a leitmotif across town. On hoardings rented out by the Ahmedabad Municipal Corporation at a fraction of their commercial cost, in thick glossy brochures sponsored by corporate houses, in newspaper advertisements and in clips on You Tube too, the chief minister looms large, a relentless presence. Political sycophancy and the cult of the leader are common phenomena in the fraught Indian landscape but the publicity surrounding Modi is unusual in its attention to presentation. Narendra Modi appears to his public in a variety of moods, poses and avatars. Thoughtful, smiling, determined, combative with his fist raised, humble with folded hands, gracious with arm upswept, these are some aspects of the leader. He likes to dress up. Indeed starting out with an image of Spartan simplicity, he has become something of a clotheshorse, dolling up in sharp suits, designer kurtas, stylish turbans, sporty track suits and Pathani outfits. The anachronistic detail—a cravat, for instance—

or occasional excess—such as a striped shirt-hat-scarf ensemble which he wore while inspecting the Sabarmati Riverfront Development Project—suggest a deliberate theatricality but also an unctuousness which enhances his glamour in the eyes of his provincial audience.

The production of images of Narendra Modi is an ongoing affair. A few select photographers in Ahmedabad are used to getting sudden calls from the chief minister's home or residence asking them to come over to make new stills. Modi has a penchant for portraits though he is often photographed full length and as if caught in the act, of gardening, or making a notation on a file, or pointing on a map, or talking on the phone, or playing with children and so on. He is his own stylist and production manager, judging his best angles, visualising props, taking care to edit out details such as a brand logo or a carelessly placed bottle of mineral water, remembering to remove a dental clip if the picture is to show him laughing, and posing with practiced naturalness, fingers in place, eyes appropriately dreamy or focused, and coordinating the colour palette.

The chief minister vets every part of the publicity juggernaut, from a lowly government advertisement to an invitation card. Government officials scurry to send him two copies, hard and soft, for approval wherever he may be. An incident involving a photograph that is reported to have taken place out in the picturesque desert area of Gujarat is extremely revealing of the place of image-making in Narendra Modi's world. It was the time of the camel festival. The day's work was done but the chief minister asked a photographer to follow him into the desert. After walking for a kilometre and a half, he stopped, pointed at a spot and described how he wanted to be photographed: hands raised in wonder, the light in his face, a trench coat flapping at his ankles, alone, on the silver sands. He told the photographer that some years before he had chanced upon the spot and thought it would make a suitable showcase for the glory of Gujarat. Modi is a brand. Modi is not just a leader, a politician. He is an object of desire. An object of consumption.

A luxury multiplex, in one of the malls at the Satellite Crossroads, is running a film by Sudhir Mishra. His last film, *Hazaaron Khwaishein Aisi*, the title a line from a famous poem by the great Urdu poet Mirza Ghalib, means 'a thousand desires', a passionate, self-annihilating, all-consuming longing. The film was a love story but an unusual one, set in the Emergency, the twenty-one-month period between 1975 and 1977 when Indira Gandhi formally suspended civil liberties across India in response to a perceived internal threat. It was about the strength and deceptiveness of human passion and the bludgeoning arbitrariness of state violence.

It felt very much like the Emergency in Gujarat in 2002. In April, when I travelled to the Saurashtra coast in western Gujarat, the violence that had unleashed itself like an enraged tidal wave across the state had receded. Yet the land seemed to tingle underfoot as if recoiling from a tremendous blow and the salt-tinged breeze of the Arabian Sea felt like a reproach. Gujarat's Hindu holy men, commanders of vast congregations at home and across the diaspora, apostles of piety, had gone strangely mute. In the small town of Mahuva I met Morari Bapu. The preacher, whose powerful rendition of the Ramayana had won him a large following in the Gujarati-speaking world, was reputed also to be a man with a practical mission, being involved in projects of social work and avidly sought after by politicians. Swarthy, bearded, solemn-eyed, in open-toed sandals and a black ash mark on his forehead, the celebrated preacher gave me a gracious welcome. Speaking in the vernacular, though his website described him as a former teacher of English, he spouted philosophical verses, quoted liberally from the epics. But he remained determinedly and mellifluously firm in refusing to be drawn into a discussion on the recent savagery.

Leaving Morari Bapu I stopped at the office of the region's largest circulated newspaper in the town of Bhavnagar. There I talked to a correspondent who boasted about how his paper had fanned anti-minority violence in the town. Bhavnagar, part of the former princely region of Saurashtra, was not communally sensitive and remained calm even when south and central Gujarat exploded into anti-Muslim violence in March 2002. 'We asked, why is Bhavnagar not reacting? Are the men wearing bangles?' the correspondent narrated gleefully, 'and then the violence broke out here as well!'

*

'Gujarat is not like that,' said Kamleshbhai, waving a pudgy hand, 'it is peaceful.' It was February 2003, almost a year after the violence. Kamleshbhai, who I was interviewing in his office at the National Cloth Market in Ahmedabad, was telling me that the episode that was perceived as the most serious outbreak of communal violence in post-Independence India did not actually take place. 'It was nothing ... all a media creation ... the English media wanted to malign Gujarat,' he looked at me with a hint of accusation. 'There was nothing much. Nothing happened.' He swerved his head to indicate his environs, the offices strung out in long straight lines. 'We were all working. I did not lose a day's work.'

'It was all a political drama. Modi was the main player and Godhra was the "magic stick",' Alok Kumar, a 41-year-old dyestuff exporter had an air of triumphant satisfaction as he analysed the events of 2002. Excitedly pacing the length of his small, modishly appointed office on Ashram Road, Alok, in jeans, in leather shoes, with paan-stained teeth, a mobile phone ringing on his table all the time, looked every bit the arriviste entrepreneur. His office was closed for as long as eight weeks during the violence. But he was not concerned about the lost business. 'It was time to teach the other community a lesson,' he said jauntily. 'For years they have been controlling us, now they have to learn to behave as a minority!'

For a substantial part of the first five decades following Independence, Gujarat was ruled by the Congress. The Hindu revivalist lobby, though it joined non-Congress coalition governments, was not a political force in the state. The first time the BJP won the state assembly elections was in 1995. The speed with which it subsequently consolidated its hold over the state led the national media to suggest that the Hindu revivalist lobby had made Gujarat a laboratory for its experiments. Analysts observed how the Sangh Parivar's yatras, politico-religious pilgrimages in the 1980s and 1990s, had been used to attract the lower castes in Gujarat. How the yatras had left a series of communal riots in their wake. They described how Hindutva-led groups, riding on the institutional damage wrought over previous decades by Indira Gandhi, had insinuated themselves into centres of power and patronage in Gujarat. By the early 2000s the Sangh Parivar controlled the government, the bureaucracy, the judiciary, local authorities, universities, the police and even state-owned boards and consultative committees, such as the Police Advisory Committee and the Social Justice Committee. In 2002 it could mobilise large, armed hate groups across the state and procure the co-operation of the police, the bureaucracy and sections of the judiciary in enabling or covering up atrocities against Muslims.

The metaphor of a laboratory was clearly relevant. At the same time the manner in which it was applied, with the focus being on the strategies and activities of the revivalist lobby, produced a skewed representation of the phenomenon. It did not ask why Gujarat should have been perceived as a suitable site for running a trial for instance. Nor did it attempt to understand why the state should have proved spectacularly hospitable for the same.

A survey of Gujarat's history for the greater part of the twentieth century reveals that the state, and Ahmedabad in particular, has always been prone to flamboyant and extremely militant mobilizations. In the 1940s, during the Quit India Movement, bomb attacks and hartals were organized against the British. During the statehood agitation in the 1950s, a rhetoric of extreme hostility was whipped up against the central government in New Delhi. In the 1970s, college students launched an unruly protest against corruption. In the 1980s, the possibility of expanding the scope of affirmative action in universities brought the upper caste to the streets. In the 1990s, Gujaratis united to support the building of the Sardar Sarovar Dam with a fervid aggressiveness. In the 2000s, the bogey of the fearsome Muslim provoked the country's ugliest bout of communal violence. Recurring features provided a sense of uniformity to these disparate agitations. An anxiety about material advancement was a common spur, giving rise to a bourgeois leadership which, in turn, brought a high level of managerial skill and gimmickry to the campaigns. A persistent tendency to vilify the Other was another noteworthy feature, the identity of the Other constantly shifting to settle variously on the colonial ruler, the centre, lower castes, the environmentalist and, in 2002, the Muslim.

Media interviews with perpetrators of violence in 2002 revealed men and women inhabiting a world of historical victimhood with a pathological unconcern for the sanctity of present life or personhood. In my conversations with ordinary middle-class non-Muslims who had not participated in the violence I found a similar proclivity towards paranoia and selective callousness. There was a woman doctor who expressed deep anguish for a brutalised tribal woman patient but asked her tenant, a Muslim woman professional, to leave her house because friends insinuated that she could be a terrorist. There was another woman, a former journalist who, in covering earlier episodes of communal violence, had figured that such episodes were politically motivated. Yet, in 2002, when her son expressed admiration for the chief minister's stern 'action' against Muslims, she would not argue with him.

'How did you feel about the crimes against Muslim women?' I asked her.

'I cried,' she said, '... but.'

'... but' was as close to empathy as I was to find in Ahmedabad. Outside of a small group of committed liberals and professional human rights activists, most people enforced a silence or they doubted themselves. The consensus was enormous, vicious and forceful. I, just a visitor, found myself keeping my counsel. Partly to avoid long and deeply unpleasant encounters such as this one at the home of an elderly Brahmin schoolteacher who harangued me for hours after I referred to India as a secular country, harangued me with vicious determination even as his wife, tennis shoes on her feet, waited for him to join her on their daily walk and it grew dark outside. The other reason I found myself increasingly disinclined to speak was because there was no one listening or willing to enter into a discussion even to persuade me about the validity of their perspective. The view was a fait accompli.

*

'Any time,' she says. 'Four o'clock? Five?' She is mistress of her time. 'We will have a cup of coffee,' she says decidedly. 'I will come to pick you up in a red Santro. *Self-driven* ...' she emphasises, and in explication she adds: 'my driver is off today.' She is an upper-class Hindu businesswoman, a relative of someone I know. She is on my list of people to meet in Ahmedabad, to widen the scope of my forays into the mind of the city.

At 4.45 a text arrives to say she will be late. A quarter of an hour later another text appears on my phone asking for more time. By and by, though, we are cruising past the open grounds of the university in her red Santro. *Self-driven.* Her eyes are firmly on the road, except for sidelong glances and a direct, stern look to tell me she doesn't have much time, a wedding to attend, she names the host, an important name. At the cafe she bustles me into a seat, her eyes still not meeting mine. 'Have you interviewed X?' she asks, referring to a wealthy person about town. I say I have. 'We were to meet him the other day,' she says with studied casualness. The cafe is noisy with young people. She is petite, a dainty woman in her forties, youthful in appearance. She leans forward. 'I must tell you something about Ahmedabad.' Her manner is grave. There are worry lines on her forehead. 'Here, even if a person becomes very rich and successful, he will not stop seeing his childhood friends. Even a *very* ...' her gesture indicates status on a grand scale, 'will still keep old friends. In Delhi and other places I am told it is not so.' Her eyes flicker over me mildly enquiring but not tarrying for a response.

'Here it is okay sometimes even to travel in an auto-rickshaw. If your car has a problem, or your driver has not come, you can arrive at an event in an auto-rickshaw. And then you explain, of course, what has happened ... that your car had a problem. But it is possible. In Delhi it would just not be! Of course in Ahmedabad also you do things like taking out your *good* car for a big event and all that but it is *so much more* ...' She breaks off abruptly and swivels her head this way and that for a waiter. 'Eat something ...' she urges. 'You must eat something!'

I demur. She has a wedding to attend. She will be late.

'I ... we will drop you,' she says. 'We can drop you at least part of the way.'

The darkening road is lit by the pallid glow of the streetlamps. Her husband is at the wheel. A florid, laconic man. Her disembodied voice comes to me from the front seat continuing a conversation begun in the cafe. It had started with her telling me that the wife of one of her Muslim employees had run away with another man. 'What will he do now?' she had asked with an expression that said 'look at that!' And then as if one followed the other or perhaps because she thought that was what any visiting journalist would be wanting to talk about, she had started talking about the 2002 violence. 'And let me tell you!' she had said, her eyes wide and her small frame tightening with anger. 'What happened was bad, and too much, but *you have to understand*!'

What she wanted me to understand, she said, was that Gujarati Hindus had ben provoked. I assume at first that she is referring to the gruesome killing of Hindu train passengers in Godhra. From the beginning the lethal fire had been cloaked in mystery. That a mob of Muslims had surrounded the train and were pelting it with stones was not in dispute. But how the fire started, who set it and for what reason was not immediately clear. Official agencies would explore various possibilities including a stove fire, an escalation of a conflict, and conspiracy.[1]

But I realize this is not what she means. At the time, journalists investigating the incident had reported that the harassment of local Muslims at the station by Vishwa Hindu Parishad activists had caused Muslims from the slums alongside the tracks to attack the coach that was ablaze minutes later. It is these media reports my companion is referring to. To her mind, they appeared to 'justify' the fire. She was outraged. '*I* myself felt, kill them all!'

In the car, now feeling the need to return to the subject she describes how tense it was the day after Godhra, when the bodies of the victims were brought to a fraught Ahmedabad. The words rush from her, eager, jagged, a hammer flailing for a nail. 'In those days we lived in A—. It was a colony of good people, all good cars. All were rich in the colony, even one or two professionals, *a CA*.' Her tone urges me to imagine the plush income of a CA. 'On that morning when the bodies were being brought into the city, our neighbour ... he is a rich person ... not, you know, someone on the streets ... he came to call my husband out—"come on, S! Let's go and teach the bastards a lesson!"' She has been turning in her seat, occasionally inserting her face between the two tall front seats to face me as she talks. Now I see her profile extending excitedly towards her husband. 'Don't you remember, S, how he came? He was banging on cars and shouting for you to come out!' Her husband nods, a little unsure, I think, in my presence. 'Then when the media tried to justify it *I* wanted to kill them all...!' A tight control had characterized her demeanour so far; it has snapped like a twig. She begins a litany: 'they needed to be taught a lesson'; 'it was time for the Hindus to hit back'. Her face reappears, with its now deeply puckered forehead, in the gap between the seats. 'I am *right*,' she says. 'I am right!'

*

At 3 pm I am on roads lined with powdered chalk marking the route the chief minister will be taking, or it is a decoy route, perhaps, to throw a potential assassin off his mark. Fire engines are parked at the Sanskar Kendra, the city's cultural centre, housed in a long Le Corbusier Modernist cube from the 1950s. Outside the gate now is a small black statue of the Hindutva ideologue Vinayak Savarkar. Dhoti-clad and with an umbrella, a cap, his raised finger accompanies the fiery declaration: 'Hey Ma Bharati, without you life is like death. To sacrifice for you, that is true life'. Policemen hover around it, looking busy and concerned. The man of the moment, Zaverilal Mehta, the 81-year-old photographer with the newspaper *Gujarat Samachar*, whose book release function is due to commence in a few minutes, waits anxiously outside the doors of the hall, cutting an outlandish figure in a maroon shirt, dyed pencil moustache, dark glasses, and a hat from which a mane falls to his shoulders. The men around him have toupees on their heads.

Inside, the high-ceilinged 700-seater auditorium, designed by the leading Ahmedabad architect B.V. Doshi, is gradually filling up. My friend Binit, a public relations man, is a regular at such dos, but for this event, his wife, Shilpa, his mother and his father have come along as well, eager to see the chief minister. We find good seats in one of the middle rows. Security men in black with ID cards round their necks, security men in grey safari suits, a sniffer dog, an eager brown Alsatian, scour the stage looking for suspicious packages amidst the props: ornate chairs, a Ganesh idol, a lamp, clumps of flowers and satin trimmings against which an announcement of the event appears in bold type: 'Flashback Lokarpan [release of *Flashback*]', to be inaugurated by Narendra Modi. The emcee announces that the CM is due to arrive in 'six and a half minutes'.

A posse of Swaminarayan monks in saffron robes and small turbans makes its way down the steps. The monks file into the front row on the left and take their places, turbans rising like small peaks. One of them films his colleagues with a weighty video camera. The song playing on the loudspeaker is a Swaminarayan bhajan performed by a chorus of callow voices: 'we are bapa's children, we will make a *tilak* and wear a *mala*.' A security man with an AK47 saunters across the stage. Local celebrities occupy the front row centre: a nephrologist, a health columnist who runs a chain of health clubs, a television-soap actor, a distinguished novelist and humorist. Shilpa points them out, whispering that a 'big writer and a *sant* [religious leader]' are a 'minimum' requirement at such events. As if on cue, Acharya Shri Purushottampriyadasji Swamiji Maharaj, head of one of the important factions of the Swaminarayan sect, appears, benignly acknowledging reverential bows from the celebrity row and posing for photographers.

The Swaminarayan sect, known by its ornate faux-medieval sandstone and marble temples, was founded by an early nineteenth-century preacher, a reformer welcomed even by the colonial administration because of his highly disciplinarian bent. As Jainism did once, the Swaminarayan creed now does, insinuating itself into the city's dry air, its detailed *Shikshapatri* providing prescriptions for every aspect of living.

My followers shall get up daily before sun-rise, offer prayers to Lord Krishna and then shall go to answer call of nature. SHIKSHAPATRI RULE 49

Male followers shall not here (sic) religious or philosophical discourses from females nor shall they enter into arguments with them or with a king or with his men. SHIKSHAPATRI RULE 34

They shall never enter into any transaction regarding land and/or money even with their own sons and friends, without putting it in writing with proper attestation. SHIKSHAPATRI RULE 143

The lights go off suddenly. The video recorder is being tested. The darkness is punctuated with coughs, tinkles and snatches of film music from cellphones. A woman in our row is telling a caller that she is at 'saheb's function'; saheb being a commonly used appellation for Narendra Modi. There are two functions today, she informs the person at the other end. Earlier Modi was naming a bridge after a former army general.

As visibility returns I recognize the familiar, tall, stooped figure of Shreyans Shah, managing editor and publisher of the Ahmedabad-based Lok Prakashan Group which owns *Gujarat Samachar*, the state's highest-circulated newspaper. Silver-haired, kurta-clad, Shah has his headquarters in a building of faded art deco elegance in the Khanpur area of the old town. His closest rival, Falgun Patel, Managing Director and Chief Editor of the Gujarati media group The Sandesh Ltd, customarily clad in leather loafers with a dusting of holy vermillion on his throat, sits across town, in a granite- and glass-fronted tower. The two are chief gunslingers in Ahmedabad, where newspapers have traditionally enjoyed tremendous influence. Unabashedly provincial and overwhelmingly commercial in their orientation, these dailies could be said to have anticipated the Murdoch era and its reverberations. In 2002, a visiting investigative team of the Editors' Guild was shocked by their gravely provocative misreporting and sensationalism. But this emotive pro-majoritarian coverage, one could have told them, was merely a node in a long narrative.

Swaminarayan bhajans play on in the background. There is a sudden frisson in the air, an excitement rippling through the hall. Photographers dash to their stations. The master of ceremonies has a smile as wide as his arm. A whisper goes up, 'Modi has arrived!' Heads swivel. Nervous titters are heard. A bustle on the left confirms the news and, all at once, the air turns electric, buzzing and zinging with anticipation. Modi appears in a brown khadi short-sleeved kurta and churidaar, and the hall is suffused with joy. Wave after wave of exultation peppered with laughter and indulgent chuckles wash over the room. Binit's mother gives me a hard nudge. Her eyes are shining. I am reminded of Janmashtami, the birthday of Krishna, of the moment, at midnight, when the temple doors open and the jostling, eager crowds get their first glimpse of the newborn god.

The emcee makes fatuous remarks about the rewards of patience which are drowned out as the audience continues to cheer. I can hear the word 'Nano' being tossed around on the unruly swell. It has been a few weeks since Tata Motors decided to manufacture its low-cost car Nano in Gujarat, after Narendra Modi unfurled the red carpet, promising land and soft loans. A bold shout breaks through the hubbub: 'Nano!' And the audience breaks into a frenzy, cheering and clapping wildly.

Studies in neuroscience have established the powerful role of the mass media in shaping the contemporary human mind; the television industry even describes commercials slots as 'brain time'. Marketers in a post-capitalist world know that to sell a product or a message they must persuade consumers not just to buy but to involve them in a story. The middle class, fed on a steady diet of television soaps, wants the story to never end. In his speeches, Narendra Modi speaks of the Other. He speaks of the Pride of Gujarat. He talks of 'development'. These few themes form the narrow ambit within which he roams. Like traditional oral narrators or advertising copywriters he deals in well-worn tales. There is no ambiguity in his speech. His rhetorical flourish—a loud rousing challenge followed by drizzling sarcasm—is as anticipated as the Indian musician's *tanna* and *bol*. His favoured stock phrases, acquire, through repetition, the lulling sway of a mantra: Gujarat as a 'leader', Gujarat as a 'model', Gujarat as a 'beacon'. Yet, like the child-god Krishna, he introduces an element of mischief, of minor anarchy. There is no saying what he will wear, who he will target, how far he will go. Like the hook at the end of an episode of a television soap, this minor trick keeps the audience guessing, wanting more. Narendra Modi ascends the stage. The emcee shouts: '*Nano!*'

Two boys, wielding a gold-handled brush and a gold mace, flank the saffron-draped chair on which Acharya Shri Purushottampriyadasji Swamiji Maharaj is seated. The Swamiji leads the assembly into prayer. The audience rises to its feet, clapping. The master of ceremonies tells the audience to sit. A candle is lit. A small tableau with models of Zaverilal's camera and cap, a quill and a scroll, is displayed. Two monks parade a copy of Zaverilal's photographic memoir, ceremoniously draped in pink. The cameras furiously record the moment. A friend of Zaverilal's is called to the mike. 'Not all politicians are as influential and handsome as Narendra Modi,' he says. Modi's smile is partially obscured by his hand. He talks about prominent Gujarati politicians of an earlier era. Modi nods as if to say: 'you are talking about *that* time!' More speeches. When speakers make distasteful personal remarks about his rivals (referring to their lack of photogenic quality), Narendra Modi grins widely. When the emcee says he knows married and single women, 'like his friend Heena, an executive, earning Rs 90,000 a month', who are in love with him, Narendra Modi smiles modestly, his fingertips twirling and stroking the fabric of his sleeve.

Modi's charisma builds on salience, a perpetual feed in varying affective modes, over various media. On the nightly news in Gujarat, Narendra Modi's stern portrait stands for durability at a time of relentless criticism from national media, for stoicism during the vicissitudes of court strictures. On hoardings he appears in his full form, and alongside him are the floating faces of eminent Indians such as Sardar Patel and Swami Vivekananda. Sometimes Modi urges Gujaratis to grow trees, or to care for their daughters, or to read. He gifts his state festivals, massive, extravagant fests. He is a constant presence, looming, poised, in gestures of benediction. Now the celebrated nephrologist is comparing Narendra Modi to the legendary political strategist Chanakya. But, 'to appreciate Chanakya,' he says, 'you need a certain class of people.' Narendra Modi brings a finger to his forehead in acknowledgement.

As the event unfolds in its slow, slapdash way, I find myself wondering about the motive that would have induced the chief minister to take time off his hectic schedule on a working afternoon. Friendship? Diplomacy? Perhaps. And then there is the matter of his artistic inclinations. Modi dabbles in photography. At public events he is liable to talk shop with attendant photographers and a picture in a daily newspaper shows him fiddling with a mediaperson's Canon. He also writes pedantic poetry. His last book, a coffee table book of his poems called *Aankh aa Sagar che* (The Eyes are the Sea) has brief verses in Gujarati ('*Zindagi aa Dhanya Che*'—Life You are Blessed), accompanied by glossy full-page pictures of the poet traipsing in colour-coordinated outfits through flower-filled meadows.

Here, now, Narendra Modi is on his feet affectionately patting Zaverilal's blushing grandson on the back. 'Narendra Modi—happy like always,' the emcee comments. Zaverilal attempts to garland Narendra Modi and there is some brotherly grappling as Modi tries to put the garland around the photographer's neck instead. The audience shouts. The audience laughs. The emcee laughs too. And returns to his preferred subject, the Nano. 'Today we have the affordable car, tomorrow we will get small, small affordable planes!' From his seat, Acharya Shri Purushottampriyadasji Swamiji Maharaj starts singing again. On either side of him, the monks take up the chorus. A boy–monk gently flaps the ceremonial brush. About me the women sing too. Narendra Modi stands, arms akimbo, feet crossed. His head slumps; then, as the bhajan ends, it jerks up. 'Narendra Modi is Gujarat's *sutradhar*. Because of him Gujarat got a gift of the Nano car,' the Swami says. 'God please bring honour to Narendra Modi saheb!' Another bhajan commences. Everybody sings along. The doctor claps softly. Narendra Modi twiddles and taps his fingers. The hall resounds: 'Akshardham ni jai!'

*

I am standing outside the Freeway Mall at the Satellite Crossroads. Across the road to my left, where the diffident flare of the new Gallops mall battles the bleak shadows of the beginning countryside, a cluster of people in dusty, windblown village attire is waiting at a bus stop. A bus approaches. They hurry towards it. There is a brief exchange between one of the group and the bus driver. The bus departs without them. I see them falling back, scattering and calling out to each other with urgent, indecipherable cries. The hull of a half-built flyover looms like a giant vulture at the crossroads. The city is in flux. Across town one can see the fissures in the tar, the mounds of sand and stone, chains, stagnant water pools, the paver blocks, axes, rollers, cranes and other paraphernalia required to crack a city open and stretch it. Stretch it sideways. Stretch it to the right and to the left and upwards, vaulting it high into the sky. Surgery is not pretty. It is even less so for those in the way. Every once in a while one sees the knocked-down remains of tin and loose brick shanties. The story is the same: a notice and then the bulldozers. And people, hundreds and thousands of people wafted, like the cottony seeds of the Calotropis in the summer breeze, from their shacks to make way for the developing city.

Cities across India are being broken, rattled and knocked to fit into the contours of a neoliberal economy. China, the leading Asian superpower, aims for an urban population of one billion by 2020. India, belatedly but with growing determination, is following in China's footsteps with an expectation of 600 million by 2030. In getting there it will need to add another 700 million to 900 million square metres of urban floor space and 350 to 400 kilometres of metropolitan railways and subways every year, not to speak of roads, houses and shops. I breathe in the warm, papery, early March air. A couple with a child brushes past me, heading for the McDonald's at the corner. The boy with silky hair cut like a pineapple top darts ahead of his parents and flings a thin arm around the fibreglass mascot. The father stops, automatically raises his arm. Click! Not far from McDonald's is the Choice Snack Bar, a popular eatery with branches all over the city. The SG Road outlet, a pricier version, smells of disinfectant and room freshener and has Hawaiian-shirted waiters hanging listlessly around the counter. Their parents probably worked in the textile mills. Ahmedabad is a city that is constantly making and remaking itself.

I realize I have lingered too long in the cool, chimerical spaces of the Freeways mall: the buzzing, bright expanse of the Crossword bookstore suffused with the aroma of freshly brewed coffee and the opaque, cavernous interiors of Bandhej, its silks and gold threads glowing in the dim light. By the time I emerge into the real world it is the time of day people call 'godhuli', when the cows come home from pasture. In a city it is that melancholy hour when the Marutis, Hondas, minivans, auto-rickshaws, buses and cycles wend their way homewards. The traffic pours in from all four directions to meet in the battlefield at the centre. The neon lights on the multiplex hoardings jump on.

In the sickly ochre light of the street lamps, headlights engage and horns communicate with each other like in some primitive mating ritual. In between there is the whistling sigh of tyres, the put-put-put of running engines and the head-spinning hit of diesel. The sidewalk I am standing on rises roughly two feet from the ground. It is abutted by a rough trough-like patch about eight feet wide, strewn with loose sand and gravel. I descend carefully feeling the rough bumpiness of gravel underfoot as I walk towards two parked rickshaws. My destination, Ramdev Nagar, is less than a couple of kilometres away; too close to be an attractive fare. Both refuse my custom. I begin to walk away. From the corner of my eye, however, I see the clumsy vehicle that locals call a *chakhdo* approach and stop close to the rickshaws. A chakhdo is a retrofitted rickshaw used to ferry the poor to and from the outskirts and also to connect a few chosen points in the city. I can see it disgorging passengers. It occurs to me that it could get me across to the other side and then I could walk the short distance that would remain. I run back, stumbling over the loose sand but the vehicle has started up and by the time I get near it has already joined the thick stream of traffic.

SIX
New York Tower

IT SEEMS THAT THE night before he left India for the last time, not long before his fatal heart attack at New York's Penn Station on March 17, 1974, Louis Kahn had dinner in Ahmedabad with B.V. Doshi. Speaking about his celebrated colleague in a film made by Kahn's son, Doshi would say that Kahn's preoccupations were unusual and 'guru'-like. 'Nothingness, spirituality of material, enigma of light mattered to him ... Kahn had reached a stage of super consciousness. Everything was alive and in a stage of transition.'

One can see the meaning of this abstraction in the stunning austerity of the Salk Institute for Biological Studies at La Jolla, California, in Dhaka's Parliament building shimmering over water, the inspirational centerpiece of an emerging democracy, and in the Indian Institute of Management in Ahmedabad (IIM-A)—another signature work of the American architect. Kahn was invited to build the IIM-A by the local elite in the 1950s. The imposing neo-gothic structures that are a hallmark of colonial cities such as Mumbai and Kolkata are conspicuously lacking in Ahmedabad. The absence of an overpowering British signage was probably an important factor in freeing the aesthetically inclined Jain and Hindu burghers to look toward the rising superpower of America, to individuals such as Kahn, Frank Lloyd Wright, Charles Eames and Buckminster Fuller, and in imprinting Ahmedabad with the fluidity and clean lines of the Modern movement.

In keeping with Kahn's preference for simple, economical materials that were reflective of the environment, the IIM-A was built of local red brick. The ruddy buildings loom over the bare campus grounds monumental as the Egyptian pyramids that stirred Kahn's creative impulses in late age, but punctured by absences, geometrical and equally monumental. 'When did the idea of teaching emerge? When did the idea of a library emerge?' These were the sorts of queries running through Kahn's mind when he designed the IIM-A. He was keen on excavating 'Volume Zero', his term for the history preceding recorded history. The beauty of architecture, he used to say, was that it dealt with the recessions of the mind, which yielded 'that which is not yet said and not yet made'. The IIM-A buildings reflect Kahn's deeply profound explorations. They are futuristic and old, heavy and light, changing appearance as the sun moves over them like a slow-panning camera.

*

Driving south on SG Road in 2009, the clean, flat rooftops of private clubs come into view. The clubs have tennis and badminton courts, swimming pools, cafes, jogging tracks and soccer stadium-sized parking lots. They alternate with the skyrocketing, coruscating facades of malls, showrooms and office buildings with names like 'Acropolis', 'Titanium', 'New York Tower', names indicating classicism, ruggedness, style; names suggesting an erasure of local, provincial and disorderly inclinations. Private grounds between this stretch of SG Highway, from Thaltej to Prahlad Nagar, and the river, are coated with iron rods and Reinforced Cement Concrete. Public roads shine with new bitumen and paver blocks. The Sabarmati is hedged between even lines of concrete. In a global economy, where money and its handlers zigzag across the world like laser beams and South East Asian cities have jumped through hoops to catch the florescence (building the world's 'tallest tower', for instance, or establishing an international cultural complex), creating anodyne city parts is just a necessary first step to giving the international businessman a soft landing. Cities have to be gentrified in the same way that exotic places were once equipped with hamburger joints to provide a feeling of comfort to the moneyed tourist.

The gentrification proceeds in stages. City's resources focus on providing the best infrastructure, power and communications; private developers build airports, glass towers, malls, green islands. Slowly, very slowly, 'development' spreads to the rest of the city. Those who cannot climb onto the inexorable train of progress for lack of resources or social acceptability are pushed out by rising real-estate prices and the high cost of living in these spaces, sanitized and dressed up to resemble a global anywhereness. Sometimes they do not leave easily and violence becomes necessary. 2002 was an episode of communal violence. By facilitating the removal of a people considered socially undesirable from upwardly mobile neighbourhoods, it dovetailed into the making of a neoliberal city.

*

The imagination of the twenty-first century city rests on scale. In February 2006, the Gujarat government brought surrounding areas within Ahmedabad's municipal boundaries, increasing its size from 198 square kilometres to 500 square kilometres and its population from 3.64 million to 5 million. The Sabarmati Riverfront Development Project is touted as the country's biggest urban transformation project. The website for the Gujarat International Finance Tec-City (GIFT) claims this hub for financial services coming up on Ahmedabad's outskirts will be double the size of Paris's La Defense and eight times more built up than the London Docklands. Science City is hailed as one of the 'largest projects in Asia'. The charitable Civil Hospital, slated for restructuring as a super-speciality hospital catering to the needs of medical tourism with a World Bank loan of nearly Rs 1000 crore, may become the world's largest hospital. The city's International Kite Festival aspires to set a *Guinness Book* record for the number of participants.

The seventeenth-century Moghul, Jahangir, called Ahmedabad the abode of dust. Narendra Modi promises to make the city 'dust free'. The desire for newness and muscularity, drivers of a neoliberal imagination, sometimes coincide with the RSS's predilection for rewriting history. In the eastern part of the city is the Hauz-e-Qutb, also known as Kankaria, a lake from the Sultanate era, a vast manmade reservoir, measuring over a kilometre across and sporting tiers of cut-stone steps, square cupolas, an exquisitely carved sluice and a garden island which travellers describe as having once housed a great fish pond and an unusual species of palmyra. Between 2006 and 2008, the Ahmedabad Municipal Corporation took over the fifteenth-century monument and refashioned it into an amusement complex with ticketed entry, rose and grey granite flooring, tall ornate gates, piped music, proliferating commercial signage and a toy train imported from the United Kingdom. Lamps, secreting from the lake rim, throw up tall steeples into the night air.

*

In January 2008 I spend a few weeks off CG Road, the city's commercial centre, in an apartment leased by Trishala, a young

America-born Gujarati Jain woman, and her mother. A mere 3 per cent of Ahmedabad's population, Jains have traditionally exercised a significant influence on the socio-cultural ethos of the city because of their wealth and dominant status, but also because the severely ascetic tenets of Jainism correspond to the strong reformist streak in Ahmedabadi society. Gandhi too derived much from his association with the Jain scholar Srimad Rajchandra in his youth. It is my first close encounter with this highly rule-bound religion.

The house empties out early and most mornings I have the large drawing room with its white walls and big, square, white floor tiles to myself. I sit at the small dining table and read the newspapers. I try to switch on the television set with the remote but it does not come alive. I realize it has been shut from the mains. I find that the lights are always kept off in the apartment unless someone is actually in a room. Since the 1,200 square-foot apartment is not well served by daylight, one is perpetually in a state of penumbral shadow. Once, entering a room and turning on the light, I hear a loud protesting yell and realise I have unwittingly disturbed the family retainer, also a Jain, at prayer. I retreat apologetically and become accustomed to gloom.

The apartment is on the third floor of a large colony of identical multi-storeyed apartments, with the inevitable Ganesh shrine at the entrance, a concrete playground and a parking lot. It is at the end of a small lane which gives it a certain quietness and privacy. At the other end of the lane, on the bustling CG Road, are a polyclinic, banks, tall office blocks, a mini mall, and a gaggle of shops and small commercial centres. At less than a kilometre is a railway crossing. Passing through the crossing every time I notice a young man holding up a sign. 'IMPOSSIBLE AS POSSIBLE', it says. And another time: 'THERE'S NEVER A WRONG TIME TO DO THE RIGHT THING'. Living downtown offers a new perspective on the city. To see the sweepers at dawn and the mothers in rumpled clothes depositing kids on bright school buses against the sleepy silhouettes of malls and office buildings is to feel a certain vulnerability at the heart of a metropolis.

One morning I head for Law Garden, a park in one of the earliest settled neighbourhoods west of the river. I see elderly couples from Ellis Bridge and Navrangpura in mufflers and jackets slowly walking along the concrete paths and young men struggling at the exercise bars. Great big peepal and gulmohar trees spread their bare branches over faux Romanesque structures. Mynahs and doves hop about squat banana trees. A young girl takes pictures with her camera phone of a white mongrel puppy. I hear a song, *Ding dong ding bole*, being played on a cellphone and snatches of a conversation in Hindi. On a morning like this, in 2003, the bullet-ridden body of former state Home Minister Haren Pandya, a longtime legislator from Ellis Bridge, was found in his car outside Law Garden. The previous year, Pandya had secretly deposed before a fact-finding team of retired judicial officers offering information that suggested an active collusion at the highest levels of the state administration in the violent attacks on Muslims in 2002.

Trishala's mother has returned from a trip to Palitana, a town with over nine hundred Jain temples. In photographs I have seen whitewashed spires clustered thickly on a hillside and devotees climbing the 3,750 stone steps to the summit of the Shatrunjaya Hill, barefoot, murmuring the name of the Lord. Induben is a petite woman with a sprightly, youthful energy which she appears to expend on religious duties and on ministering to the needs of her many relatives in the city. Her solicitude extends to me, particularly in the matter of food. She herself seems to eat little, taking her dinner before sunset, on a small mat on the floor. But large, wholesome meals are prepared for her daughter and me. And jars of dry snacks are placed on the table. Home-cooked:

'We do not eat food from outside.' Needless to say, the fare is strictly vegetarian. Jains are fanatically wedded to the principle of non-violence, taking elaborate precautions to avoid, even unwittingly, the taking of a life. The taps in the house are tied with a muslin cloth to prevent small insects from climbing up the nozzles and being drowned by the gush. One day, I find the maid distraught over the clogged sink in which two large cockroaches are floating on their backs, their feathery legs bent against their brown shellac wings. 'This is not allowed in our religion,' she says furiously.

The days pass. Slowly and determinedly, like a wave flattening out over the sand, the life of the house seeps into me. I am not bound by the rigorous customs and the severe restrictions by which my hosts choose to live their lives. Nor does the atmosphere of piety in the cold rooms make anything but the lightest demands of me. And yet I feel heavy with trepidation.

The newspapers lie scattered all over the dining table. There are now four English-language newspapers in the city, and every upper-class household appears to order at least two. The stories in the lifestyle sections reveal a fast transforming Ahmedabad. They talk about dog and pony shows, art openings and golf. The front pages take up local issues.

'Anger & Outrage' is the bold headline in the *Ahmedabad Mirror*. Over the last couple of weeks, one of the newspapers has been conducting a campaign to sensitize readers to the vulnerability of birds during the approaching kite festival. The anger and outrage is over the fact that the voluntary organisations which had made such a to-do about their efforts at rescuing maimed birds during the festival went on to dump them at a carcass depot. The photographs show a large-winged bird hopping pitifully on the ground. The traditional ethos of Ahmedabad's Hindu–Jain populace stresses *karuna*, or compassion, towards animals and birds but the current campaign, in its tone, its rendering and evident tokenism, seems to reflect a more recent, a more Westernized concern. Indeed, altruistic faddism appears to be a growing trend among people in their twenties and thirties. I hear of whimsical initiatives in the city. Of a group of do-gooders that offers free tea and bananas to cyclists; of another group that hopes to spark off chain reactions through acts of kindness such as helping the elderly cross the road; and yet another group that feeds two hundred people every Sunday in the old city. Some initiatives are more ambitious and purposeful. On the notice board at the large Crossword bookstore an advertisement from an organisation called Indiacorps for instance, talks about the 'change you can make happen'. I look up Indiacorps on the Net and find it is a 'non-partisan, non-religious, non-profit' organisation founded to provide 'Indians from all over the world with a channel to reconnect with India and with the means to contribute to its development, while fostering a new generation of socially conscious global leaders.' Its India operations are based in Ahmedabad.

*

Ahmedabad is rife with courses in spoken English. The manager of a beauty parlour on Satellite Road, in purple lipstick and black tights, tells me how much she too wants to learn to speak in *phataphat* English. Behind the new, massive Exhibition Hall, in the tall building housing the Gujarat Mineral Development Corporation, glass-bubble lifts surge up an atrium dressed in foliage, perfumed by agarbattis and maintained by staffers uniformly dressed in dark-blue trousers and light-blue shirts. Less than 200 metres away, the few square kilometers that surround the Gujarat University and include colleges under the newly started Ahmedabad University are awash with announcements and promises:

CAREER OPPORTUNITIES FOR GRADUATES DIPLOMA IN BUSINESS MANAGEMENT WITH E-COM IN BUSINESS FINANCE. SUPPLY CHAIN AND LOGISTICS MANAGEMENT
PARELLEL EDUCATION: WE HELP BUILDING ATTITUDE/SKILLS REFINEMENT/IMAGE ENHANCEMENT

*

The aunts arrive, doughty Gujarati matrons from Cleveland, Ohio. They squat on the black sofas in the drawing room and on the white-tiled floor and talk in American-accented Gujarati about the looming recession back home. They ask me to join them, quiz me about the things they have read in the local newspapers.

'Oh Ambani is going to do so well with his public issue.'

'India is going great guns.'

'But what is being done for the poor?'

Trishala tells me she has arguments with her family about the communal issue. 'They do not like Muslims,' she tells me, 'I do not understand it, they will not kill an insect but they will not condemn what happened in 2002.'

I have an SMS from a man I was introduced to the previous evening at the walking track of the Karnavati Club. 'Buy RNRL', it says. RNRL. Reliance Natural Resources Limited.

The stock market has crashed. Till yesterday it was boomtime and the housewives and young mothers at home and men crouching on stools in little makeshift cabins were clicking away on keyboards. Buy, sell, buy, sell. According to the newspapers, investors in Gujarat have lost Rs 3 lakh crore. I think about this as I ride down the Nehru Circle, all broken up to make a path for the BRTS and the dust hanging like fine mist in the air. Policemen have been posted at the Kankaria Lake to prevent victims of the stock-market crash from drowning themselves.

The Muslim owner of the Italian Bakery at Lal Darwaza tells me that sometime, about twenty years ago, Ahmedabadis stopped eating eggs. This and competition led to a decline in business for him. He is not bitter. 'Times change,' he shrugs. I buy a packet of biscuits from his store and leave it on a plate on the dining table when I get home. I wake up uneasy in the middle of the night, run into the dark, silent living room, thrust the 'food from outside' into my handbag and scrub the plate before returning it to its usual place on the rack.

*

The temple is on a small, low plateau overlooking a lake. Many years ago, a priest brought the sacred lamp from another town and placed it amidst a pile of bricks. His sons built the marble walls and the clay painted lion, and now, though modest by the standards of contemporary temple architecture, it still dominates the landscape. A thin girl opens the glass doors behind which the idol is placed. Outside, across the flat ground, I see the young priest approaching with a small boy by his side. Around us lies the village. They describe the layout to me by pointing one by one at the various caste-based localities: 'Patel vaas', 'Waghri vaas', 'Rajput vaas', 'Thakur vaas'.

Lying west of the Sarkhej–Gandhinagar Highway, Shilaj is less than twenty kilometres from Sanand, the site of the new Nano factory. It is at the centre of the fastest-escalating piece of real estate in Ahmedabad. The brash, newfound prosperity of the Socially and Educationally Backward Communities, the official name for the category to which many of the town's residents belong, is challenging the puritanical and abstemious upper-caste Hindu–Jain ethos of the city. But money has also stirred up the torpid, bucolic landscape, infecting it with big-city nightmares.

We have driven through roads narrow and squelchy, like interstices, not even paths. Barbed wire marks off parcels of unbuilt property. A new, unoccupied multi-storey apartment block faces a tall brick wall with a signboard for 'Royal Retreat'. Tall potted plants await delivery outside the brown gate, ludicrous in the middle of the luxuriant wilderness. Land hereabouts costs Rs 1.5–2 crore per *bigha* and Shilaj's landowners are selling off.

'What do people do with the money?' I ask.

'They buy,' the priest says.

'Cars, bikes and television sets,' his boy says.

The girl laughs. 'Bigger and better than their neighbour's.'

Yes, but two crores!

The priest laughs. 'It goes. And then,' he adds, 'they have to get jobs.'

The elders are on a charpai under an awning, motionless gents in white plaited turbans and short jackets. A small shrine raises its pink arc by the side of a road cracked and waterlogged in the middle. I am told that the residents deliberately damage the road to make the traffic slow down. A new tall, arched gate formally announces the Shilaj village. Behind it a camel nuzzles a bale of grass next to an electrical transformer. Entering the main street we find narrow doorways topped by signboards advertising cement, electricals, groceries, tailoring and feminine products. Every single shutter is down. No reason is immediately apparent for the shutdown; there are no buntings or flags that might suggest a festival. And the desolate streets are filled with indolent able men squatting on the road and in doorways, eerily silent. I stop to take a photograph. As I put away the camera I notice one of the men I have just photographed, a man in a purple shirt, signalling wildly for me to take another one. He has put on a pair of dark glasses and wants to be photographed all by himself. He looks drunk and so do his companions.

At a junction where the road forks, on a small rise, I spot a small house with a Ganesha printed on a tile at the gate. A man and a woman in late middle age are on a swing in the tiled, handkerchief-sized courtyard. The scene of middle-class gentility, so ubiquitous in the settled neighbourhoods of the city, looks somewhat forced here. Impulsively I make my presence known over the gate nailed with an upside down signboard to hide the broken grille and, despite a frosty reception, open it and walk in. The man, small-built and sallow-skinned, makes no sign of acknowledgement. Neither does his wife, a stout woman in glasses with one eye almost completely shuttered by the eyelid. But they offer laconic responses to my queries. The man was a farmer till fifteen years ago when he sold his land. 'At a low price,' he says with resentment, 'not like it is now.'

'So you don't farm anymore?'

'How?' he gives a derisive snort. 'I sold the land.'

'Do you do other work?'

He shrugs. 'I am ill.'

He does look unwell. His children go to work in the city, he tells me dourly.

The young men of the emergent castes are in love with the motorcycle. All the new jobs they have come into—loan recovery, couriering—are made doubly attractive because they run on wheels. Muscular Rabaris and Thakurs are in demand as drivers and security guards, particularly on these open stretches of unbuilt land. Our way out is clogged with motorcycles. A sea of Hero Hondas and Pulzars, some with two or three astride. Young swarthy men in cheap tee shirts with Playboy Bunny logos and flared, stained denims.

The protective galvanized iron barricades have come down at the Ramdev Nagar Crossroads. When I visit the city in September 2010, the Marriot Courtyard is revealed in all its glory with water splashing down a 30-foot wall and a banner advertising a soup and salad deal for Rs 250. The Bajrang Dal's 'Hindu Rashtra' board no longer glowers opposite. I do not know when or by whom it was removed. In fact, even the fencing that propped up the board has disappeared and been replaced by a smart, green island. Around the island, however, a new primitivism has taken over. At peak hour, traffic clogs the new roundabout making movement a slow, tortuous process. One evening I watch as a traffic policeman sticks out his arm and whistles to halt the eastward movement while beckoning forth the southbound vehicles. Suddenly, from behind him, a motorcycle ridden by two young men with long sideburns and open-necked shirts, surges forward almost grazing the cop. 'Get out of the way. Don't you see me?' the rider in front snarls into the turbid air.

The newspapers write frequently about these daredevil traffic offenders. One morning I experience one first hand when my auto rickshaw streaks past a red light on the Drive-In Road, ignoring the policeman at the centre whistling energetically. 'Can a moving target be stopped?' the driver asks, triumphant, as he sails to the other end. At Bodakdev, I see a man pushing a Maruti 800 across the street. The man is in a striped shirt, one hand on the steering wheel, the other clamped on the metal side. He pushes across the busy road, stops for the traffic to surge past him, then starts pushing again. Nobody stops to let him pass. Nobody comes forward to help him.

*

'He is ... *sleeping*.'

I look at my watch. Ten-thirty in the morning.

'He woke up early to go to the gym and then he went back to sleep and *I can't get him out of bed*.'

Her tone is exasperated, the tone of a mother at the edge of her patience. I had been to their home a few days before to meet her husband who was departing on a business trip abroad. 'Don't ask me when I will be back in front of my children,' he had cautioned. 'I want to keep them guessing. You know how it is, when the cat is away ...'

They are a couple in their late forties, living in a mansion in one of the upcoming areas in the west. Their affluence and aspiration shows in the fashionably elevated ceiling and the quicksand of carpeting. They have used their enterprise and their influence in the right circles to make good in the new economy. But the native inflexion of his speech and their parental despair suggest that they are products of a more homey, more conservative, upbringing.

In *Fear of Falling,* the American sociologist Barbara Ehrenreich writes about the anxiety that besets the middle class: 'a fear of inner weakness, of growing soft, of failing to strive, of losing discipline and will. Even the affluence that is so often the goal of all this striving becomes a threat, for it holds out the possibility of hedonism and self-indulgence.' I wonder how this anxiety plays out beyond individuals, beyond families. How does the Ahmedabadi identity, a hardy, canny, parsimonious thing grown in resistance to the sapping winds from the Thar desert, to political adversity and natural disaster, how does it respond to the sudden release? How does the long-accustomed habit of cautious pragmatism, of slow, calculated expenditure, respond to a trend of lavish expense and flamboyant celebration? How does the puritanical, assiduous instinct relate to the indolence of the leisure era? Is there not, hidden from the conscious eye, perhaps, some acceleration of pulse, some tightening of heart, some unnamed, vague apparition of dread and loss of control? And the sleeping son, small-built, frail, in the manner of upper-caste Ahmedabadi men, pumping iron at the local gym, who or what will he become?

A retired top corporate executive describes his latest project, a civil society initiative called 'United India': 'A—J—, a director of Gujarat NRE Coke, suggested and we thought why not?

For a sense of national integration, patriotism, to work against corruption and indiscipline—a spark, a catalytic force was needed. We called a meeting at the Ahmedabad Management Association, which is a hub of such activities. Fifteen of us—among them academics, advocates, doctors—discussed ideas on how to inculcate better values in the minds of the young. We had heard of Singapore—so much propaganda was done there by the authorities that it became a model both for a city state and for public behaviour. So we decided we would pick a few issues and start experimenting, influencing minds. Maybe insert advertisements such as one with a son asking his father why he does not pay taxes. We will start with the family itself. We are in the process of formulating a theme song. Next we will identify young leaders to be change agents in schools. We will organize debates on topics like "how good values will help". We will talk to the state government and ask "why have you taken away moral studies, civics?"'

I watch three films made by an advertising agency that works closely with the state government: *Gujarat Glimpses of Glory* is a succession of touristy scenes. Skimmed sunrises, birds, temples, mosques, fairs, craft and acts of piety threaded together by the strains of a gently plucked sarod; *The Bitter Truth* depicts prisoners, illegal migrants awaiting repatriation to Bangladesh at a Kolkata jail to make the point that the central government is not paying attention to border security; *Endangered Women* is about the horrors of rape, foeticide and female circumcision and recalls with admiration figures such as Florence Nightingale.

Under the blaze of recessed lighting the Gujarati visitor from Australia asks, 'how can we market Gujarat state to my state?' The light bounces off wood, leather and granite. A photograph of Gandhi shares wall space incongruously with the seal of the Gujarat Chamber of Commerce. Bunches of fake sunflowers and bad pottery are scattered about the room.

The half-a-dozen men and a woman scattered in padded chairs debate the question in Gujarati-American accents. The mood is upbeat. The President, a tallish lean man in a blue shirt and blazer with white streaking his moustache and hair, informs me that, apart from the export-led industries, the recession has not had a severe effect in Gujarat. Central and state packages have kept the growth rate stable, he says; agriculture is booming. All this, he believes optimistically, should make Ahmedabad, with the advantages but not the high cost of Mumbai, extremely attractive to new global investors. I ask him about the problem of communal violence. A sharply rueful expression comes over his face. 'That is really *sonani thali ma lodha ni mekh* [an iron nail in a plate of gold].'

*

The Imam of Ahmedabad's Jama Masjid came from Bihar in 1981. He has seen the communal violence of 1985–6, of the 1990s and of 2002. He meets me in a small official room by the side of the mosque. A child lolls on a chair covered in gaudy print, watching us. I ask him about a recent newspaper interview in which he is quoted as having said with reference to the communal violence of 2002 that the past should be forgotten. 'The press has misreported me,' he says. 'It should not have.' He has a thin, severe face. 'What happened in 2002 was *zulm* [torture] without limit. You cannot put a purdah on it.'

'In the interview you praised the chief minister Narendra Modi?'

'I did not do that. I just said that there has been peace after 2002 and progress. Both Hindus and Muslims have progressed.'

Muslim Id and Hindu Ganesh Chaturthi have coincided. At Brand Factory, a mall in Prahlad Nagar near the SG Highway, a female voice urges customers to avail of 'great discounts' in exaggeratedly cheery Gujarati-inflected tones. I see two men, unmistakably Muslim, in Pathani suits, wandering amidst the richly dressed customers. My Ahmedabadi Muslim friend Qamar tells me this is becoming a familiar occurrence, that Muslims prohibited by an informal majoritarian consensus from living and working in large parts of the city west of the river are nevertheless becoming a visible presence in the shops and malls of the west. Not just that, he says, often entire colonies hire buses to commute to new parks such as the Prahlad Park, located in a posh Hindu neighbourhood, with food for the day. Consumption and leisure are the materials with which social fissures are being filled.

Amidst the stark ghettoisation in the city, attempts at a rapprochement between the two communities are being seen. The newspapers report a proposal for 'hundreds of Muslims' to participate in one of the city's most flamboyant (and divisive) Hindu religious events, the Lord Jagannath Rath Yatra. And then, an astonishing sight. At an event to commemorate the fiftieth anniversary of the 1960 Mahagujarat Movement, a photograph of Chief Minister Narendra Modi, smiling uneasily, and clumsily hugging an elderly Muslim gentleman.

2010: Surakshit Gujarat Nirbhay Gujarat Swarnim Gujarat (2010: Secure Gujarat Fearless Gujarat Golden Gujarat), is the title of a booklet released by the Gujarat government. A graphic of a rifle over a map of the state is repeated on every page. On the cover Narendra Modi, fist clenched, shares space with the chubby-cheeked visage of his right-hand man Amit Shah. In Shahibaug, the old British cantonment area, now the location of the state's security machinery, including the anti-terrorist cell, paths lead into compounds filled with dull, official buildings and low bungalows with military-green jeeps and Sten-gun-wielding guards in the porch. The threat of attack is palpable and yet has the feel of a conjuring trick, for a raft of senior police officers and the man in charge of the Home Ministry, Amit Shah, are in jail for reportedly inventing threats to the chief minister's life and killing the alleged conspirators.

*

Kanaji Thakore twists his small hand into a fist to demonstrate the working of a press dye punch. Kanaji is from a backward caste. In his childhood he worked for a rupee a day. Affirmative action has recently elevated him to the office of city mayor. Unusually he has refused the perks of his position, including official accommodation and transport. He explains that in doing so he is influenced by the humanistic teachings of the Hindu right wing ideologue Deen Dayal Upadhyaya. I am curious about what someone of Kanaji's persuasion would make of the extravagantly mounted projects taking shape in the city under his guardianship. I broach the subject. He smiles shyly saying everything that is happening is good for the city. I prepare to quiz him further, to ask him how he perceives the displacement caused by the attempted beautification of the city, for example. But before I can ask him any more questions, he is summoned to the door. He will be back, he says, after seeing off the chairman of the municipal corporation's Standing Committee.

I wait. The mayor's office is imposing. The names of distinguished aldermen rain down from the high walls. Visitors and staffers fill the chairs. The mayor's assistant, a lean man with a notebook, sits alongside me at the table. I sensed his resentment earlier when I bypassed him to talk to the mayor. But when Kanaji began to describe the difficult circumstances of his early life in response to my questions, I noticed his attitude change, become less hostile, more curious. Minutes pass. I consider asking the mayor's staffers what they think of the recent projects of urban transformation and decide against it. I know that their response is unlikely to be anything but overwhelmingly enthusiastic, not just because they are public servants but because there is widespread concurrence among the middle and upper classes on the subject.

The conformity surprises me. The disinclination to critically engage with the nature of the new civic projects seems out of sync with the traditional Ahmedabadi persona. One would have expected an unpretentious, commercially minded citizenry to be skeptical of the soaring ambitions of the Modi government, to subject the billowing expenditure and appropriation of public land to intense scrutiny. One can imagine the horror with which an older generation might have responded to instances of profligacy, the lavishly mounted, telephone-directory sized souvenirs advertising the government's achievements, for example; even the state government's commitment to the Gujarat Fiscal Responsibility Act 2005 unfurls on expensive art paper in blocks of navy blue and turquoise. It is possible that Ahmedabadis have grown less thrifty, more flamboyant. It is more likely that the approval of the economically privileged is based on a realization of how much neoliberal policies are calibrated in their favour. In a past era the elite led the city's progressive battles, for freedom from colonial rule, for a better deal for labour, for women's education, for public health, for breaking caste barriers and a host of other public issues. Now those with a voice have no interest in rocking the boat.

The mayor has not returned. I think of a way to elicit a less conventional response from his subordinates. 'What will remain of the old Ahmedabad in the new city?' I ask them. The men appear bemused. Then I hear the mayor's assistant say: 'The *jusso*, the carefreeness, the spirit of enjoyment! Yes,' he asserts, 'definitely!'

SEVEN

Bombay Hotel

IN THE GLOOMY PERIPHERAL realm that is the last stretch of the city before the Narol Road merges into the country's busiest highway, the NH 8, snuck in between one-night lodges and diesel shops is the Bombay Hotel, a dhaba back from the days when the city ran on octroi and the daily pile-up at the Chandola Octroi Naka a few kilometres down ensured a steady flow of hungry truckers. The food wasn't special, just the usual omelette, nihari, bhuna gosht that one could expect to find on the roads spooling out of the back of any Indian city. There was just the matter of its name, a tantalising mirage of urbanity in a provincial town. According to the owner, Izaz Khan, it gave his establishment cachet, made it an easy point of reference for denizens of the road and for those wishing anonymity such as meat-seeking youths from vegetarian Gujarati families. With the demolition of many of its unlicensed establishments by a tough new municipal commissioner in the 1990s the character of the strip began to change. Computerisation of octroi collection, and later the abolition of octroi altogether, meant that traffic flowed through with little need for a halt. Fashionable youngsters in the city found more salubrious non-vegetarian restaurants closer home. At some point in the 2000s, Bombay Hotel shut down. All there is now is a small dark room with sooty walls, a few small tables and chairs and a counter behind which a manager might have stood.

A brooding transience brews in the charred air. The tinkle of the mechanic's wrench and the gasp of swelling tyres rise above the incessant traffic. The road trembles underfoot. Barrels, mountains of barrels, are piled up in the godowns across the road. And in the scrap shops beside them a variety of merchandise awaits dismemberment: steel cupboards, ceiling fans, table fans, sagging rubber tyres stacked like doughnuts, canvas sacks tipsy with bulge. A heaving refrigerator sways on a scale. The air is suffused with the corrosive smell of burning. This is the place where society's refuse finds its way. It is the junkyard of Ahmedabad. The place where waste is scalped, disemboweled for its last vestige of use before it finds its way to the dung heap of history.

It is hard to locate the opening on Narol Road. The gap is narrow and appears to lead nowhere. Entering it one finds oneself on a rough, stony path that extends for about a hundred metres or so at the end of which one sees two bleak houses looking out on a vast, dusty, open field. Thin white squares, like a tramp's shrunken trousers, are painted on the walls. A bent, scaly palm tree is visible to their left. Ahead, a long, straight dirt path billows like a levee cutting through the sandy sea. The loose soil seems to scatter and blow over the bare expanse. Half-a-dozen autorickshaws are parked side by side at the end of the path. Children in ragged clothes frolic around them. The path gives way to a wide embankment. Sly-eyed young men, local toughs known as *bhai log*, sit there, next to parked motorcycles, passing the time and keeping an eye on the comings and goings of people. Behind them extend rows and rows of thin brick and plaster houses. A bird's-eye view would reveal a water body, a large ditch marking the edge of the settlement. Beyond it, beyond the chimneys and the saw-tooth roofs of warehouses, lie the nether parts of the city: the slaughter house, the old carcass dump and the Pirana Sewage treatment plant.

Here, just twenty years ago, the pochia grass grew high and free, trapping the overflow from the dyeing and chemical workshops. Snakes slithered among the vegetable plants. And at night the foxes could be heard, howling in the eerie moonlight. There were no shops, no lights, just a dim glow from a solitary hut. The land was owned by a Hindu Patel woman, or so I am told; jungle land, far from the city centre, of little use apparently to anybody except a Muslim widow from Shahpur working as a servant in an office close to the main road, who had made a home in it for herself and her three children. But as the city extended its limits, surely and steadily like an ink blot, the outskirts came to have a perceptible potential value. More significantly, the heightened degree of insecurity resulting from communal violence created a new form of migration from the city.

This swathe of land, off the Narol Road, was parcelled out among a host of small-time, would-be developers. Through the fraught nineties a steady trickle of Muslims arrived from the city. Some even bought a plot as an investment. Bit by bit, the jungle was cut down. 'Bombay Hotel' is what the new residents called it. 'Bombay Hotel', after the dhaba that once was on the Narol Road, except that they shortened the 'o' and emphasised the first syllable of both words so that it lost its sheen becoming, instead, something hurried over, something mumbled: 'Bombe Hottel'. After 2002, the trickle turned into a flood. From all over town and the adjoining villages, from Gomtipur, Daryakhan Ghumat, Ramol, Naroda Patiya, Saraspur, Asarwa, Chamanpura and Behrampura, they came. Leaving neighbourhoods with schools, roads, street lights, hospitals, transport and markets, scalded by fear, they came, seeking safety in numbers. And the houses proliferated like weeds in this arid landscape.

The houses are set cheek by jowl and vary in shape and size. Some are rooms that are a step off the lanes. Some have a single storey with a thin balcony running alongside and an otla, except that nobody here sits outside for a bit of air and a chat. Nobody has the time, perhaps, or maybe they are afraid because in this makeshift town of outcasts people have brought their wounds, their nightmares, and their insomnia. People are touchy. Violence flares over any small thing and the *talwars* come out. The builders have their offices in caravan-like shacks, right up front, at the head of the hamlet, where the dirt path ends and the bhai log sit around shooting the breeze. In this burgeoning settlement the builders are the doyens, the captains determining the course, the direction, the scope of the enterprise. Under their entrepreneurial gaze, the rash of construction spreads further afield and every few days a new clutch of houses erupts, called something 'Nagar', something 'Park' or something 'Society', in an ironic jab at urbanity. Second to the builders in hierarchy in this emerging community are the water kings. Rafiq, Raju and Anwar have bore wells on their property and supply water, brackish and yellow (probably from gallons of overflow from the dyeing workshops trapped in the pochia grass over the years), every alternate day, for Rs 125 a month. Next in line are the men who supply electricity, stolen from an official line. These are the frontiersmen in this town.

In a lane, near a mosque that rises surprisingly solid and rooted between the lightweight houses, a bazaar has materialized. A couple of vendors with handcarts sport scanty pieces of bruised fruit and vegetables. Flies buzz around thin shanks of meat straining on hooks in a butcher's shop. The *azaan* for *namaz* sounds out. A loud wailing call. And an acrid odour hangs in the air. Despite the despair that shadows its origins, there is something unreal, something unconvincing, about the basti. Perhaps it is the suddenness of its emergence that gives it the character of a carnival. One expects to find acrobats and clowns swaggering down the path. The possibility that any moment now the whole community will get up and move on to the next town.

*

Bombay Hotel is where Meraj and his family have moved after 2004. The family owned a small plot in one of the colonies known as Faisal Nagar. They had bought it in the late 1990s or so as an investment with no thought of living there. After their fraught return to Asarwa–Chamanpura following 2002, however, they were forced to reconsider. Meraj and his brother's in-laws helped with money to build a house and both families and their father moved into it. It is hard to miss the Ansari house even in the higgledy-piggledy pile of houses. The electric-blue walls, perched on wide steps, convey a measure of durability and spaciousness, relatively speaking of course, in the squalid lane. I have just seen it from the outside, though, never entered. And when I do drop in on him, unexpected, in Bombay Hotel, some months have passed since Meraj and I visited his childhood home in Chamanpura. I find him bent over a sewing machine in a small room on the right that he appears to have converted into a workshop. On a chair against the wall, a woman in a salwar kameez, snub-nosed and pretty but with tired eyes behind a pair of glasses, runs a needle through a hoop. The room is awash in men's shirts. Checked, lined, plain, they lie, stacked, or in heaps, spread with outstretched arms like disembodied scarecrows on the floor and teetering dangerously on stools and tables. Snowy peaks of fabric, glowing with newness, a cocoon against the harsh heat of the afternoon.

Meraj is startled to see me. 'Oh sister!' he says in his customary manner of welcome. But I notice my presence has unusually flustered him. The feeling persists as he jumps to his feet and moves about, agitatedly clearing up, shifting piles from here to there, a flurry of movement ostensibly to make a place for me to sit, but also, I sense, to buy time, make an internal shift to accommodate my unforeseen appearance. A few minutes later he seems to recover his equanimity and faces me, now seated on a recently emptied stool, with a smile and introduces the woman in the room as his wife Shamshad. I start and he, anticipating my surprise, says in explanation, 'She has joined me in work. I have taught her the trade and she is picking up fast.'

'But ... your workers?' The question escapes my lips even as it dawns on me that this is most likely the cause of his embarrassment: the shrunken scale of his operations. In the past that he had described to me, he was an entrepreneur, with investment in space, machinery; he was a manager, overseeing professional workers. In Bombay Hotel he is back to where he began, or even worse, thrown farther away from the city, away from the markets and forced to call on the services of his wife, a novice. I amend my question. 'They don't come to visit?' Instead of causing him further embarrassment as I fear, the question seems to put him at ease and he replies in the open, confiding tone that I am familiar with from our previous meetings.

'The Muslim workers used to come,' he says. 'But they are all scattered now ... everyone went here and there, some quite far ...' He leans against the wall, arms akimbo. 'The Hindus come occasionally. But they don't stay long because they are worried about getting home from here.' There is a pause. 'It is just the two of us now,' he says. There is a note of resignation in his tone. It contrasts so sharply with the alternating states of effervescence and bitterness, the quicksilver moods that he had displayed some months before, that I look at him in surprise. Something has changed. Some anger has dulled. Some acceptance has occurred.

Or perhaps I am wrong. Perhaps the hurt has not abated but merely been overlaid by a thick layer of preoccupation. Perhaps he has grown through the trauma. Or perhaps he just has too much to do.

The profusion of *maal* in the room clearly suggests that there is a lot of work on hand. With an increasing revival of his old enthusiasm Meraj begins to pull out things from the clutter to demonstrate his new designs. He displays georgette salwars embroidered with dainty rosebuds and shirts embellished with jagged lines and letters. He flourishes logos he is developing on pieces of fabric which he hopes will please his trader clients. One says 'Dragon' in the style of an ornamental Chinese motif; another has 'America' written like a motorcycle. And the last one says 'WROLD' (sic). He tells me how he looks around the market, gauges the current mood and then uses his imagination.

'*Hamesha nava design* [always a new design]', Shamshad intervenes with confident pride.

Meraj smiles modestly. 'It is difficult you know, sister,' he says. 'There, in Chamanpura, I was in a certain environment where people were talking business. You could get tips and ideas about loans and movements and trends. Here there is nobody to talk to. Just bhais.' He comes to the door to see me off. 'But it looks like Allah has picked up our hand again. So let us see.'

The garment embroiderer next to Meraj's house lives in a thin-walled one-storeyed structure with a grille running around it. On the ground floor is his workshop, a large room, bare, save for a computer on a table and an embroidery machine, a China-made Feiyata long and powerfully gleaming in the centre like a multi-armed deity. A director from the Bombay realistic cinema movement of the seventies is being interviewed on the radio. I ask the workshop employees to show me how the Feiyata works and they obligingly slip a piece of khaki fabric into the machine and press a button. On the computer the letters appear and a split second later they are replicated in blood red on the fabric that emerges out of the shuddering metal ... T-R-A-D-E-L-I-N-K.

The *kutcha* lanes of Faisal Nagar are a mosaic of glass, cloth, string, plastic, brick, stone and goat droppings. Here and there are open squares in which rubbish has collected. In one a dead mongrel pup lies on its back, hind legs severed, front legs raised, as if to beg, its young, fawn coat crawling with flies. The flies and mosquitoes are everywhere, a low-winged fog, forcing me to flail my hands before me as I walk. Scholars observe that the new economy has engendered a state of 'degenerated peripheralisation' where pollutant industries and poor migrants are obliged to locate in the hinterland where the quality of life is poor. It is hard to imagine conditions worse than these. And yet, even here, in these spindly lanes spotted with excrement and dirty puddles, the rancid air hums with industry. Machines drone. Spindles whir like Tibetan prayer wheels. Under bright tubelights and dirty wires, striped paper-stiff wings turn into shirt collars, gold *zardosi* patterns appear on silk, handkerchiefs newly edged and scooped lie in soft heaps, ready for delivery to the traders.

I have stopped to watch two women, a matriarch and her daughter-in-law, plaiting wool. Their arms work like pistons, twirling the wool around a post stuck into the ground five feet away. Each plait takes about half an hour to complete for which they will be paid a rupee. I have been waiting awhile for a chair which the matriarch has asked her other daughter-in-law to fetch. Every time I try to squat on the ground she stops me saying 'wait for the chair'. Finally a woman's face appears at the door sheepishly admitting that the chair has gotten wedged somehow and cannot be pried away. There would, of course, be no other chair. These hardy women, who plait wool, paste gold thread and beads for *rakhis*, shell peas and stuff them into plastic pouches, melt wax to make candles, weave nylon ropes, embroider, stitch, pull apart old fabric for threads, make agarbattis, brooms and a million other trifles for middle-class life, are virtually at the bottom of the food chain.

The conventions arising from the contemporary way of doing business, which is to combine lavish spends on brand building with cost cutting on labour, ensures that their work will be meagerly compensated and also that they have to contribute towards manufacturing. In *Rethinking Informalization: Poverty, Precarious Jobs and Social Protection*, labour scholars Lourdes Beneria and Maria Floro describe how global firms and domestic enterprises seeking to lower production costs have successfully tapped into an abundant female supply of labour by creating new forms of 'putting out systems' whereby workers produce goods or perform tasks in their homes and also absorb costs of production such as electricity and rent.

Narol Circle is a mess. The concourse of grinding, screeching, thundering vehicles is a significant point on the 1,483-kilometre Delhi–Mumbai Industrial Corridor being built at a cost of $90 billion in collaboration with Japan and linked to the Golden Quadrilateral, a network of highways that connects the country's major metropolises. There is a fire in one of the open godowns on Narol Road. I see angry wisps of smoke billowing and people shouting and running towards it.

Amidst the dismal housess of Bombay Hotel, the white dust rises. From somewhere comes the ratatat of a wooden post, the putter putter of a van, a woman shouting. City sounds are absent here. No buses. No honking cars. No television. Or hardly any because there is no money for cable and the lights go out often. It is a tent city made of brick. Here are Shaikh, Pathan, Kasai, Saiyed from Gujarat, Rangrej and Ansari from Uttar Pradesh, Chippa from Rajasthan; people of diverse dialects and one religion. It is the edge, where the loose sand shifts in waves and every once in a while a foul bitter wind rises and overwhelms you with its fetid breath.

*

'*K kamal no k, kh khatara no kh, g gadheda no g, gh ghar no gh, ch chakli no ch, chh chhatri no chh* ...' Shahnawaz in black sawed-off jeans, a belt and long hair like his favourite actor Salman Khan in the film *Tere Naam*, recites the Gujarati alphabet in his high, whiny voice. Behind him, his friends play with a stationary rickshaw, riding it like a horse, hurtling against its metal frame. A passing drunk stops suddenly and grabs Shahnawaz by the shoulders. The boy wriggles away. The drunk stumbles back, hunched and glowering, then shambles away muttering to himself. A cluster of white goats goes by like priests late for a convention. A rickshaw parked in the next lane blares an old Hindi film song. A woman with long, waist-length hair approaches, eyes black and suspicious. She chews on her dirty ochre dupatta, swaying slightly, regarding me with frank curiosity. Kamlaben next to me greets her gently, 'How are you Sameena Aapa?'

Sameena's bright eyes flicker between us. She has a striking face, moon-shaped with dimples, but there is a peculiar vacancy about her look. 'I want to ask you if there is something I can do to reduce my stomach.' She rests a palm on her belly.

'Why, what is the matter?'

'Three kids and the operation ... my stomach has bloated. My man says I am fine but my stomach is not.' She laughs, rubbing her swollen abdomen. There is anxiety in her laughter.

'Eat less,' Kamla suggests.

Sameena breaks into dimples. 'I can't do that!'

Her glittering eyes turn to me then abruptly she looks away, calling out to one of the kids on the auto rickshaw.

'Get me a Kuber!' She orders, slipping him a coin.

'What are you doing!' Kamla protests.

Sameena laughs. 'It keeps my stomach down.'

'Ku-*ber*,' Shahnawaz whispers in the way children do when they refer to something they deem immoral. Kuber is a chewing tobacco, highly addictive, a known stimulant. No, Shahnawaz says, they do not sell it at the stall his nine-year-old sister Rumanna and he run. It is not much of a stall. There are just a couple of jars of sweets and savouries. They open up a jar and offer me a toffee. A motorcycle goes by with three young men on it. The hot dust rises in its wake. Rumanna opens her shiny handbag to reveal her most precious possessions, a pair of glass bead earrings, a gilt necklace and two photographs, one a studio shot of herself and Shahnawaz with their mother, and a black-and-white passport picture of their father. Rumanna's Abba, a cycle-rickshaw puller, looks grim and older than his thirty-five years. There is no photograph of their elder brother whom they adore. Fifteen-year-old Javed, away at a *madarsa* in Kheda, is the clear family favourite. 'They teach him computers and English and Arabic. He speaks all these languages so well we don't even understand him,' his mother Meherunissa says, her eyes shining with pride. 'He wants to work but I think it is too soon, he should wait till he is a little older. He says he wants to take care of us all.'

*

'My father-in-law,' says Shamshad Bano, identifying the elderly man shuffling along the unlit passage. I detect a trace of wistfulness in her voice, the reason for which becomes clearer a little later. The house is empty except for the two of them. Meraj has gone to the city to get the maal. The workshop door is ajar. And the house is shrouded in an afternoon stillness. Shamshad beckons me to follow her through the large, gloomy passage, bending to pick up a squished tomato off the floor. 'My brother-in-law and his family live there,' she says, replacing the chunni that has slipped off her head, and waving to the right, 'this is our side.' At the rear of the house are rooms that can be rented out. The large sunlit kitchen has two identical platforms and shelves with vessels, facing each other. The two brothers have had a falling out necessitating a division of the living space. Her father-in-law has sided with the other son. Shamshad tells me all this with a sadly resigned air.

While we talk in a small living room, the children come home from school. The two sallow-faced girls in faded uniforms disappear into the shadowy passage. Thirteen-year-old Saahil, however, stops at the door for a peek. Shamshad laughs gaily, revealing a gap between her front teeth. 'He is curious about you.' I ask Shamshad how the kids spend their leisure time. 'The girls do their homework, a little housework. They used to go out to learn the Koran earlier but now I read to them at home. If there is time, they watch a little TV. I can't send them out to play in this *mahaul* [environment].' Saahil, a high-spirited boy who has become 'such a bully and keeps beating up kids at school', is artistically inclined. 'Here let me show you,' she says, pulling down a small model made by Saahil with cues from a television show called 'Art Attack'. It is a box pasted over with black cardboard strips to resemble a coffin. She pulls a lever, opening the lid and causing a doll-like figure to pop up. She bursts into giggles.

The afternoon lengthens. Shamshad opens a steel cupboard, giving me a glimpse of neatly arrayed clothes, to fish out the family photographs. From an envelope she takes out some loose snaps, pictures from the house in Chamanpura. There are shots of Meraj and his brother enacting the ritual fight with wooden swords on Mohurram watched by an appreciative crowd; pictures of the family at Saahil's birthday party; the proud father Meraj lovingly observing his baby son. It is quiet in the room. The jagged disorder of the street does not percolate the innards of the house. We flip through the pages of Shamshad's wedding album. She tells me about the young men self-consciously posing in sharp loud shirts and suits, her brothers and cousins. They are all scattered now, running garages in far-flung places like Saudia Arabia and Bijapur. Her father too had owned a big garage in Mehsana but it was at a town crossroads and went in a 'cutting'.

I had noticed a photograph displayed on top of the TV, a composite of pictures of Shamshad and Meraj taken individually on their wedding day. In it Meraj looks thin with sunken cheeks and eyes large and full of anxious intensity. He is wearing a flat-topped cap of dark velvet or fur, a white jacket on a white shirt with a smart narrow tie. She has a red-and-gold dupatta draped over her head. Her mehendi-adorned hands are folded under her chin displaying the ample gold on her wrists. The make-up and jewellery obscure her demure rounded features giving her a hard, apprehensive look. 'We are distantly related,' she tells me when I ask her how the marriage came about. 'I had seen him at weddings. My mother and I had even visited the house at Chamanpura when I was a child.' In the wedding album are photographs of Shamshad preparing for the ceremony. She is dressed in a light salwar kameez and is surrounded by smiling girlfriends. 'I had just passed my twelfth with 60 per cent,' she says proudly. 'I was a good student. But when the *rishta* came, my family said "she is not going to work in a job, so there is no point in her studying further."' Seven years after the wedding the 'dhamaal' occurred. 'It is sad,' she says softly. 'All this is new. Now the day goes in business.'

*

A dark, narrow staircase leads up to the Centre run by the NGO Sanchetana in Faisal Nagar. The long room has been arranged for the weekly Wednesday meeting with thin mattresses lined up against the walls. Gaudy charts depict various vegetables with their names and similarly identified parts of the female anatomy. Anwar Tirmizi holds court at one end of the room. A mass of women sits around him, documents contained in plastic or cloth bags which they all carry. Some have their papers laminated, a necessary precaution, perhaps, in an environment that offers little protection from the hazards of nature. One by one they tell him their problems. A tall Chippa woman wants her ration card transferred from her old neighbourhood Jamalpur to Bombay Hotel.

'Cancel the old one and fill out a form for the new.'

'I've done that,' the woman protests, 'but they are driving me away in both places!'

A dank-haired woman in a maroon salwar kameez wants to know how she can get a ration card that identifies her as 'Below Poverty Line'.

'Don't waste your time,' Anwar says, 'the government doesn't want to show poverty, so it is against issuing BPL cards.'

A widow newly arrived from Jhansi where her husband was killed in a farming dispute says she wants to buy a house in the neighbourhood but is scared it will go in 'cutting'.

'Say "Bismillah" and buy it,' Anwar advises.

Kamla and Farzana tut-tut in sympathy. Their houses on the bank of the Sabarmati are slated for demolition to facilitate the beautification of the riverfront. 'With this mega city there is so much "cutting" taking place.'

More women bring up problems with ration cards. Altering the address after relocation seems to be a common problem. Anwar is a master of rules and regulations. After identifying the solutions he advises the women to commute together in a chakhdo to the municipal office since there is no affordable public transport available from Bombay Hotel. The buzz of conversation continues. I see a slightly built woman in pink dazedly circumambulating the room telling anyone who will listen that if she doesn't find a thousand rupees urgently to put down as deposit on a room her belongings will be out on the street. Someone complains of dizziness because of Copper T, a common intrauterine device. A woman grabs my arm and points to a stained page on her bank passbook to indicate the piffling compensation her family received for its losses in the 2002 violence. Anxiety, overwhelming, unbearable, rides on the soft gurgle of voices.

Haseena smiles when she says she is depressed. She makes a moue and flashes her teeth making it hard to believe her. But the light goes out in her eyes when she says that her neighbours will not let her live in peace. 'They watch everything I do. If anyone comes to visit they ask: "Who's come? Why come?" If my daughter goes down to play they call her a prostitute. If I go out, they say she is up to no good. My previous neighbours had a free mind; these people are newcomers, they have a bad mind. They talk in each others' ears—not openly. I say "talk loud!", such is my chaali.' She rests her head on her knees.

*

The *saliya* is a thin rod, the talwar a long sword, the *chhuri* a knife, the *china* a mutton chopper, the *dharia* a hooked knife with a mean curl at the end. Salma Aapa's fingers stretch and curl eloquently mimicking the form of the weapons that she says are stock in trade for the toughs of Bombay Hotel. Salma Aapa is a big-boned woman, with a rich brown skin and a scar on her forehead. Her voice has the raspy quality of dry leaves in the wind.

'So,' she says, 'the policeman's second wife was in the business of giving *do numbri* light to houses in Bombay Hotel and the arrangement was that my son Laiq would go around collecting the money, hundred rupees per house.

'Laiq wanted to give me some income from the business so he told the policeman's wife: "Aunty, I am keeping these four houses for Ammi, so don't take anything from them."

'But she double-crossed him and gave the four houses to Pappu's brother-in-law. Then she made an allegation of rape against Laiq. So he hit her.

'He threw that huge woman against the wall. He beat her and dragged her to the masjid. The public was all there. But no one did anything. I ran for help to save her.

'I found Majid. He came. And Munnabhai Pathan came. I stood trembling in front of the woman and said: "don't beat her, my son!"

'Then I bathed her and took her to the clinic. Someone took Rs 1,200 from her purse and Majid broke her mobiles.

'Laiq attacked Pappu's brother-in-law. The cops said we will put both in jail.

'Pappu's side gave the cop Rs 10,000 and said "don't intervene in our fight". And then Pappu went and freed Laiq on bail even though he had hurt his brother-in-law. Why? Because they are friends. *Friends?*'

She pauses, incredulous laughter welling in her wise, mean eyes.

'Pappu's brother-in-law bribed the cops to make Laiq *tadi paar*. The cop that took it has a house in Bombay Hotel, and also one in Behrampura.

'When the court order for externment came, Laiq tore it up and said "*now I will cut him up!*"'

The migrants keep coming. A continuous flow now, not of Ahmedabad's violence-affected, but of the poor fleeing violence elsewhere or seeking work in a dynamic city. The construction in Bombay Hotel continues apace giving rise to fresh colonies: New Faisal Nagar, Hariyali Nagar, Salam Nagar, Rahim Nagar (1, 2, 3), Karima Park, Sanjay Park (1, 2, 3), Ashiana Row House ... The lines of brittle houses have almost reached the pond that marks the western perimeter of the settlement. Around it the factories rise spilling black smoke into the sky. That familiar corrosive odour rises again, giving me the queasy sensation that might result from swallowing a bottle of nail polish remover. And then it fades away. I continue to stand on the shifting white sands at the edge of the dank, unmoving water and unexpectedly realise that the feeling stealing over me is what I would describe as peace.

*

On a late morning in the month of Ramzan in 2009, I pass Meraj worriedly conversing with two men from the electricity company on the steps of his house and head for the workshop expecting to find Shamshad there. The room is empty and the machines idle. But more surprising for me is the fact that it is bare. There are no mountains of garments, swathes of fabric, piles lying clumsily atop each other. The floor is clean. The tops of the stools and tables are visible for the first time that I can remember. The walls, the skirting, the floor tiles seem ablush in their newfound nakedness. If I hadn't seen Meraj standing outside I would have wondered if he had decided to suddenly up and leave. Shamshad appears with a baby—her brother-in-law's son—at her hip, and ushers me into the living room. She is wearing glasses and has a dull look from fasting. 'What happened?' I ask, indicating the emptiness.

'Oh it's very bad. It's a state of *mandi*!'

She uses the term widely used in north and west India for a business downturn, the same as used by the diamond workers for the recession-led depression in the industry. Just then Meraj comes in, having settled with the electricity men in the usual way, I suspect. I ask him, 'How is business?'

'O sister, the Titanic is sinking!' He says laughing, flashing his white teeth.

I laugh with him. 'Why, what's going on?'

He shrugs. 'Normally at this time, with Ramzan and with Diwali approaching, business would have been thriving but this time there is no work. Maybe it is the rains coming so late ... And these computerised machines! They are everywhere.'

'Really?'

'Yes. One computer does the work of twelve men. And the embroidery is of a consistent quality you know, not like what you get by hand. By hand there is an inconsistency of at least 20 per cent.'

'Why don't you get one?'

'I've thought about it,' he confesses, 'but the investment is about 4.5 lakhs and with the inflation these days and the kids' fees ...' He falls silent. 'Maybe,' he says as if he has not made up his mind. 'Let's see how it goes. Leave it to the *malik*.'

*

At first it appears to me as if the round tray carried by the withered woman emerging from a doorway in Karima Park is piled with human flesh. Then I realize it is a clutter of dolls. Not whole dolls, just the heads. Decapitated poly bubbles lying atop each other, their perfect irises blankly observing or shuttered and fringed by stiff eyelashes. Now that I have noticed them once I seem to spot them everywhere. Flushed cheeks scattered on gritty sand, always the heads, never a limb or a torso, though sometimes an accessory remains: a whistle between rosy lips or a bead necklace strangling the neck. It is the elderly women with their gnarled fingers that specialize in this work. Ancient Anjum squatting outside her gate, one leg curled expertly, skins and tosses heads on a growing pile. Her granddaughter, in an unbuttoned oversized party frock, plays in the sand as Anjum works with her scissors. She cuts through the soft luscious mouth, the dainty nose, and turns the face inside out. She presses a pair of protuberances to deftly detach the eyes. The eyeballs roll on the floor. She shears the flaxen blonde hair with a curved knife, pulling out the remaining threads by hand and tosses the eyeless, bald mask on a pile. It looks like a pig's skin and in time it will be melted and recycled. It takes four days to work her way through ten kilos for which she will be paid Rs 30. The sand is pitted with eyeballs.

I am keen to see the 'factory' in Salamgir from which the old women of Bombay Hotel tell me they get their maal. Farzana says she will come with me. We discuss the possibilities. I imagine a factory would be out on the main road somewhere. Farzana laughs and says it is just here, across the vast open field, among the line of houses rising jaggedly on the horizon. Walking there takes longer than I expect. My feet slip and slide in the hot sand. I think of the old women carrying loads of twenty or thirty kilos across this terrain. Some, if they are lucky, manage to cajole their grandsons to ferry their consignments on a bicycle.

The buxom woman at the door regards us with tawny eyes half closing with sleep. When she learns we have come to talk about the dolls' head business, the languor is instantly replaced by a sly alertness. 'What can I say?' she says in a complaining tone. 'I make no money. I pay them what I make. Luckily I have a husband who earns enough for us. I just do this on the side. There is no profit ... hardly anything.'

'She is lying,' Farzana hisses in my ear. 'All lies.'

I ask her if we can come in. She shrugs and opens the door wider. The effluvium trails out almost knocking me out. Covering my nose I enter the shadowy darkness. In the foul gloom dolls' heads loll vacantly on the shelves. There must be tens and hundreds of heads, dumb and frozen in their fatuousness and in the unfeeling perfection of their sleek rubbery skin. More heads are stuffed in sacks on the ground. There are heads on the floor, spilling silken tresses on the dirt. Baby heads, sultry seductress heads, Barbie heads, glamour-girl heads, little girl-next-door heads, Goldilocks heads—all with the cold unseeing eyes of the insensate.

In the auto-rickshaw a pair of eyes, large as lamps and lined with kohl, regards me from the back. 'It is my grandson,' Abdul Hafiz says. 'He won't bother you.' It is true. The child, almost a baby, lies curled and so silent he could almost not be there but for those bright orbs. Abdul Hafiz is a hefty man, bearded and dressed like a pious Muslim in a *jhabho-lehngo* and a white cap. He tells me he wasn't always religious. In fact he confesses he was a tough guy, a bully, who moved to Ahmedabad from Uttar Pradesh some twenty years ago. 'Gujarat *sudharaoed* [reformed] me,' he says. But moving to Bombay Hotel from his previous home in Jamalpur spoilt his three sons. One son is in jail. 'His father,' he says, meaning the child at the back. 'So I am looking after him.' The little boy pokes his head out of the rickshaw and immediately withdraws it, mumbling that the street is 'very crowded'. Lately, Abdul Hafiz says, he has discovered religion. He reads the Koran, prays regularly and dresses as required by the proselytizers. It has given him great calm, he says. As he drops me at my destination Abdul Hafiz asks: 'Why do you come to our poor peoples' basti?' I tell him that I am writing a book about Ahmedabad. He looks puzzled. I say I want to try and describe the basti and its people for a better understanding of the city. He nods, says it is good of me to try.

*

A strip for the BRTS runs through the centre of the Narol Road. So much has changed in the year that I have been away that I almost miss the gap in the wall through which I usually enter Bombay Hotel. When I find it I realize why I have had such a hard time locating it. For now the hitherto unobtrusive space between two walls is abutted by a BRTS Workshop. The workshop appears to be spanking new, not even in use yet. But it is not just the sparkling freshness of it that attracts and holds the gaze. It is the futuristic, ultra-chic form, the vast arc of moulded metal, the grille underpinning it. My jaw drops when I catch sight of it. I cannot stop looking, and twist my head to keep it in view even after passing it by.

But it is not the only new development at the mouth of the basti. The small shops at the entrance, the frozen meat storage depots and shops with chicken coops are still there but new ones have opened up alongside. Packets of wafers in shiny foil hang like pennants. Further up I see a glittering readymades shop, a chemist, a doctor's clinic and a flour mill. Every vacant slot seems to have come to be occupied and the dusty open sandy ground is surrounded by a host of small-scale factories or workshops. The Hindu driver of the rickshaw I have hired is enraged when I direct him straight ahead to the familiar strip where the builders' offices still stand next to the bhai log's quaffing station. '*Why have you brought me here? To this ruffian quarter!*' he shouts. I pay him hurriedly and tell him he can go but I hear him still cursing me as he speeds away.

Nothing has changed in the small residential lanes. In fact the recent rains have washed off the soil from the pathways. I can feel the stones hard underfoot through my shoes. Here and there are puddles, occasionally a long trough of black water. The stench of rotting garbage hangs in the air and I put a scarf to my nostrils as I walk through Faisal Nagar. Meraj's house, the house with electric-blue walls, is in one of the lanes. As I approach it appears to me that it does not stand out as it used to. Perhaps it is the light, the fading light of early evening, or the ravages of time, but it seems to be one now with the rest of the lane. I find the couple at home. The interior seems jaded just like the exterior, the walls stained, the sparse furnishings faded. The mandi has lifted a trifle but the business environment, they tell me, is still uncertain. Yet for all that, Meraj and Shamshad seem not unhappy. It is Ramzan again. They invite me to come and celebrate Id. Or better, they say, stay in Ahmedabad till Diwali. I tell them I will try. But somehow I feel it is time to say goodbye.

In my last meeting with Meraj in September 2010 I asked him something that had not occurred to me to ask before. I asked him if he had ever gone back to visit his native village in Uttar Pradesh. 'Oh yes,' he said, 'we go occasionally for weddings or a family event.' The Ansaris, he told me, were traditionally weavers. His grandfather always had a big loom in the house on which he wove Banarasi saris and a hand loom for preparing the thread. The family had a patch of land on which it grew rice. But tilling the soil was laborious and the results heavily dependent on the rains. The elder son had left what was increasingly an insecure livelihood to work in an Ahmedabad mill. The other son, Meraj's father, had followed him but left the mill to open a paan shop instead. 'It is a village of about a hundred or hundred-and-fifty houses, a Muslim village but with many Hindu settlements around. The two communities have very old relations so there are no tensions between them. The village is quite remote. There was no road till recently and electricity only for a few hours. There are no shops and you would have to walk four kilometers to find a restaurant so you have to eat whatever is given and however much. It is very pretty, very green with a river in the middle. But when we go we want to leave soon because it is boring there. We have become used to the pleasures of the city. Who would want to leave Ahmedabad?'

(Coda) The Kite

THE VODAFONE HOARDING LOOMS over a Jain Snack parlour at a small traffic junction in the old city. Small black birds are massed on the awning of the food shop. A man throws a fistful of grain on the road and the birds swoop down like alert paratroopers. The new slogan on the hoarding is 'KAPYO CHE! (I CUT IT!)', the war cry of the kite festival.

A giant kite, spread-eagled across the façade of a two-storeyed building on a commercial street in Jamalpur, flashes greetings for the new year. A lanky man in white with a skull cap sells kites on the footpath. In Ahmedabad kites are made and sold mainly by Muslims. In the shop across the street run by a burly man with an ash mark on his forehead and a henna-dyed beard, kites lie in heaps, a profusion of styles: silver kites from waste turmeric packaging paper with the logo and picture clearly visible, kites screaming nationalistic slogans ('Mera Bharat mahan') or the latest catchy tunes ('Aa to prem che'), white quadrilaterals painted with birds or pasted with coloured cut-outs, small kites known as the *chewali*, oversize *cheels*, the rocket, the *dhal* and the season's showstopper, the mightiest prize in the sky, the heavy eight-*gat* moon-shaped kite. The rickshaw driver pulls a tangle of *manjha* off his rearview mirror. I pass pickets of uniformed men, a cluster under a tent, a lone man with his slung rifle and two men in chairs reading a newspaper. I feel sorry for them, at work on a festival day.

Last night Baubhai Jodhpurwala was on the pavement at Dilli Darwaza amidst the thousands of kite vendors and canopied stalls selling cheap dark glasses, floppy hats and baseball caps. Now, though he is dropping off from exhaustion, he has opened his shop, the only one to do so in the lane. A couple of boys come by on a scooter and ask for plain kites. 'Plain kites look decent,' one of them says decidedly. Two men come by, in gaudy shirts and a little drunk. 'Give a proper price,' one says threateningly. A two-wheeler goes by, the pillion rider has a cheel in his hand, golden on one side, scarlet on the other. 'Don't buy it,' Baubhai is admonishing a customer who is eyeing an automated *phirki* in the shop. The object of his desire has a press button and a bulb. 'It is too costly. Here,' he pulls out an ordinary wooden spindle wound with string. 'Hold it in the wind and the current will come.'

They say there is a special wind on January 14, the day of Makar Sankranti, the kite festival, a wind that whips and circles with a fierce forcefulness. The special wind holds the kites in the sky. Coloured swallows, paper squares on taut pink manjha. The kite fliers are on every terrace in the pols of the old city, on rooftops at an arm's length from each other. Faces all turned up to the sky. And beyond them, a clock-tower, a hoarding, a mall, a cellular tower, a chimney and a minaret. The kinetic energy is all about me, both arms, all arms moving simultaneously, bent at the elbow, tugging, reeling. Laughter and urgent shouts of 'reel it in!' as a kite comes close. Boys with plastic dark glasses, band-aids over fingers coating pretend-wounds, boys opening their arms wide to catch the eight-gat moon. Dull music comes from another neighbourhood, now a-boom, now fading. Figures dance on a water tank. The kites surge, twirl, dip, hold, plunge, brighten. Thick-hipped women become agile as the girls they once were, and the grey falls away from middle-aged men. The peee-petta-peeee of a paper flute pierces the air; cymbals jangle. And voices gather like a swarm, flying in harmony under a damp winter sky. The kites turn black in the blue-gold-orange expanse. In the fading light, there is a soft distant glimmer and burst of a firecracker. Figures blur. The kites drop off one by one. And the *tukals* come out, large kites trailing lanterns, glowing steady, bold in the still night. From the ground comes the metallic clanging of vessels for the feast.

*

In the late afternoon on the streets a vagrant girl striding by in toy dark glasses and a dirty sari brandishing a torn olive-coloured cheel stops to yell at a policeman following her. The crows alight on Delhi Gate and flutter away. Under a blue winter sky, threaded with wool the kites are stuck on branches and on electric cables like coloured post-its.

On Kasturba Gandhi Road I stop to watch a street urchin play with a white kite and a discarded phirki. He has tied the kite and now he runs about fifteen feet away and attempts to lift it from the ground. The kite resists. It rises by a few inches and flops. The boy, clutching the phirki between his knees, tries again; and again. Each time, the kite holds, just a few seconds, swaying like a lush before crashing to the road. But the boy does not give up and goes through the same motions, tugging and hoisting, the intentness never leaving his small, taut dark face. Then, suddenly, he is distracted. A blur overhead signals a falling kite. His eyes light up as he races about, moving this way and that, arms spread to catch the falling gift. Then suddenly the kite crashes. It lies face down on the road. The traffic races past it. The boy reels it in. The paper has all but come away from the light wooden frame. He tugs, trying again to raise it. It hops, like a man on a pogo stick, then splat, on the road. A car goes over it. He reels it in, a shredded, autumnal thing.

Notes

PREFACE TO THE PAPERBACK EDITION

1. Number of households in India with a disposable income of $10,000 or more according to Euromonitor International. Euromonitor International from national statistics/UN on the World Economic Forum website: '6 Surprising Facts About India's Exploding Middle Class', https://www.weforum.org/stories/2016/11/6-surprising-facts-about-india-s-exploding-middle-class/
2. Much has been written about the impact of televised Hindu epics (A. Rajagopal, *Politics After Television: Hindu Nationalism and the Reshaping of the Public in India*, Cambridge University Press, 2001) and the 'seamless blend of Hinduism and capitalism' in the hugely popular series of Ekta Kapoor at the end of the 20th century (T. Chatterjee, 'Era of the Individual Viewer? Taste, Value, and Creative Media Work in India's Streaming Industries', *Television & New Media*, 25(8), 796–813, https://doi.org/10.1177/15274764241235603). A content analysis of characters' surnames in the visual media (Rakesh Kumar Maurya, 'Do Hindi Cinema & Television Serials Propagate Caste Stereotypes Through Surnames of Characters: A Content Analysis', *The International Journal of Indian Psychology*, 3 (3), DOI: 10.25215/0303.055, DIP: 18.01.055/20160303) revealed that out of 135 leading characters selected from 45 TV serials, 111 characters (82 per cent) carried a surname belonging to upper caste/ general category, 6 characters (5 per cent) carried a surname belonging to

Other Backward Classes (OBC), 6 characters (4 per cent) carried a surname belonging to Muslim and 12 characters (9 per cent) carried no surnames.
3. Zoya Hasan, *Democracy and the Crisis of Inequality*, Primus Books, 2014, 141.
4. Justus Uitermark and Jan Willem Duyvendak, 'Civilising the City: Populism and Revanchist Urbanism in Rotterdam', *Urban Studies* 45, no. 7 (2008): 1485–1503, http://www.jstor.org/stable/43197834.
5. Ajay Gudavarthy, 'The Majoritarian Circus on India's Streets Has Entered Parliament', *Scroll.in*, 21 December 2024, https://scroll.in/article/1076955/indias-colosseum-politician-gladiators-spar-over-manufactured-conflict
6. Nitin Kumar Bharti, Lucas Chancel, Thomas Piketty and Anmol Somanchi, 'Income and Wealth Inequality in India, 1922–2023: The Rise of the Billionaire Raj', https://wid.world/www-site/uploads/2024/03/WorldInequalityLab_WP2024_09_Income-and-Wealth-Inequality-in-India-1922-2023_Final.pdf
7. Figures from a 2023 report of the People Research on India's Consumer Economy (PRICE) and India's Citizen Environment. 'Indian Middle Class Will Nearly Double to 61% by 2046-47: PRICE Report', *Business Standard*, 24 October 2025, https://www.business-standard.com/economy/news/indian-middle-class-will-nearly-double-to-61-by-2046-47-price-report-123070500864_1.html

1. MERAJ

1. The mass violence had been preceded by the gruesome murder of fifty-nine Hindus, many of them volunteers for the Vishwa Hindu Parishad (VHP), in a fire on a train believed to have been set by a throng of Muslims on 27 February 2002, in the town of Godhra, 150 kilometres east of Ahmedabad. Hindu revivalists claimed that the statewide attacks on Muslims were a response to the incident.
2. Bus Rapid Transit System.

2. THE RIVER

1. Photograph of Delhi Darwaza, *Ahmedabad* ed. George Michell and Snehal Shah, Marg Publications, 1988, 2003.

3. OLD CITY

1. S. Balakrishnan, 'Chiman', *The Illustrated Weekly of India*, February 16–17, 1991.
2. James Forbes, *Oriental Memoirs*, from *Ahmedabad: From Royal City to Megacity*, Achyut Yagnik and Suchitra Sheth, Penguin Books India, 2011.
3. Rashtriya Swayamsevak Sangh, a volunteer organization committed to a Hindu nationalistic agenda and perceived as an umbrella organization of various pro-Hindu groups, particularly the BJP.
4. Brenda S.A. Yeoh, 'The Global Cultural City? Spatial Imagineering and Politics in the (Multi)cultural Marketplaces of South-east Asia' (*Urban Studies*, 42.5–6, pp. 945–958, 2005).

4. WORKING CLASS

1. The huddle of hovels around factories transmogrified into barracks-like walk-throughs.

5. HIGHWAY DREAMS

1. The Gujarat government had described it as an act of terror, wrongly as it turned out. In February 2011, a special court hearing the case supported the theory of a premeditated plot by convicting thirty-one local Muslims for criminal conspiracy and murder but sent a confusing signal with its acquittal of sixty-three others including persons described as key conspirations by the police.

Select Bibliography

Ackroyd, Peter, *London: The Biography*, Chatto & Windus, London, 2000
Adorno, Theodor, *Minima Moralia: Reflections from Damaged Life*, Verso, London, 2005
Agarwal, P.K., and Singh, V. P., 'Tapi, Sabarmati and Mahi Basins' in *Hydrology and Water Resources of India*, Springer, May 16, 2007
Ahmad, Irfan, *Islamism and Democracy in India: The Transformation of Jamaat-e-Islami*, Permanent Black, New Delhi, 2010
Aiyar, S. P. (ed.), *The Politics of Mass Violence in India*, Manaktalas and Sons, Bombay, 1967
Akbar, M.J., *Riot after Riot: Reports on Caste and Communal Violence in India*, Penguin Books India, New Delhi, 1988
Allchin, B. and Goudie, A., 'Dunes Aridity and Early Man in Gujarat, Western India', *Man*, New Series, Vol. 6, No. 2, pp. 248–265, Jun., 1971
AMC, AUDA with Technical Support from CEPT University, 'Jawaharlal Nehru National Urban Renewal Mission: City Development Plan Ahmedabad 2006–2012'
Anderson, W., and Damle, S., *The Brotherhood in Saffron: The Rashtriya Swayamsevak Sangh and Hindu Revivalism*, Vistaar, New Delhi, 1987
Appadurai, Arjun, *Fear of Small Numbers: An Essay on the Geography of Anger*, Duke University Press, Durham and London, 2006
Banga, Indu (ed.), *The City in Indian History: Urban Demography, Society and Politics*, Manohar Publishers, Delhi, 1994
Bates, Crispin (ed.), *Beyond Representation: Colonial and Postcolonial Constructions of Indian Identity*, Oxford University Press, USA, 2006

Baudrillard, Jean, *Simulacra*, University of Michigan Press, Ann Arbor, 1994

Beattie, Alan, *False Economy: A Surprising Economic History of the World*, Penguin Books, London, 2010

Benjamin, Walter, *The Arcades Project*, Belknap Press of Harvard University Press, Cambridge, Massachusetts, 1999

Berenschot, Ward, 'Political Fixers and the Rise of Hindu Nationalism in Gujarat, India: Lubricating a Patronage Democracy', *South Asia: Journal of South Asian Studies*, 34:3, pp. 382–401, 2011

Bose, Sugata, *A Hundred Horizons: The Indian Ocean in the Age of Global Empire*, Permanent Black, Delhi, 2006

Bhaumik, Saba Naqvi, 'Birth of the Septic Fringe', *Outlook*, Aug. 11, 2008

Bhattacharya, S. (ed.), *The Mahatma and the Poet: Letters and Debates between Gandhi and Tagore 1915–1941*, National Book Trust India, New Delhi, 2008

Bhatt, Anil and Yagnik, Achyut, 'The Anti-Dalit Agitation in Gujarat', *South Asia Bulletin* pp. 45–60, Vol. IV, No. 1, Spring, 1984

Bhatt, Ela, *We Are Poor but So Many*, Oxford University Press, New York, 2006

Bhatt, Purnima Mehta (compiled and translated), *Reminiscences: The Memoirs of Shardaben Mehta*, Zubaan, New Delhi, 2007

Brass, Paul R., *The Production of Hindu–Muslim Violence in Contemporary India*, Oxford University Press, Mumbai, 2003

Bridge, Gary, and Watson, Sophie (eds), *The New Blackwell Companion to the City*, John Wiley & Sons, Oxford, UK, 2011

Breman, Jan, *The Making and Unmaking of an Industrial Working Class: Sliding Down to the Bottom of the Labour Hierarchy in Ahmedabad, India*, Oxford University Press, New Delhi, 2004

Breman, J., 'Communal Upheaval as Resurgence of Social Darwinism' *Economic and Political Weekly*, Vol. 37, No. 16, pp. 1485–1488, April 20, 2002

Breman, Jan, and Shah, Parthiv, *Working in the Mill No More*, Oxford University Press, New Delhi, 2004

Brosius, Christiane, *India's Middle Class: New Forms of Urban Leisure, Consumption and Prosperity*, Routledge, New Delhi, 2010

Bunsha, Dionne, *Scarred: Experiments with Violence in Gujarat*, Penguin Books India, New Delhi, 2006

Burleigh, Michael, *The Third Reich: A New History*, Pan Books, London, 2001

Caro, Robert A., *The Power Broker: Robert Moses and the Fall of New York*, Knopf, New York, 1974

Castells, Manuel, *Communication Power*, Oxford University Press, USA, 2009

CEPT, *Interactions with River Sabarmati*, Interactive Workshop 08–09, Ahmedabad, Dec., 2008

Chandhoke, Neera, et al., 'The Displaced of Ahmedabad', *Economic and Political Weekly*, Vol. 42, No. 43, pp. 10–14, 27 Oct., 2007

Chatterjee, Ipsita, 'Violent Morphologies: Landscape, Border and Scale in Ahmedabad Conflict' *Geoforum*, Vol. 40, No. 6, pp. 1003–1013, Pergamon, 2009

Chatterjee, Partha, *The Nation and Its Fragments: Colonial and Postcolonial Histories*, Princeton University Press, Princeton, 1993

Chaudhury, Anasua, 'Sabarmati: Creating a New Divide?' *Economic and Political Weekly*, Vol. 42, No. 8, pp. 697–703, Feb. 24–Mar. 2, 2007

Chua, Beng-Huat (ed.), *Consumption in Asia: Lifestyle and Identities*, Routledge, London, 2000

Chitralekha, 'Everyday Killers', *Sunday Hindustan Times*, April 19, 2009

Citizens' Initiative, Ahmedabad, 'How has the Gujarat Massacre affected Minority Women? The Survivors Speak', April 16, 2002, http://cac.ektaonline.org/resources/reports/womensreport.htm

Commissiariat, M.S., *A History of Gujarat (With a Survey of Its Monuments and Inscriptions)* Vols. 1 and 2, Orient Longman, Mumbai, 1938 and 1957

Coverley, Merlin, *Psychogeography*, Pocket Essentials, Harpenden, 2006

Dabhi, Parimal, '2 Fidayeen have left for Ahmedabad ... they and Javed aim to kill Modi' *The Indian Express*, Ahmedabad, November 23, 2011

Dasgupta, Manas, '31 convicted, 63 acquitted in Godhra train case', *The Hindu*, Feb. 23, 2011

Das Gupta, U., *Rabindranath Tagore: A Biography*, Oxford University Press, New Delhi, 2004

Dave, V.S. (Justice), *Report of the Commission of Inquiry into the incidents of Violence and Disturbances which took place at various places in the state of Gujarat since February, 1985 to 18th July, 1985*, Vols 2, Government Central Press, Gandhinagar, 1990

Davis, Mike, *City of Quartz: Excavating the Future in* Los Angeles, Vintage Books, New York, 1992

Debord, Guy, *The Society of the Spectacle*, 1931, Nicholson-Smith, Donald (tr.), Zone Books, New York, 1995

Debroy, Bibek, *Gujarat: Governance for Growth and Development*, Academic Foundation, New Delhi, 2012

Deshpande, Satish, *Contemporary India: A Sociological View*, Penguin Books India, New Delhi, 2003

Desai, Radhika, 'Gujarat's Hindutva of Capitalist Development', *South Asia: Journal of South Asian Studies*, 34:3, pp. 354–381, 2011

Desai, Renu, 'Governing the urban poor: riverfront development, slum resettlement and the politics of inclusion in Ahmedabad', *Economic and Political Weekly*, Vol. 47, No. 2, pp. 49–56, Jan. 14, 2012

Dharaiya, R.K., *Gujarat 1857*, Gujarat University, Ahmedabad, 1970

Directorate of Economics and Statistics, Government of Gujarat, *Socio-Economic Review Gujarat State 2007–2008*, Gandhinagar, Feb., 2008

Divya Bhaskar Team, *The Dollar Kings: Leading Exporters of Gujarat*

Ehrenreich, Barbara, *Fear of Falling: The Inner Life of the Middle Class*, Pantheon Books, New York, 1989

Erikson, Erik H., *Gandhi's Truth*, W. W. Norton & Co. Inc., USA, 1969

Erikson, Joan, *Mata ni Pachedi: A Book on the Temple Cloth of the Mother Goddess*, National Institute of Design, Ahmedabad, 1968

Forrest, George, *Cities of India*, A. Constable and Co. Ltd, Westminster, 1903

Fernandes, Leela, 'The Politics of Forgetting: Class Politics, State Power and the Restructuring of Urban Space in India', *Urban Studies*, Vol. 41, No. 12, pp. 2415–2430, Sage Publications, New Delhi, Nov., 2004

Fernandes, Leela, *India's New Middle Class:Democratic Politics in an Era of Economic Reform*, University of Minnesota Press, Minneapolis, 2006

Gandhi, M.K., Mahadev Desai (tr.), *The Story of My Experiments with Truth*, Navajivan Publishing House, Ahmedabad, 1928, Reprint 1948

Gandhi, Rajmohan, *Mohandas: A True Story of a Man, His People and His Empire*, Penguin Books India, 2006

Gandhi, Rajmohan, *Patel: A Life*, Navajivan Publishing House, Ahmedabad, 1990

Ganesh, S., and Mody, Mrudul, 'Ahmedabadi Youth: What Causes Moral Amnesia?' *Economic and Political Weekly*, Vol. 37, No. 21, pp. 1969–1973, May 25–31, 2002

Gayer, L. and Jaffrelot, C.E., *Muslims in Indian Cities: Trajectories of Marginalisation*, Harper Collins Publishers India, New Delhi, 2012

Ghassem-Fachandi, Parvis, *Sacrifice, Ahimsa and Vegetarianism: Pogrom at the Deep End of Non-Violence*, PhD Dissertation, Cornell University, 2006

Giddens, Anthony, *Human Societies: A Reader*, Polity Press, Cambridge, 1992

Gillion, Kenneth L., *Ahmedabad: A Study in Urban History*, University of California Press, Berkeley, 1968

Gopal, Sarvepalli, *Jawaharlal Nehru: A Biography*, Vol. 1, Oxford University Press, Bombay, 1976

Gourevitch, Philip, *We Wish to Inform You that Tomorrow We Will be Killed with Our Families: Stories from Rwanda*: Picador, New York, 1998

Guha, Ramachandra, *India after Gandhi: The History of the World's Largest Democracy*, Picador India, 2008

Gupta, Geeta (tr.), 'If there was any evidence against me, I would have been hanged long ago': Narendra Modi, *Indian Express*, Oct. 26, 2008

Gupta, N. L. (ed.), *Communal Riots*, Gyan Publishing House, Delhi, 2000

Hansen, Thomas Blom, *The Saffron Wave: Democracy and Hindu Nationalism in Modern India*, Princeton University Press, Princeton, 1999

Hardiman, David, 'Penetration of Merchant Capital in Pre-Colonial Gujarat' in Shah, G., et al. (eds), *Development and Deprivation in Gujarat*, Sage Publications, New Delhi, 2002

Hardiman, David, 'The Quit India Movement in Gujarat' in *Histories for the Subordinated*, Seagull Books, London, 2007

Hardy, P., *The Muslims of British India*, Cambridge University Press, 1972, Foundation Books, New Delhi, 1998

Harvey, David, *The New Imperialism*, Oxford University Press, Oxford, 2003

Harris, Nigel, *The End of the Third World: Newly Industrializing Countries and the Decline of an Ideology*, Penguin Books, Harmondsworth, Middlesex, 1986

Haynes, Douglas E., 'Artisans and the Shaping of Labour Regimes in Urban Gujarat, 1600–1960' in Shah, G., et al. (eds), *Development and Deprivation in Gujarat*, Sage Publications, New Delhi, 2002

Herbert, Bob, 'The Worst of the Pain', *New York Times*, Feb. 8, 2010

Hesselberg, Jan (ed.), *Issues in Urbanisation: Study of Ahmedabad City*, Rawat Publications, Jaipur, 2002

Hirway, Indira, 'Identification of BPL Households for Poverty Alleviation Programmes', *Economic and Political Weekly*, Vol. 38, No. 45, pp. 4803–4808, Nov. 8, 2003

Hobsbawm, E. J., *The Age of Capital*, Vintage Books, New York, 1996

Jaffrelot, Christophe (ed.), *The Sangh Parivar: A Reader*, Oxford University Press, Delhi, 2005

Jain, Jyotindra, (ed.) *India's Popular Culture: Iconic Spaces and Fluid Images*, Marg Publications, Mumbai, 2007

Jalal, Ayesha, 'Exploding Communalism: The Politics of Muslim Identity in South Asia' in Bose, S. and Jalal, A.E., *Nationalism, Democracy & Development: State and Politics in India*, Oxford University Press, New Delhi, 2008

Jasani, Rubina, 'Violence, Reconstruction and Islamic Reform: Stories from the Muslim "Ghetto"', *Modern Asian Studies*, 42.2–3, pp. 431–456, 2008

Jawaharlal Nehru National Urban Renewal Mission, 'Overview: Report from Urban Ministry Government of India' http://jnnurm.nic.in/wp-content/uploads/2011/01/UIGOverview.pdf

Jha, Prem Shankar, *Crouching Dragon, Hidden Tiger: Can China and India Dominate the West?* Soft Skull Press, New York, 2010

Jones D. and Jones R., 'Urban Upheaval in India: The 1974 Nav Nirman Riots in Gujarat', *Asian Survey*, Vol. 16, No. 11, pp. 1012–1033, Nov. 1976

Juergensmeyer, Mark, *Terror in the Mind of God: The Global Rise of Religious Violence*, Vol. 13, University of California Press, Berkeley, 2003

Kalia, Ravi, *Gandhinagar: Building National Identity in Postcolonial India*, University of South Carolina Press, Columbia, 2004

Kakar, Sudhir, *Colours of Violence*, University of Chicago Press, London, 1996
Kanwar, Kamlendra, *Trailblazers of Gujarat*, Harmony Publishers, Ahmedabad, 2008
Kamath, M.V. and Kher, V. B., *The Story of Militant but Non-Violent Trade Unionism: A Biographical and Historical Study*, Navajivan Trust, Ahmedabad, 1993
Kamath, M.V. and Randeri, Kalindi, *Narendra Modi: The Architect of a Modern State*, Rupa & Co., New Delhi, 2009
Khan, Saeed, 'Muslims can prosper under Modi: Imam', *Times of India*, Ahmedabad, Mar. 1, 2009
Khetan, Ashish, 'Conspirators & Rioters', *Tehelka*, Nov. 3, 2007
Khilnani, Sunil, *The Idea of India*, Penguin Books India, New Delhi, 1998
King, A.D. and Dovey, Kim (eds), *Framing Places: Mediating Power in Built Form*, Routledge (Architecture Series), London, 2014
Klein, Naomi, *Fences and Windows: Dispatches from the Front Lines of the Globalization Debate*, Picador, New York, 2002
Klein, Naomi, *No Space No Choice No Jobs No Logo*, Picador, New York 2000
Kleinenhammans, Sabrina, *Re-envisioning the Indian city: Informality and Temporality*, Dissertation, Department of Architecture, Massachusetts Institute of Technology, Massachusetts, 2009 http://hdl.handle.net/1721.1/49550
Kothari, Rita, 'Short Story in Gujarati Dalit Literature', *Economic and Political Weekly*, Vol. 36, No. 45, pp. 4308–4311, Nov. 10–16, 2001
Kothari, Rita, *The Burden of Refuge: The Sindhis and Hindus of Gujarat*, Orient Longman, New Delhi, 2007
Kundu, Amitabh, and Mahadevia, Darshini (eds), *Poverty and Vulnerability in a Globalising Metropolis: Ahmedabad*, Manek, New Delhi, 2002
Kudva, Neema and Beneria, Lourdes (eds), *Rethinking Informalization: Poverty, Precarious Jobs and Social Protection*, http://hdl.handle.net/1813/3716
Kulkarni, Atmaram, *Shankersinh Vaghela: Portrayal of a Charismatic Leader*, Leelavati Publication, Mumbai, 1998
Lasch, Christopher, *The Culture of Narcissism: American Life in an Age of Diminishing Expectations*, W.W. Norton & Co. Inc., New York, 1979
Le Corbusier, 'The Inefficiency of the Modern City' in Le Corbusier, and Jeanneret, Pierre, *Oeuvre Complete 1934–1938*, Dakin, A. J. (tr), Bill, Max, Editions Girsberger, Zurich, 1958
Lobo, L. and Kumar, S., 'Development-induced Displacement in Gujarat (1947–2004)', Summary of a report for the National Workshop by the Centre for Culture and Development, Mar. 10, 2007
Macwan, J., Kothari, Rita (tr.), *Angaliyat (The Stepchild)*, Oxford University Press, New Delhi, 2012
Mahadevia, Darshini, 'Communal Space over Life Space: Saga of Increasing

Vulnerability in Ahmedabad', *Economic and Political Weekly*, Vol. 37, No. 48, pp. 4850–4858, Nov. 30, 2002

Mahadevia, Darshini (ed.), *Inside the Transforming Urban Asia: Processes, Policies, and Public Actions*, Concept Publishing Company, New Delhi, 2008

Malabari, Behramji, *Gujarat and the Gujaratis: Pictures of Men and Manners Taken from Life*, W.H. Allen, London, 1882

Malhotra, Inder, *Indira Gandhi*, Hodder & Stoughton, London, 1989

Mangaldas, Leena, *Akhand Divo*, Shreyas Prakashan, Ahmedabad, 1979

Mehta, Makrand, *The Ahmedabad Cotton Textile Industry Genesis and Growth*, New Order Book Co., Ahmedabad, 1982

Mehta, Makrand, 'Gandhi and Ahmedabad 1915–20', *Economic and Political Weekly*, Vol. 40, No. 4, pp. 291, 293–299, Jan. 22–28, 2005

Mehta, Mona G., 'A River of No Dissent: Narmada Movement and Coercive Gujarati Nativism' in Mehta, Nalin, and Mehta, Mona G. (eds), 'Gujarat beyond Gandhi: Identity, Conflict and Society', *South Asian History and Culture*, 1:4, pp. 509–528, Taylor & Francis, 2010

Mehta, Nalin, 'Ashis Nandy vs. The State of Gujarat: Authoritarian Developmentalism, Democracy and the Politics of Narendra Modi' in Mehta, Nalin, and Mehta, Mona G. (eds), 'Gujarat beyond Gandhi: Identity, Conflict and Society', *South Asian History and Culture*, 1:4, pp. 577–596, Taylor & Francis, 2010

Miabhoy, N. M., *Prohibition Policy Inquiry Commission Report*, Government of Gujarat, Gandhinagar, 1983

Michell, George, and Shah, Snehal (eds), *Ahmedabad*, Marg Publications, Vol. 39, No. 3, Bombay, 1986, Reprint 2003

Mishra, Neelesh, 'The Prime Minister of Gujarat', *Hindustan Times*, Ahmedabad, Jan. 23, 2009

Moraze, C., *Triumph of the Middle Classes: A Political and Social History of Europe in the Nineteenth Century*, Anchor Books, New York, 1968

Mukta, Parita, 'On the Political Culture of Authoritarianism' in Shah, G., et al. (eds), *Development and Deprivation in Gujarat*, Sage Publications, New Delhi, 2002

Mumford, Lewis, *The City in History: Its Origins, Its Transformation, and Its Prospects*, Harcourt, Brace & World, Inc., New York, 1961

Munshi, Kanaiyalal M., *Gujarat and Its Literature: From Early Times to 1852*, Bharatiya Vidya Bhavan, 1935, Reprint 1967

Myrdal, Gunnar, *Asian Drama: An Inquiry into the Poverty of Nations, Volume One*, Allen Lane, The Penguin Press, London, 1968

Morris, Meaghan, *Ecstasy and Economics: American Essays for John Forbes*, Empress Publishing, Sydney, 1992

Nag, Kingshuk, *The Namo Story: A Political Life*, Roli Books, Delhi, 2013

Nagarkar, Kiran, *Cuckold*, HarperCollins Publishers India, New Delhi, 1997

Nair, Janaki, *The Promise of the Metropolis: Bangalore's Twentieth Century*, Oxford University Press, Oxford and New York, 2005

Nanda, Meera, *The God Market: How Globalisation is Making India More Hindu*, Random House India, New Delhi, 2009

Nandy, Ashis, 'Obituary of Culture', *Seminar*, No. 513, Delhi, May, 2002

Nandy, A., et al., *Creating a Nationality: The Ramjanmabhoomi Movement and Fear of the Self*, Oxford University Press, Delhi, 1995

Narayan, S., *Those Ten Months: President's Rule in Gujarat*, Vikas, Delhi, 1973

Nasar, Sylvia, *Grand Pursuit: The Story of Economic Genius*: Fourth Estate, London, 2011

Orwell, George, *Down and Out in Paris and London*, Penguin Books, UK, 2001

Pandey, Gyanendra, 'Can a Muslim be an Indian?' *Comparative Studies in Society and History*, 41.04, pp. 608–629, Oct., 1999

Pandya, Yatin (ed.), *The Ahmedabad Chronicle: Imprints of a Millennium*, Vastu-Shilp Foundation, Ahmedabad, 2002

Panikkar, K. M., *A Survey of Indian History*, Asia Publishing House, London, 1963

Patel, Bhailalbhai, *Bhaikakana Smarano*, Sahitya Vardhak Karvdaya, Ahmedabad, 1970

Patel, Dilip, 'Amdavad Rising', *Ahmedabad Mirror*, Ahmedabad, July 6, 2009

Patel, Sujata, 'Urbanization, development and communalisation of society in Gujarat' in Shinoda, Takashi (ed.), *The Other Gujarat: Social Transformations among Weaker Sections*, Popular Prakashan, Mumbai, 2002

Patel, Sujata and Masselos, Jim (eds), *Bombay and Mumbai: The City in Transition*, Oxford University Press, New Delhi, 2003

Piramal, Gita, *Business Legends*, Penguin Books India, New Delhi, 1998

Pow, Choon-Piew, *Gated Communities in China: Class, Privilege and the Moral Politics of the Good Life*, Routledge, London, New York, 2009

Prasad, Sunand, 'Le Corbusier in India' in *Le Corbusier: Architect of the Century*, Raeburn, M. and Wilson, V. (eds), Hayward Gallery, London, 1987

Rajput, Vipul, 'Police Chowkies to go Corporate Way', *Ahmedabad Mirror*, Ahmedabad, Aug. 17, 2010

Raychaudhuri, Siddhartha, 'Colonialism, Indigenous Elites and the Transformation of Cities in the Non-Western World: Ahmedabad (Western India) 1890–1947', *Modern Asian Studies* 35 No. 3 pp. 677–726, Jul., 2001

Ray, Raka and Katzenstein, Mary Fainsod (eds), *Social Movements in India: Poverty, Power and Politics*, Rowman & Littlefield Publishers Inc., USA, 2005

Reddy, Jaganmohan (Justice), *Report of the Commission of Inquiry into the Communal Disturbances at Ahmedabad and other places in Gujarat on and after 18th September 1969*, Government Central Press, Gandhinagar, 1990

Rivett, Kenneth, 'The Economic Thought of Mahatma Gandhi', *The British Journal of Sociology*, Vol. 10, No. 1, pp. 1–15, Mar. 1959

Rizzolatti, Giacomo and Sinigaglia, Corrado, 'The Mirror Neuron System', *Annual Reviews*, Vol. 27,pp. 169–192, Jul. 2004

Routledge, P., 'Voices of the dammed: discursive resistance amidst erasure in the Narmada Valley', India, *Political Geography* 22, pp. 243–270, 2003

Rudolph, Lloyd I. and Rudolph, Susanne, *In Pursuit of Lakshmi: The Political Economy of the Indian State*, Orient Longman, Hyderabad, 1987

Sassen, Saskia, *The Global City: New York, London, Tokyo*, Princeton University Press, Princeton, 2001

Sassen, Saskia, *Territory, Authority, Rights: From Medieval to Global Assemblages*, Princeton University Press, Princeton, 2006

Sbriglio, Jacques and Pande, Alka (curators), *Le Corbusier from Marseilles to Chandigarh 1945–65*, Exhibition, Ahmedabad, Jan. 5–22, 2008

Schneider, Jane and Susser, Ida (eds), *Wounded Cities: Destruction and Reconstruction in a Globalised World*, Berg, New York, 2003

Sennett, Richard and Cobb, Jonathan, *The Hidden Injuries of Class*, Knopf, New York, 1972

Sennett, Richard, *The Uses of Disorder: Personal Identity and City Life*, W.W. Norton & Co. Inc., New York, 1992

Sennett, Richard, *The Culture of the New Capitalism*, Yale University Press, New Haven, 2006

Sereny, Gitta, *Albert Speer: His Battle with Truth*, Picador, London, 1996

Shaban, A., 'Ghettoisation, Crime and Punishment in Mumbai', *Economic and Political Weekly*, Vol. 43, No. 33, pp. 68–73, Aug. 16–22, 2008

Shah, Amrita, 'Knife Edge: Why Ahmedabad Burns', *Imprint*, Jun. 1985

Shah, Amrita, *Vikram Sarabhai: A Life*, Penguin Books India, New Delhi, 2007

Shah, Ghanshyam, 'Middle Class Politics: Case of Anti-Reservation Agitations in Gujarat', *Economic and Political Weekly*, Vol. 22, No. 19–21, pp. 155–172, May 23, 1987

Shah, Ghanshyam, 'The 1969 Communal Riots in Ahmedabad: A Case Study' in Engineer, Asghar Ali (ed.), *Communal Riots in Post Independence India*, Sangam Books, Hyderabad, 1984

Shah, Kirtee, 'Riverfront Development Scheme: Will It Remain a Blueprint?' *Amdavadma*, Issue 11, Ahmedabad

Shani, Ornit, 'Bootlegging, Politics and Corruption: State Violence and the Routine Practices of Public Power in Gujarat (1985–2002)' in Mehta, Nalin, and Mehta Mona G. (eds), Gujarat Beyond Gandhi: Identity, Conflict and Society, *South Asian History and Culture*, 1:4, pp. 494–508, Taylor & Francis, 2010

Shaw, Annapurna (ed.), *Indian Cities in Transition*, Orient Longman, Hyderabad, 2007

Sharma, S. and Suhrud, T., *M. K. Gandhi's Hind Swaraj: A Critical Edition*, Orient BlackSwan, New Delhi, 2010

Sheth, Chimanlal Bhailal, *Jainism in Gujarat*, Shree Mahodaya Press, Bhavnagar, 1953

Sheth, D. L., 'Politics of Communal Polarisation: A Precursor to the Gujarat Carnage', *Manushi*, No. 129, 2002

Sheth, Pravin, *Indians in America: One Stream, Two Waves, Three Generations*, Rawat Publications, New Delhi, 2001

Singh, K.S. (ed.), *People of India: Gujarat*, Vol. 22, Parts 1–3, Anthropological Survey of India, Popular Prakashan, Mumbai, 2003

Sivaramakrishnan, K.C., *Re-visioning Indian Cities: The Urban Renewal Mission*, Sage Publications, New Delhi, 2011

Smith, Neil, *The New Urban Frontier: Gentrification and the Revanchist City*, Routledge, London, 1996

Smith, Neil, *Uneven Development: Nature, Capital, and the Production of Space*, University of Georgia Press, Athens, 2008

Sontag, Susan, *Regarding the Pain of Others*, Picador, New York, 2003

Spodek, Howard, *Ahmedabad: Shock City of Twentieth-Century India*, Orient BlackSwan, New Delhi, 2012

Srivastava, Sanjay, 'Urban Spaces, Disney-Divinity and Moral Middle Classes in Delhi', *Economic and Political Weekly*, Vol. 44, No. 26–27, pp. 338–345, Jun. 27–Jul.10, 2009

Steele, James, *The Complete Architecture of Balkrishna Doshi: Rethinking Modernism for the Developing World*, Thames and Hudson, London, 1998

Steger, M.B. and Roy, R.K., *Neoliberalism: A Very Short Introduction*, Oxford University Press, Oxford, New York, 2010

Streefkerk, Hein, 'Casualisation of the Workforce: Thirty Years of Industrial Labour in South Gujarat' in Shah, G., et al. (eds), *Development and Deprivation in Gujarat*, Sage Publications, New Delhi, 2002

Subramanian, K. S., *Political Violence and the Police in India*, Sage Publications, New Delhi, 2007

Sud, Nikita, 'Secularism and the Gujarat State: 1960–2005', *Modern Asian Studies*, Cambridge University Press, Vol. 42, No. 6, pp. 1251–1281 Nov. 2008, 2007

Sud, Nikita, *Liberalization, Hindu Nationalism and the State: A Biography of Gujarat*, Oxford University Press, New Delhi, 2012

Suhrud, Tridip, 'Modi and Gujarati Asmita' *Economic and Political Weekly*, Vol. 43, No. 1, pp. 11–13, Jan. 5–11, 2008

Suhrud, Tridip, *Writing Life: Three Gujarati Thinkers*, Orient BlackSwan, New Delhi, 2009

Tagore, Rabindranath, *Nationalism*, Penguin Books India, New Delhi, 2009

Tambs-Lyche, Harald, 'The Quest for Purity in Gujarat Hinduism: A Bird's-Eye View', *South Asia: Journal of South Asian Studies*, Vol. 34, No. 3, pp. 333–353, 2011

Thapan, Meenakshi, 'Imagining Citizenship: Being Muslim, Becoming Citizens in Ahmedabad', *Economic and Political Weekly*, Vol. 45, No. 3, Jan. 16, 2010

Thapar, Romila, *Somanatha: The Many Voices of a History*, Penguin Books India, New Delhi, 2004

Tribunal, Concerned Citizens, 'Crime against Humanity: An Inquiry into the Carnage in Gujarat', Three Volumes, Mumbai, Citizens for Justice and Peace, Mumbai, 2002

Tripathi, Dwijendra (ed.), *Business and Politics in India: A Historical Perspective*, Manohar, New Delhi, 1991

Varshney, Ashutosh, *Ethnic Conflict and Civic Life: Hindus and Muslims in India*, Oxford University Press, Delhi, 2002

Wai, Albert Wing Tai, 'Place Promotion and Iconography in Shanghai's Xintiandi' in *Habitat International* Vol. 30, No. 2, pp. 245–260, Jun., 2006

Weizman, Eyal, *Hollow Land: Israel's Architecture of Occupation*, Verso, London, 2007

Williams, Raymond Brady, *An Introduction to Swaminarayan Hinduism*, Cambridge University Press, New York, 2001

Wood, John R., 'Extra-Parliamentary Opposition in India: An Analysis of Populist Agitations in Gujarat and Bihar' *Pacific Affairs*, Vol. 48, No. 3, pp. 313–334, Autumn 1975

Yagnik, Achyut, and Sheth, Suchitra, *The Shaping of Modern Gujarat: Plurality, Hindutva, and Beyond*, Penguin Books India, New Delhi, 2005

Yagnik, Achyut and Sheth, Suchitra, *Ahmedabad: From Royal City to Megacity*, Penguin Books India, New Delhi, 2011

Yajnik, Indulal Kanaiyalal; Devavrat N. Pathak, Howard Spodek, John Wood (tr.) *Athmakatha*, Vol. 1–6 (1955–1973), Van Pelt Library, University of Pennsylvania, Pennsylvania, 1986

Yeoh, Brenda S.A., 'The Global Cultural City? Spatial Imagineering and Politics in the (Multi)cultural Marketplaces of South-east Asia', *Urban Studies*, Vol. 42, No.5–6, pp. 945–958, May, 2005

Zakaria, Fareed, *The Post-American World*, W.W. Norton & Co. Inc., New York, 2009

FILM

Bringa, T. and Christie, D., *We Are All Neighbours*, UK, 1993
Cohen, Peter, *Architecture of Doom*, Sweden, 1989

Gandhi, H., and Dhruv, S., *Suno Nadi Kya Kehti Hain?* DVD of filmed play, Samvedan Cultural Programme, Ahmedabad, 2003

Kahn, Nathaniel, *My Architect: A Son's Journey*, USA, 2003

Krishnan, Akhila, *Words in Stone*, NID Student Film, Ahmedabad, 2005

Sharma, Rakesh, *Final Solution*, India, 2004

Acknowledgements

To the New India Foundation for a fellowship in 2008; to its Managing Trustee Ramachandra Guha for being patiently encouraging through the years it took to finish the book and for commenting on the manuscript.

To the United States–India Educational Foundation for a Fulbright–Jawaharlal Nehru Doctoral and Professional Research Fellowship in 2009. To esteemed professors, Richard Sennett and Craig Calhoun for inviting me to spend my fellowship year at the Institute for Public Knowledge at New York University. To the generous and brilliant Saskia Sassen, for recommending my inclusion in the BMW Foundation Initiative on Changing Behavior and Belief at Lake Tegernsee in 2008 and in the panel on Emergent Research and Theorization Agendas at the first World Social Science Forum in Bergen in 2009, invaluable opportunities that introduced me to cutting edge thinking on contemporary urban processes.

To the Homi Bhabha Fellowships Council for a fellowship in 2010 and to its Honorary Executive Director, S. M. Chitre, for his gracious support. To the Indian Ministry of Culture for a Senior Fellowship in Literary Arts in 2011which allowed me to give thought to the form of the book.

To Raghavendra Gadagkar, accomplished scientist, for creating an environment suited for contemplative work on the humanities at the Centre for Contemporary Studies at the Indian Institute of Science, Bengaluru, and for inviting me to be a part of it. To Geetha Gadagkar, to Ponnanna K.A., Maheshwari Satheesh, to my colleagues Srinivas Raghavendra, Bitasta Das, Uday Balakrishnan and particularly to the redoubtable Rajan Gurukkal for commenting on the manuscript.

To my father Nalin Shah whose instinctive approach to scholarship permeates this book. To my brother Hemal Shah for helping with research inputs and so much else. To Indira Chowdhury for recommendations and introductions. To Ayisha Abraham for rescuing me from writer's block. To Ishar Satyapal for his robust scepticism. To Yogesh Chandrani, fellow traveler on the research trail. To Yashdeep Srivastava for a top notch reading list on cities. To Ajay Sharma for being a bulwark in tough times.

To Diya Kar Hazra, my editor, for believing in the manuscript and nurturing it with care and skill. To my agent Shruti Debi, my comrade in arms.

To Achyut Yagnik, wise historian, for sharing his deep knowledge of Gujarat and for commenting on the manuscript. To Professor Neelkanth Chhaya at CEPT for helping out with workspace and library access. To Hanif Lakdawala for facilitating my exploration of the city. To Sujata Patel, Ghanshyam Shah, D.L. Sheth, Makrand Mehta and Tridip Suhrud for helpful conversations. To Ahmedabad, to its people, especially to Urvish Kothari, Binit Modi and Pravin Mishra for good food, laughter and companionship.

Since its publication, *Ahmedabad: A City in the World* has been widely presented including at the Indian Institute of

Science, New York University, the University of Witwatersrand, the University of Cape Town, Parlement Populaire and Oxford University. It won the inaugural 'Tejeshwar Singh Memorial Award for Excellence in Writing on the Urban' from SAGE in association with the Indian Institute for Human Settlements in 2017. Thank you, Dilip Menon, Ruchi Chaturvedi, Amrita Pande, Parenivel Pillay Mauree, Nikita Sud and Arpita Das for facilitating the above and Itty Abraham for inviting me to present the book in its formative stage at the University of Texas at Austin in 2009.

Thank you, Manish Sabharwal and the New India Foundation for your continued support. And for breathing new life into the book with a striking 2025 edition, a warm thanks to my editors R. Sivapriya and Jaishree Ram Mohan and to Rahul Srivastava, Managing Director, Bloomsbury. And thanks also to Kanishka Gupta for his sage advice.

The responsibility for any inadvertent errors is mine alone. I thank you all, sincerely.